DISAVOWED KNOWLEDGE

This is the first and only book to detail the complicated and often tumultuous history of the century-long relationship between education and psychoanalysis. Relying on primary and secondary sources, it provides not only a historical context but also a psychoanalytically informed analysis. In considering what it means to think about teaching from a psychoanalytic perspective and in reviewing the various approaches to and theories about teaching and curriculum that have been informed by psychoanalysis in the twentieth century, Taubman uses the psychoanalytic concept of disavowal and focuses on the effects of disavowed knowledge within both psychoanalysis and education and on the relationship between them. Tracing three historical periods of the waxing and waning of the medical/therapeutic and emancipatory projects of psychoanalysis and education, the thrust of the book is a plea for psychoanalysis and education to come together as an emancipatory project but one that does not forsake the therapeutic project.

In his discussion of psychoanalytic concepts, Taubman is careful to define their meanings and give examples, and to make them accessible to readers. A distinctive aspect of the book is the integration of Taubman's own relationship to both professions into his reconstruction of the history of the relationship between psychoanalysis and education. As psychoanalysis insists, one's own psychic investments, one's family, and the intimate dead, however irrelevant they may seem to one's scholarship, are always close at hand. Psychoanalytic theory offers a particular way, however, to interrupt the seamless personal narratives that in education often constitute autobiographical work or narrative inquiry. This book performs a particular kind of autobiographical work, one informed by psychoanalysis.

Disavowed Knowledge supplements the recent work of the increasing number of educational scholars who use psychoanalytic concepts to understand teaching, education, and schooling. In the academy, particularly in teacher education, it works to articulate the stranded histories—the history of what could have been and might still be in the relationship between psychoanalysis and education.

Peter M. Taubman is Professor of Education in the School of Education, Brooklyn College, City University of New York.

STUDIES IN CURRICULUM THEORY
William F. Pinar, Series Editor

For additional information on titles in the Studies in Curriculum Theory series visit **www.routledge.com/education**

DISAVOWED KNOWLEDGE

Psychoanalysis, Education, and Teaching

Peter M. Taubman

Routledge
Taylor & Francis Group

NEW YORK AND LONDON

First published 2012
by Routledge
711 Third Avenue, New York, NY 10017

Simultaneously published in the UK
by Routledge
2 Park Square, Milton Park, Abingdon, Oxon OX14 4RN

Routledge is an imprint of the Taylor & Francis Group, an informa business

© 2012 Taylor & Francis

Library of Congress Cataloging in Publication Data
Taubman, Peter Maas, 1947–
Disavowed knowledge : psychoanalysis, education, and teaching / Peter Maas Taubman.
p. cm. -- (Studies in curriculum theory series)
Includes bibliographical references and index.
1. Psychoanalysis and education. I. Title.
LB1092.T38 2011
370.15--dc22

ISBN: 978-0-415-89050-2 (hbk)
ISBN: 978-0-415-89051-9 (pbk)
ISBN: 978-0-203-82950-9 (ebk)

Typeset in Bembo
by Taylor & Francis Books

Printed and bound in the United States of America on acid-free paper
by IBT Global.

CONTENTS

PREFACE

One might well wonder whether there could be a less auspicious time to publish a history of the relationship between psychoanalysis and education. Given the current drive in the United States to align public education with various corporate agendas, and equate teaching and curriculum with scripts, scores, and job preparation, and given the transformation of psychoanalysis into pharmacology and short term therapies, a history of the relationship between these two professions may seem as relevant to educators, as, say, the history of the relationship between midwifery and spiritualism is to today's obstetricians. Quaintly interesting? Certainly. But pertinent to current educational approaches and policies that aspire to the control, predictability, and objective standards associated with the medical profession? Well, perhaps not. But that is exactly why I believe that now more than ever we need to revisit the relationship between psychoanalysis and education—its history as well as its possibilities.

At a moment when there appears no outside or beyond to the new educational order, when there is a desperate need for a new understanding of how we came to the state we are in and for a new rhetoric that can free us from the vicious circle of educational reforms in which we have been spinning for almost a century, studying the long neglected history of the relationship between education and psychoanalysis may offer a way to rethink our current state and articulate alternatives.

I started to write this book as a way to recover a subjectivity that is increasingly ignored in current discourses on and approaches to teaching and education. Comparing teaching to medical protocols and the curriculum to a vaccine against ignorance, today's educational reformers imply that the inner life of the student or teacher is as irrelevant to student learning as a doctor's or patient's psychic state is to the efficacy of antibiotics on a patient's health. The subjectivity that has been excised from current educational approaches, policies, and reforms, and that I sought to recuperate is inextricable from an unconscious that psychoanalysis has done so much to illuminate. Gradually, I came to believe that part of such a project of reclamation required me to study and reconstruct a past shared by psychoanalysis and education.

With such work of remembrance, I hoped not only to find a way off the merry-go-round of educational reform but also to recover other ways to think about teaching and education, ways that keep alive the spark of subjectivity, that acknowledge the presence of the unconscious and that remind us of the work of others who tried to resist the mechanization of the human spirit.

ACKNOWLEDGMENTS

This book would not have been possible without the generous support of a Wolfe Institute Fellowship which provided me with a year off to research and write this book. The Wolfe Institute and Brooklyn College provided the funding for that fellowship, and I am grateful to them.

The ideas for the book have been forming for several decades but without the wisdom, questions, and support of several individuals, this book would have been impossible. There are several people I wish to thank directly. I thank Robert Viscusi, the Director of the Wolfe Institute for his support, friendship, and keen suggestions. Talking to him about his own creative struggles and reading his work has been for me a humbling experience, and I owe him my gratitude for inspiring me to listen more carefully to "the voices of what you remembered and what you imagined."

Deborah Britzman also made this work possible through her enormous scholarly contributions to thinking psychoanalytically about teaching, teacher education, and curriculum. No one has done as much as she to remind educators that the unconscious is intimately involved in our life in classrooms and always and forever disturbs our educational efforts.

I want to thank the three analysts with whom I worked over the course of almost twenty-five years. Fred Wright awakened me, sometimes abruptly, from a restless sleep, taught me to listen to my unconscious, and led me to see my mother in a very different light. Mark Epstein helped me loosen my identification with my feelings and thoughts and led me to watch my reactions to them rather than act out of them. Ken Eisold helped me re-construct a past with my father and to appreciate the passage of time.

I am also grateful to the Wednesday night group and in particular I want to thank Ann, Ellen, Joanne, Mary, Michael, and Sue, for their unsettling but deeply caring insights.

In anything I think or write about education, I must always thank William Pinar. Not only have I borrowed phrases and ideas from him, but I have always counted on his voracious intellectual appetites to point me in new directions. His courage in reclaiming, remembering, and preserving an endangered subjectivity continues to inspire me as does his friendship. He has been a mentor and is my very close friend.

Madeleine Grumet was never far from my mind as I engaged in this project. I often turned to her *Bitter Milk* to remind myself of what it means to write beautifully and thoughtfully about teaching, education, and curriculum. Her comments were extremely helpful in working through the issues raised in this book.

I want to thank some of my colleagues in curriculum theory whose work and conversation over the years have influenced this book, in particular Gail Boldt, Terry Carson, Susan Edgerton, jan jagodzinski, Jo Anne Pagano, Alice Pitt, and Jonathan Sillin.

Lad Tobin's work in composition theory, his knowledge about the history of psychoanalysis, and his support for this project were very important in its realization. And I appreciate his friendship.

I want to thank a few friends and colleagues who over the last three decades engaged me in conversations about psychoanalysis and education: Dermot Dix, Sherry Giles, Melissa Hammerle, Tom Jackson, Hugo Mahabir, John Rankin, and Jessica Siegel all challenged me to question my often controlling ideas.

My editor, Naomi Silverman, deserves particular thanks for having faith in the project. Her support continues to be very important to my work.

As always my daughters, Zoe and Una, and my step daughters, Ali and Lily, showed their incredible patience, humor, and support as I remained glued to the computer and lost in the library.

And finally, and most important, I want to thank Paula Salvio. Her close reading of this work, her helpful questions, and her deep and compassionate support enabled me to complete this book. I love her deeply.

1

INTRODUCTION

A Troubled Relationship

> The relation between education and psychoanalytic treatment
> will probably before long be the subject for a detailed investigation.
>
> (Freud, 1925b, p. 274)

Forty two years ago, in an article entitled "Psychoanalysis and Education," written for *The School Review*, Bruno Bettelheim (1969) described the relationship between education and psychoanalysis as having been from the beginning "neurotic." Comparing the relationship to a marriage, in which communication had broken down and the partners respectfully ignored one another, the offspring, he wrote, resembled "a bastard child ... too sickly to thrive, too schizophrenic to realize the inner split that ails them" (p. 73). It's quite an image—a frozen marriage, illegitimate children, psychosis. Could such a persistently troubled relationship really have had a future? Especially one outside the normative arrangements presupposed by Bettelheim's analogy? If we consider the relationship between education and psychoanalysis from today's standpoint, we might well conclude that its future was indeed bleak.

With the exception of a few departments in the humanities, psychoanalysis in the United States has been banished from the academy, its disturbing knowledge disavowed. As a form of treatment, psychoanalysis increasingly looks to the pharmaceutical industry and cognitive behavioral therapies to treat the psyche. The inner life of the patient or client frequently appears as scripts that can be re-written or as chemical configurations that can be adjusted. In the field of education, other than in the small field of curriculum theory, psychoanalysis exerts no influence. Its absence is particularly glaring in teacher education and in educational policy, where the learning sciences, neoliberal agendas, and business models determine the dominant approaches to education and provide the terms to describe teaching and curriculum. Those terms and approaches replace the inner lives of teachers and students with behavioral techniques and quantifiable outcomes. Ignored or disparaged are the very theories constitutive of psychoanalysis, theories that work on the border between the socio/cultural and the intrapsychic, that explore the mysteries of subjectivity, and that can illuminate the dreams, desires, ideals, and terrors that shape our understanding of education.

It is, indeed, a dismal state of affairs, especially given the auspicious beginning of the relationship announced by Freud's honored presence at Clark University in 1909 and the initial embrace of psychoanalytic ideas by early progressive educators. How did a relationship that Freud considered "so rich in hopes for the future" (1933a, p. 146) deteriorate into what it is today? Was it ever really feasible? If Bettelheim was right and the relationship has always been neurotic, and if neurosis suggests the compulsive repetition of a repressed history, its acting out rather than its working through, how, we might ask, could the reconstruction of that history interrupt that compulsion? And, how might knowing the history of the relationship allow us to think differently about our work as educators, particularly in an age when various educational agendas, such as the professionalization agenda, the social justice agenda, and the de-regulation agenda (Zeichner, 2003, p. 491), seem increasingly to ignore the teacher's and the student's subjectivity and with it the unconscious? These are the questions around which I have organized this book.

It seemed to me that if we were to gain any insight into the current relationship between education and psychoanalysis and especially if we were to imagine a future for that relationship, we would need to understand its history. It also became clear to me that if we were to envision a future for teaching that was more than job training and test preparation disguised as educational reform, the reconstruction of the history of that relationship might offer alternatives to the dominant educational culture of "teaching by numbers" (Taubman, 2009).

In good psychoanalytic fashion, I have tried to move into the past of these two "impossible professions," as Freud so often called them (1925b, p. 273; 1937b, p. 248). I have done so to get a sense of what troubled their relationship, to imagine a different relationship, and to try to bring forth from that reconstructed history the basis for a new rhetoric for teaching and education, one not caught in the vicious cycle in which education has been trapped for over a century.

Offering a straight, linear history of the relationship, while necessary, seemed, however, contradictory to or perhaps a defense against the unsettling presence of the unconscious. The unconscious led Freud to label psychoanalysis and education impossible professions, since its *unheimliche* proximity and intimate alterity, as well as its eruptions, resist and disrupt the closure, transparency, and causal narratives that education and psychoanalysis often pursue. Not only do the enigmatic workings of the unconscious create unexpected shifts and unanticipated feelings in the relationships between patient and analyst and between students and teachers, but they make a shambles of efforts to predict and to control, two projects that many educators and psychoanalysts have made priorities in today's culture of measurable outcomes and accountability. The unconscious also interrupts or complicates any straightforward historical narrative of the relationship between education and psychoanalysis, unless of course, one has already disavowed the disturbing knowledge of and from the unconscious. How then to proceed?

Reconstructing a History

In reconstructing the history of their relationship, I have combined a psychoanalytic approach with an historical one. I have sought to explore the disavowed knowledge within both psychoanalysis and education and its effects on their relationship. But in piecing together the history of the troubled relationship between education and psychoanalysis, I deemed it important to include, from a psychoanalytic perspective, not only the odd twists and turns of that relationship but also my own relationship to both professions and the ways these two professions resonated with my own family dramas. All too often those who write about education and psychoanalysis ignore their own psychic investments and autobiographically overdetermined involvement in their work, but as psychoanalysis insists, those investments, one's family, and the intimate dead, however irrelevant they may seem to one's scholarship, are always pressing close. Certainly they have shaped this work. My father was a doctor of Jewish, German-Austrian descent and was a professor of medicine. My mother was a high school teacher whose background was Protestant. Both my parents, like Freud and like, at least sometimes, public education, practiced a secular humanism. While my father's and mother's religious and professional backgrounds were tied respectively to the "Jewish science" of psychoanalysis and to the pre-dominantly Christian teaching force, I was never sure which parent would resonate at any given time with which profession, and thus how my own affective histories would inflect the approaches I took to psychoanalysis and education and their relationship.

At certain periods in the twentieth century psychoanalysts took on the more stereotypic masculine role, exhibiting a paternalistic concern for teachers, as they informed teachers of what was in teachers' and their students' best interests. At other times educators seemed to occupy that role, as they rejected psychoanalysis for its unscientific theories and irrational ramblings. My parents' own roles in the house often interrupted more normalized arrangements; my father, for example, did dishes, my mother acted as both disciplinarian and confidant. Both acted as my teachers. While Bettleheim may have assumed particular gender roles in his metaphorical marriage between education and psychoanalysis, the history of the relationship subverted that assumption.

If, as psychoanalysis suggests, any relationship is infused with labile sexualities, genders, and libidinal currents, then the relationship between education and psychoanalysis was no different. While women analysts were prominent in the early days of the psychoanalytic movement, their numbers dwindled by the 1940s with the increasing medicalization and institutionalization of the profession and its normalization of a nuclear domesticity. Teachers, we know, have usually been women, except in the academy, where men have dominated. Men in both professions, however, have struggled at times with fears of being seen as feminized or as homosexual. Sherwood Anderson's (1983) character Wing Biddlebaum, in the story "Hands," and the popular caricature of the egghead professor exemplify the feminized teacher and the homosexual panic that haunts education. Paradoxically, Freud, himself, suggested to the members of the Vienna Psychoanalytic Society in 1910, a time when education was often still single sexed, that problems in education were "connected with the growing *proscription* of homosexuality" (my italics) at the time, because "in suppressing the practice of homosexuality, one has simply suppressed the homosexual direction of human feeling that is so necessary for our society" (Nunberg and Federn, 1910, p. 324). As recorded in the Vienna Psychoanalytic Society's minutes, Freud stated the "best teachers are the real homosexuals" (Nunberg and Federn, 1910, p. 324). We don't know why Freud made such a claim – it is the only time he did – but we can speculate. Certainly, he argued for the polymorphous nature of libidinal life. At various times he claimed that the severe repression or rigidly narrow channeling of our erotic plasticity could stunt emotional life, and that the acknowledgment of our libidinal interests in the same sex expanded our psychic capacity. We might even venture that his erotic draw at that time to Ferenczi and Jung, described by Saul Rosenzweig and George Protchnik in their detailed histories of Freud's trip to the United States, provoked such thinking. Or perhaps, too, he was suggesting that the loosening of rigid sexual definitions would increase teachers' and, for that matter, analysts' ability to more fully relate to their students and patients. But this very dissolution of normative definitions and the diffusion of sexuality into myriad ways of relating may well have posed a threat to Freud's colleagues, even to Freud himself. Indeed, perhaps out of their own panic, psychoanalysts quickly supplanted Freud's tentative acceptance of and even valuing of homosexuality with an intensified pathologizing of it. Freud's comments do raise questions, though, about the libidinized and labile gender relations implicit between and within both psychoanalysis and education.

As I explored the history of the relationship between psychoanalysis and education, and began to see my parents and the two professions as metonymical for one another, I wondered if their relationships held similarities. Was I the troubled off-spring Bettelheim had talked about? How did I hold the split to which he referred? I have been a teacher for many years, was involved in analysis for a long time, and now found myself writing about the relationship between the two. My parents never appeared to have had difficulty understanding one another, although I knew they had. In fact, my own unconscious desire to return to familial history may have contributed to my curiosity about why, at different points, psychoanalysis and education had such a difficult time communicating. So, in part, my reconstruction of the history of the relationship between psychoanalysis and education cannot be disassociated from my own history, including the history of my own sexual and gender identifications. I wanted to take account of this personal history and weave it, however lightly, into the chapters in this book, but I have also worked to present a more traditional history of the relationship between psychoanalysis and education.

In reconstructing the history of that relationship, I have tried to attend to the failed experiments, the dreams, and the symptoms that litter the history of their relationship. In doing so I wanted to see if there was another history that lay within and that might hold another future for the relationship and for how we think about teaching and education.

Extant Histories on the Relationship between Psychoanalysis and Education

As I began this project and turned to the existing historical work on the relationship between education and psychoanalysis, I found few secondary sources. Given how many histories there are of American education and of psychoanalysis, as both progressed in the United States, it struck me as odd that so few scholars had attended to the historical relationship between the two professions. There were, however, exceptions. Deborah Britzman's (1998, 2003, 2006, 2009, 2010) groundbreaking work on psychoanalysis and education has revealed the complicated relationship between these two impossible professions. In several books she has explored how the work of August Aichhorn, Siegfried Bernfeld, Anna Freud, Hermine Hug-Hellmuth, Melanie Klein, and, of course, Freud influenced and was integrated into American education. She has articulated that history, not by focusing on it directly, but by thinking psychoanalysis and education together. Thus her work exemplifies how the split between and within these two professions might look when, if not repaired, then at least thought through.

A few other writers have begun to reclaim the lost history of the relationship. Sol Cohen (1979, 1983) has written about the influence of psychoanalysis on the American mental hygiene movement, as well as about the impact on progressive education in the United States of psychoanalytically informed progressive schools in Europe in the early twentieth century. Stephen Petrina's (2004, 2006) efforts to complicate simplistic histories of the mental hygiene movement, and the place of psychoanalysis in teacher education offer some insight into the relationship, as does Bertram Cohler's (1989) shorter historical essay on psychoanalysis and school learning. A large body of work on the mental hygiene movement in the United States does exist and sheds some light on the relationship between psychoanalysis and education, but more often focuses on the public policy implications of the movement and its social conservatism (Jones, K., 1999; Richardson, 1989), or in some cases its liberal bias (de Forest, 2006, 2007).

Other than these scholars' work, I could not find any secondary accounts of the history of the relationship. My efforts to reconstruct that history were therefore based on primary sources, the few extant secondary sources on the relationship, and several histories that treat education and psychoanalysis separately. That there is so little extant work in this area suggests the extent to which psychoanalysis has been banished from schools and departments of education, and its troubling knowledge disavowed in the academy.

Disavowed Knowledge

As I began to piece together the history of the relationship between education and psychoanalysis, I came to attribute much of the difficulty in their relationship to the disavowal of the very thing that, according to Freud, made them impossible—the unconscious and its effects—and in part to the resulting inner split within both professions, a split Bettelheim, perhaps unconsciously, alluded to in his analogy, when he referred to "the inner split that ails them." That split, I argue in Chapter 2, has resulted in and been between two projects central to both education and psychoanalysis.

To describe this split I relied in part on Eli Zaretsky's (2004) description of the "dual character" (p. 4) of psychoanalysis. For Zaretsky psychoanalysis has had an emancipatory dimension as well as a repressive dimension. I shy away from such a judgment and instead see the split within psychoanalysis, as well as education, as between two projects, one of which, following Zaretsky, I label the *emancipatory project*. The other project I label the *therapeutic project*. The therapeutic project has as its goal cure—cure of illness and cure of ignorance. Such a project, which has historically been the main focus of both psychoanalysis and education, strives to help the patient or the student, who are placed at the center of all the professions' efforts, reach particular goals: for the patient freedom from stasis or suffering and for the student a change in behavior, attitude, or what he or she knows. The criterion by which the theories and practices of the therapeutic project are measured is their use value in the clinical setting, be it office or classroom, and in bringing forth demonstrable positive change in either patient or student. Within such a project teachers or analysts frequently aspire to scientific certainty, so that they can control and even predict the effects of their practices aimed at helping patient and student achieve set and demonstrable standards of health, normalcy, political rectitude, and/ or disciplinary knowledge and specified skills. Perhaps the purest form of such a project would be the medical model of psychoanalysis or teaching, which relies on protocols, clearly measurable outcomes, and experimentally proven treatments and practices. But even those educators or analysts who reject the medical model share some version of such a project, whether they are committed, for example, to assuring students become aware of specific social inequities or learn a core curriculum or whether they help patients change their life script, learn new behaviors, or gain insight that leads to a demonstrable or subjectively felt change in the patient's psychic state.

The emancipatory project, on the other hand, works toward deepening and helping us understand and articulate our inner lives without promising the result will be a happier, more beautiful, or more just life or a better job or a better relationship or a higher test score. The emancipatory project eschews efforts at control and cure, offering questions and an interminable analysis, rather than answers and solutions. Such a project never assumes it knows in advance what is best for the patient or student or what the outcomes of its endeavors will be. At the center of its efforts, the project places the teacher and analyst alongside the student and patient. It does so because the teacher and analyst know the student or patient only through the teacher's and analyst's own idiosyncratic subjectivities and through a relationship fraught with unconscious desires and shadows from the past. Thus, the teacher's and analyst's own desires must be acknowledged and taken into account. Such a project finds its voice in literature, particularly poetry, and the arts, since, as Deborah Britzman (2006) has pointed out, these carry affective knowledge without assuming to know its meaning in advance. The emancipatory project cherishes a kind of understanding for understanding's sake, a suspension on the part of teacher and analyst of immediate judgment to be replaced by curiosity, attunement, analysis, and a focus on creating conditions such that the patient or student can generate material for further elaboration or analysis. Perhaps most important, the emancipatory project asks teacher, analyst, patient, and student to recognize their own psychic complicity in what they claim to know and what they ignore. Echoes of the emancipatory project can be heard in Frank McCourt's student's comments recounted in McCourt's *Teacher Man* (2005). The student exclaims about McCourt's classroom, "In this class you never know what you're supposed to know" (p. 253). Or, to take another example, psychoanalyst Wilfred Bion's (1993) belief that "the emotional truth of a session has no psychological locus at all," that "[n]o starting or ending point can be envisioned for it [because] it is always evolving" (Eigen,1993, p. 130) suggests the emancipatory project.

While both projects are related, often in undisclosed ways, and while they blur in the hurly-burly world of the classroom, they do have different trajectories. Many educators, and I certainly include myself, feel committed to, as well as torn between, aspects of these two projects. We want to project a curriculum that ushers students into the Good, the True, and the Beautiful as we interpret these, as well as the useful, but we resist a set curriculum's standardization and the fixed pedagogical protocols that neglect students' uniqueness, agency, and idiosyncrasies, and that overlook the press of contextual factors, and the palpable ebbs and flows of class-room life. We want to advocate for particular pedagogical practices, but we resist turning them into recipes that ignore teachers' and students' subjectivities, particu-larly the vicissitudes of the unconscious. On the other hand, while we cherish the unpredictable and spontaneous, strive to attune to our own desires and those of each student, and don't want to impose an instrumentalized control, we worry about the very loss of control and the potential chaos that may ensue when we lose direction. Certainly both projects provoke anxiety, anxieties about not measuring up or failing and anxieties about loss of power, meaning, and identity. Both projects also pose dangers, particularly if either dominates to the exclusion of the other. We are witnessing such a situation today, where an extreme version of the therapeutic project has overwhelmed the emancipatory project in both education and psycho-analysis. Education is increasingly reduced to test preparation and job training and teachers reduced to following scripts that promise a good bottom line of test scores. Educational reformers tout medical and economic models for educational research, teaching, and running schools. Psychoanalysts feel increasingly pulled toward short term therapy, cognitive/behavioral therapies, pharmaceutical inter-ventions, and implementing outcome-based assessment. Neither profession seems interested in talking to the other, except about kids diagnosed with learning difficulties or behavioral problems.

The disavowal of the unconscious has not, however, only resulted in a split between the therapeutic and emancipatory projects. Coupled with the repression of the historical relationship between psychoanalysis and education, it has doomed education to a repetition compulsion. For more than a century, education has been caught in a cycle. We bemoan the rotten state of education and its damaging effects on our economy or democracy. We proceed to blame teachers or students or par-ents or schools of education for this deplorable state. Sensitive to the criticism, educators sheepishly accept the blame and rush to embrace the new reforms meant to ensure educational success or social transformation. When these fail to solve the crisis, we rush on to the next reform.

The pattern remains the same. First come announcements of some crisis: Johnny can't read, or our seventeen-year-olds don't know their history, or our students have academically fallen behind their peers in other countries, or students are not prepared for life or the workplace, or their emotional lives are neglected, or students aren't creative enough, or they have lost a civic sense or understanding of democracy. These alarms are followed by some new reform meant to solve the crisis: perfor-mance based education, higher standards, vocational education, holistic education, education for democracy, free schools, more rigorous standards. When the promised improvements are not forthcoming, for example, there is no political revolution, all young people do not grow up into more secure, tolerant, well adjusted adults, standardized exam scores do not go up relative to students' scores in other countries, kids continue to complain of boredom and irrelevant curriculum, the economy maintains its own ups and downs independently of any reforms, and graduation rates do not rise, then more hand wringing ensues and more reforms are called for. Conversely if social improvements do occur, for example, the gains achieved by the civil rights movement, the women's movement, and the gay liberation movement, or if the economy does grow or social policies produce marked success, the educators who taught all those who shaped and participated in these movements or who created the policies or who drove the economy are never seen as responsible for the success. Rather the cycle simply repeats with predictions that things will worsen or that such improvements don't compare to those of other countries. This cycle, I argue, is a repetition compulsion that results, in part, from a failure of memory. When we ignore the history of the relationship between education and psycho-analysis and the very knowledge psychoanalysis itself has at times repressed, knowledge of and from the unconscious, we doom ourselves to repeating compulsively the very efforts that keep us stuck.

Repressing the disruptive power of an unconscious that can de-rail our plans, predictions, and attempts to ensure specific outcomes, forgetting the history of the relationship between psychoanalysis and education, a history that might hold alternatives to the mechanization of teaching and learning, we rush from one reform to another, each the opposite of the previous one. Even when educators have acknowledged the unconscious and embraced the emancipatory project, they have often romanticized that knowledge and forwarded that project in the service of some greater good. The failures to achieve that good, because of education's inherent impossibility, have stoked the dreams of the next group of reformers, who then forward some more extreme version of the therapeutic project, a version that today excises any consideration of the unconscious.

Organization

I have organized the book into six chapters, including this introductory one. In Chapter 2, I lay out the theoretical architecture of the book. I rely on Freud's theorization of disavowal and splitting and suggest that the academy and teacher education were not able to tolerate the disturbing knowledge psychoanalysis revealed. That knowledge is knowledge of and from the unconscious. The unconscious and its enigmatic traces undermined the drive in the academy and teacher education to predict, control, and cure, and threatened the possibility of a unified field of knowledge, one synonymous with and transparent to itself. The disavowal of the unconscious, I argue, created a split within both psychoanalysis and education, between what I label the emancipatory project and the therapeutic project, and I discuss both of these in detail in Chapter 2. The complete disavowal today of psychoanalytic knowledge and the Freudian unconscious in the academy and teacher education and the neglect of the historical relationship between education and psychoanalysis suggest how much of a threat they may pose to current neoliberal reform efforts to regulate teacher and public education. The reconstruction of that relationship opens up possible alternatives to the current state of education and teacher education.

In Chapters 3, 4, and 5, I have worked to reconstruct the history of the relationship between psychoanalysis and education, as it unfolded over three periods of its history: 1909 to World War II, World War II to 1968, and 1968 to the present. I tried to make sense in these chapters of the disavowals and splitting and the defenses and traumas that have structured the relationship between psychoanalysis and education. The anti-intellectualism of American society (Hofstadter, 1962) has proved inhospitable to a psychoanalysis and an education oriented to anything other than expediently curing illness and ignorance and adjusting students and patients to whatever was deemed reality, be it the job market or market values. Given their own traumas and the defensive structures they developed, a relationship between psychoanalysis and education could never have been easy. It is not surprising then that its past is littered with failed experiments, recriminations, and miscommunications, and, faced with the current faith in and demands for quantifiable outcomes, a future for such a relationship is certainly in doubt. The recovery of that history can, however, remind educators of aspirations that go far beyond the test preparation, training for the global workforce, and streamlined certification that shape educational efforts today.

Chapter 3 opens with Freud's visit to the United States in 1909. The Clark Conference at Clark University constitutes in effect the primal scene of psychoanalysis's arrival in American education. I introduce in this chapter the central concepts in Freud's theory as he presented them in the Clark lectures, discuss the radical implications and questions such concepts raise for education, and trace the gradual and circuitous way psychoanalytic theory came to affect, as it was transformed by, American educators, who sought to *apply* psychoanalytic theory in the classroom. Their efforts paralleled efforts occurring in Germany and Austria at that time. I take a brief detour to those countries to look at the psycho-pedagogy that existed there, because many of the psycho-pedagogues, such as Alfred Adler, Siegfried Bernfeld, Erik Erikson, and Anna Freud, influenced how psychoanalytic theory would be integrated in American schools. Those approaches carried with them the spirit of the emancipatory project, but that spirit was often lost in the drive to apply that project and render it therapeutic.

I also suggest in Chapter 3 that psychoanalysis's ambivalent reception in the United States, its rejection by departments of psychology, its dismissal for lack of scientific validity, and Freud's own insecurities and ambitions led psychoanalysts to pursue more salvific goals and an alliance with medicine. That pursuit led, in turn, to the disavowal of its own radical knowledge, but also to its influence on schools through the mental hygiene movement. That movement opened a portal through which psychoanalysis, a particularly medicalized version, entered teacher education and schools.

Chapter 4 opens with the outbreak of World War II. Freud had died in 1939, and his death and the commencement of hostilities marked the beginning of a new phase in the relationship between education and psychoanalysis. The war not only was contemporaneous with the decline of progressive education in the United States, but also accelerated the medicalization and popularization of psychoanalysis, both of which affected the relationship between education and psychoanalysis. As psychoanalysis's alliance with medicine, its aspiration to scientific status, and its promise of a better future garnered initial success in the post World War II period, it increasingly disavowed its more radical insights and questions. As it hardened into dogma, and solidified its alliance with medicine, the number of women analysts declined. As women returned to the home and normalcy shrank into nuclear domesticity and the pursuit of material success, the nation became obsessed with mental health and mental illness. Psychoanalytically trained psychiatrists were there to help with an expanded list of mental diagnoses.

The post war years also witnessed the rise of the life adjustment movement in education, which dovetailed with a revitalized mental hygiene movement to bring a medicalized and normalized version of psychoanalysis into teacher education and discussions of schooling. The rise of ego psychology intensified the focus on developing a healthy personality and accompanied the drive in education to ensure an academically prepared nation faced with external enemies.

I suggest in Chapter 4 that the failure to work through the traumas of the war and the Great Depression led educators and psychoanalysts to focus on developing a well adjusted, contained, and well armored ego, psyche, and curriculum. If that meant expelling what was threatening, then psychoanalysis and education would work together to ensure mental health at the price of a continued splitting within both professions. Such a history may shed light on the current state of education, when that which is not measurable does not count. As educators willingly embrace or are forced to accept more medicalized models of education as well as the bottom line of performance outcomes, they may meet the same fate psychoanalysts did who rushed to embrace an alliance with medicine: eventually pharmaceutical and behavioral interventions and fixed protocols replace the art of listening and attuning to the idiosyncrasies of one's own or the other's unconscious. The inner life shrinks and disappears behind observable behaviors.

Chapter 5 begins with 1968. I use that year because it marks the surge in the open school movement and also because of the tumultuous events that occurred that year. The year also acts as a synecdoche for the sixties and early seventies, which witnessed the second and last time educators, often unknowingly, would turn to the emancipatory project of psychoanalysis and the radical knowledge of the unconscious to inform educational experiments. The failure of those experiments and the resurgence of calls for a return to basics, standards, objectivity, and performance outcomes perhaps point to the shortcomings of the emancipatory project when it is pressed into the service of the therapeutic.

By the end of the 1970s, the relationship between psychoanalysis and education would have disintegrated had it not been for Jacques Lacan's return to Freud. Chapter 5 offers a brief review of Lacan's theory and his influence in the academy and on curriculum theory. I devote the end of the chapter to those curriculum theorists who have worked psychoanalytically to sustain the relationship between psychoanalysis and education. These educators have kept alive the spark of what I label the emancipatory project at a difficult moment for both professions. I also consider, at the end of Chapter 5, why teacher education, unlike curriculum theory, has ignored psychoanalysis.

In Chapter 6, the concluding chapter, I reconsider the relationship between education and psychoanalysis in light of its reconstructed history. I suggest that in thinking back through the disavowals, splitting, traumas, and defenses that have structured that relationship, and in acknowledging and studying the unconscious and its radical knowledge, we may be able to gain a bit of freedom from the repetition compulsions in which education seems trapped and find another future for the relationship.

Psychoanalysis

I want to say something about my use of psychoanalysis throughout this book. So far I have discussed psychoanalysis as if it were a monolithic movement or theory. Clearly it is not. As Stephen Mitchell and Margaret Black (1995) point out in *Freud and Beyond: A History of Modern Psychoanalytic Thought*, there are "multiple schools of thought, technical terminologies, and forms of clinical practice" (p. xvi). Throughout the book I rely primarily on the work of Freud, although in Chapter 5 I also turn to Jacques Lacan's work.

I have used various psychoanalytic concepts in order, as Sherry Turkle (1992) puts it, "to think through" (p. xxiv) specific issues. I take "thinking through" in three senses. First, I take it to mean using the concept as a lens. The concept enables me to see or articulate what previously I had not noticed. Second, I understand the phrase in terms of Winnicott's (1968a, 1968b, 1968c) notion of using an object— destroying it, rough housing with it, chewing on it, and finally metabolizing it, such that it becomes part of one's psychic life, although it is always going through phases of destruction and resilient come-back in an altered form. And finally, I take it in the psychoanalytic, clinical sense of working through, which refers to a loosening of one's emotional attachment to, in this case, concepts or ways of thinking, including psychoanalytic concepts, and draining them of their fantasmatic attraction.

Openings

As will become clear, I want to resist applying psychoanalytic theory to practice—that is part of the therapeutic project—although I feel continually lured in that direction. My resistance, I believe is occasioned by my own family's gender politics, by my fear that collapsing education into the therapeutic project reduces teachers to robots and curriculum to skill sets, and by my belief that if we focus on applying psychoanalytic theory rather than on thinking through it, we will silence the unconscious and remain trapped in a repetition compulsion. But the question is, then, if one does not apply psychoanalytic theory, how does thinking through it affect what one does in a classroom? In part my argument is that in thinking through psychoanalytic theory, in metabolizing it so to speak, we become to ourselves and to our students different in our teaching. Such a statement, however, recalls the fact that to be a psychoanalyst one must have been psychoanalyzed. While I think that would probably be a good idea for teachers, it is not a realistic proposal. I am offering a much more modest suggestion.

I believe that in studying psychoanalytic theory and the history of the relationship between education and psychoanalysis, we might begin to shift how we think about teaching and what it means to be educated, and we might find it a bit easier to resist today's inexorable and relentless demand that we become programmed teaching machines. The reconstruction of the history between these two professions offers us the opportunity to find language that acknowledges and reclaims a subjectivity absent from current educational discourses that treat the unconscious as a relic of the past. Such a reconstructed relationship may provide teachers with a way to talk to others about the very complicated and elusive work they do and about their relationships with students and their work, without freezing or fixing these. It may provide a way of talking that incites and nourishes curiosity and that can resist the all encompassing embrace of the marketplace, the normalcy of the status quo, and the lure of causal narratives. It may help us see the narrowness of current educational reforms that accept as a given the social and political context, in which those reforms roll out, and it may help us avoid the traps into which psychoanalytically informed radical educators and early progressives fell. Finally, it may allow us to interrupt the repetition compulsion trapping education. These are the possibilities this book offers. They appeal, paradoxically, to the therapeutic project, in that they attempt to cure education of its illness. But they also appeal more substantively to the emancipatory project because such a cure is premised on the acceptance of its own radical uncertainty, and the subversive unconscious that will always and forever disrupt our best intentions, our certainties, and our securities.

For many people psychoanalysis provokes anxiety and suspicion. Certainly when it is paired with education or teaching, visions appear of imposed therapy, a "touchy-feely" curriculum, and dangerous intimacies. When I initially encountered psychoanalysis, it certainly provoked those feelings and images in me. But when I actually entered psychoanalysis to find relief from a sense of anxiety and grim stasis and to understand how I had arrived at such a place of despair, I came to find in analysis and in some psychoanalytic theories ways to make more interesting meanings out of my feelings and experiences, including my experiences as a high school teacher.

Psychoanalysis, after all, does allow us to appreciate the inseparability of our thinking from our personal and collective terrors, pleasures, obsessions, dreams, and desires. It pushes us to explore how we are responsible for the world "out there" and how that world "out there" enters and shapes who we are. If, as Freud argued, psychoanalysis is "a grave philosophy" (quoted in H.D., 1974, p. 18), it is a way of philosophizing shaped by and suffused with the body and one's idiosyncratic emotional and sexual life. After years of resisting psychoanalysis, sometimes for good reasons, I found myself drawn to this "grave philosophy." I came to realize that, as Isador Coriat, the first American born psychoanalyst, stated, "[t]he object of psychoanalysis is not artificial classification but to understand something" (Coriat, 1926, p. 24). The something this book seeks to understand is the relationship between psychoanalysis and education and its implications for teaching.

2

DISAVOWED KNOWLEDGE

Looking back over the patchwork of my life's labours, I can say that I have made many beginnings and thrown out many suggestions. Something will come of them in the future.

(Freud, 1925a, p. 70)

The psychoanalytic century was over before the 21st century had begun. Everyone knew … [p]sychoanalysis was indeed dead.

(Dufresne, 2004)

Freud is dead in America.

(Roudinesco, 2001, p. 62)

Absences

A colleague of mine in education recently told me he was interested in getting his prospective student teachers to "really talk about their feelings about going into teaching." I asked him if he was planning to include psychoanalytic theory in the seminar. Somewhat taken aback, he laughingly stated, "I am not going to do therapy with them!" A year ago, the Head of Brooklyn College's School of Education's Program in School Psychology told me that to be in compliance with NASP—the National Association for School Psychologists—she had to drop psychoanalytic theory from the courses to make room for more outcome-based approaches required for registering their program. Two years ago, during a session at the American Association of Educational Research, a respondent to a new book, one informed by psychoanalytic theory, proclaimed, "I am a Marxist and feminist, so I don't really have much to say about psychoanalysis." It is not only education professors and education programs, however, that seem to eschew or misunderstand psychoanalytic theory. High school teachers, too, seem to know little about it.

In my graduate course on Research Methods in English Education, when I ask the students, all of whom teach high school English, what they know of psycho-analysis, they report knowing some basic terms, that psychoanalysis is about sex and sleeping with your mother, that since it's all your parents' fault no one is responsible for anything, and that it has a history of racism, sexism, and homophobia. While a few have read essays by or about Freud or Lacan, none of the students have con-sidered what it might mean to think psychoanalytically about teaching and education, and none of them know anything about the history of the relationship between psychoanalysis and education. And, I suspect, these students in an urban school of education in New York City know more about psychoanalysis than most aspiring or working teachers do who live outside urban areas.

If you were to ask most teachers or professors today how psychoanalysis or psychoanalytic theory might contribute to their understanding of teaching and education, they would probably look somewhat bewildered or make a joke, or they might talk about diagnosing or counseling kids with emotional problems. I would venture that most K–12 teachers and teacher educators, and a good many professors in the liberal arts and sciences, particularly those outside the humanities, have, at best, a passing knowledge of psychoanalysis. It is likely, too, that such knowledge has come from popular culture or a course in abnormal psychology or select courses in departments of literature, film, and art history. Criticisms of the therapeutic culture and of psychoanalysis raised in the 1970s and 80s by Marxists, feminists, post-structuralists, and critical race theorists may have also provided a picture of psycho-analysis, although a negative one. And, in some instances, familiarity with psychoanalysis may derive from a teacher's or professor's own experience in therapy. If, however, some educators have internalized or are intellectually committed to psychoanalytic theorizing, chances are they have not directed that analysis toward the enigmas of teaching and education.

Absence in Education Programs

Perhaps among K–12 teachers and teacher educators the ignorance about psycho-analysis and its relationship to education is understandable. Today's relentless push to quantify outcomes, prepare students for the global workforce, close the test score gap, and master formulaic approaches to teaching elbows aside considerations of unpredictable subjectivities in the classroom and the antinomy between socio/cultural norms and psychic unruliness. Coursework on Vygotsky, Piaget, and cognitive development may promise greater certainty, generalizability, and applicability than do psychoanalytic theory's insights into the idiosyncratic eruptions of the unconscious. Even those courses that promote the social justice agenda, perhaps the only alter-native discourse to the dominant neoliberal ones of professionalization and de-regulation, collapse subjectivity and the psyche into identity and relations of power. In teacher education programs, speculative theorizing has, itself, been subjected to the criteria of use value in the classroom, and has withdrawn to courses on educational foundations. Those courses, already packed to the gills with everything that is *not* of immediate use in the classroom, pay no attention to the historical relationship between education and psychoanalysis. Nor do they approach psycho-analytic theory the way they might teach, for example, Dewey's pragmatism, that is as a living theory pertinent to understanding teaching and education.

Furthermore, given the dominance of psychology, particularly cognitive psychology, in how we educate teachers and think about teaching (Cochran-Smith and Fries, 2005; Darling-Hammond and Bransford, 2005), it is not really surprising that teachers are unfamiliar with a theory that has been banished from psychology departments. As teaching collapses into applied psychology, psychoanalytic theory, if it appears at all, appears as a revenant or relic from another time.

Absence in Psychology Departments

According to a recent study conducted by the American Psychoanalytic Association's Task Force on Undergraduate Education (Redmond and Shulman, 2008), university and college psychology departments treat psychoanalysis as "desiccated and dead" (p. 393). Analyzing course descriptions at one hundred and fifty public and private undergraduate institutions, which were highly ranked by *U.S. News and World Report*, the study found that only fourteen percent of the more than one thousand courses that referenced psychoanalysis were offered in psychology depart-ments. Redmond and Shulman's finding that in the academy psychoanalysis has been exiled to humanities departments is supported by other researchers investigating the vibrancy of psychoanalytic ideas in psychology departments (Bornstein, 1988, 2001; Gourguechon and Hansell, 2005).

If professors of psychology consider psychoanalysis out of the mainstream and doomed unless it shows "more of an appreciation of empirical rigor and testing," as Scott Lilienfeld, a professor of psychology at Emory University was quoted as stating (Cohen, p. 2007), professors of education, given their attachment to academic psychology (Labaree, 2004; Lagemann, 1989, 2000), are even less apt to turn to psychoanalysis for insights about teacher education or teaching. According to Redmond and Shulman (2008), less than one percent of references to psychoanalysis were found in education courses (p. 398). If we go by presentations at the American Educational Research Association (AERA), the leading educational organization in the United States, one whose presidents have frequently been psychologists, psychoanalysis's absence is glaring. There is no special interest group (SIG) devoted to psychoanalysis, although there are several devoted to cognition, neuroscience, the learning sciences, and aspects of educational psychology. Furthermore, psychoanalysis is not among the descriptors provided for searching for presentations. Reviewing programs from the last two decades, I discovered that out of the thousands of papers presented each year, fewer than five every year were devoted to or referenced psychoanalysis. If we turn to the prominent journals in the field of education, psychoanalysis is rarely mentioned. A search on the ERIC database matching the terms "psychoanal*" and "Freud" and "Lacan" with the terms "classrooms," "pedagogy," "schools," "teacher education," and "curriculum" turned up for each pairing an average of forty articles written between1966 and 2008—less than ten a year.

The absence of psychoanalysis from discussions of teaching and education as well as from teacher education programs is striking, but given its treatment by academic psychology and education's enthusiastic embrace of accountability and standards not surprising. The very aspects of daily life that psychoanalytic theory considers— dreams, slips of the tongue, bungled actions, unintended consequences, and ideas, actions, and feelings that seem to make no sense or disturb us—today's educational approaches ignore or pathologize. Psychoanalytic theory and the knowledge it generates have been banished from schools, from teacher education programs, and, with the exception of a few departments in the humanities, from the academy.

Presence in the Culture

On the other hand, psychoanalysis is everywhere. It has, as W.H. Auden (1940) said in his eulogy for Freud, become "a whole climate of opinion." Psychoanalytic terms and ideas, such as "Freudian slip," "Oedipal complex," "repression," "unconscious," and "phallic," circulate in public discourse, often in the service of humor or glib remarks, but also in private conversations, when we talk about how a friend represses his or her feelings or pursues rejection or about a colleague's unconscious aggression or a daughter's need to separate from her mother. We watch the popular HBO series, *In Treatment*, focused on an analyst and his patients, or Tony Soprano's tumultuous sessions with his shrink in *The Sopranos*. Therapy, in a wide range of forms, continues to draw patients, although insurance companies have shortened the covered time period. The acceptability of seeing a therapist or listening to one on the radio or T.V. suggests that we no longer feel ashamed of talking about our personal problems. Psychiatry, of course, remains an active branch of medicine, particularly now that drugs promise relief from our psychic distress. In the popular media there are the perennial articles announcing or questioning whether or not "Freud is dead," and the tabloids and supermarket magazines overflow with articles analyzing the hidden motives behind celebrities' self-destructive or scandalous acts. In no small part we owe what is seen as our sexually permissive culture and our seemingly endless burbling about feelings to psychoanalysis' breakdown of taboos and its foregrounding of emotional life.

Nevertheless, in the United States, even outside the academy, psychoanalysis and psychoanalytic theory are not widely spoken of today. So, on one hand we live in a therapeutic age. On the other hand, psychoanalytic theory, itself, remains on the culture's margins. Outside of some departments in the humanities, where it tends to exist in the language and form of Lacanian or Žižekian studies, it exerts no influence in the academy. In particular it has failed to play an important role in helping us think about teaching and education. Psychoanalysis is both everywhere and nowhere. It is part of the culture yet remains unrecognized. It is acknowledged yet denied.

Disavowed Knowledge

> [The ego] must now decide either to recognize real danger, give way to it and renounce the instinctual satisfaction, or to disavow reality and make itself believe that there is no reason to fear, so that it may be able to retain satisfaction.
>
> (Freud, 1940b, p. 275)

Now Freud has a term for a situation where something is both known and denied at the same time. He refers to it as disavowal, in German "Verleugnung." His theorization of disavowal evolved over time, but essentially he used the term to refer to a defensive splitting in which threatening knowledge is both denied and acknowledged. On one hand this seems to make no sense. How can you believe in something and not believe in it at the same time? But in fact we do it all the time. One example concerns global warming. Many of us hold that climate change is a reality and yet, in our driving and consuming habits, we act as if we did not take it seriously. Or to take another example, we know that our dog is dead, buried in the ground, but we have on the mantle his ashes and talk to him. Or, another example, we know that there is no real correlation between test scores and intelligence, and yet we act as if we believed that there was. Or, we know that if every student actually did graduate from high school, there would never be enough jobs for them, let alone good ones, but we persist in holding teachers responsible for ensuring all students learn, graduate, and enter the global workforce. Or, one final example, we know that at this very moment insane horrors are occurring in the world, young children raped and mutilated, parents forced to have sex with their kids, or watch them blown up or starve. We know this, and we may even know that our own lifestyles are connected to that suffering, yet we act as if we didn't know, and in fact we can't really hold that knowledge, because it is too de-stabilizing and threatening. If, on the other hand, we don't disavow reality and we choose to face dangerous knowledge, we not only lose the pleasurable feeling we gain from our comfortable beliefs and willed ignorance but experience the accompanying anxiety. And so we paradoxically hold contradictory views at the same time, while disavowing one.

According to Freud (1940a, p. 204), disavowal occurs all the time, but he had more to say about it. He argued that it resulted from an initial threat to a sense of unity, sameness, or oneness, and he gave as the primary example, a little boy's shock at noticing that little girls and, more importantly, the mother did not have a penis. The boy's shock over the missing phallus leads the boy to disavow reality and sustain the belief that indeed his mother or the little girl does have a penis and is like him. According to Freud (1923, pp. 143–44; 1924, pp.184–85), the little boy, during the anguish of the Oedipal drama, recalls the disavowed knowledge and experiences it as traumatic evidence that indeed castration is not an empty threat, but is a real possibility. Thus he gives up his first love, his mother.

While Freud (1925a, pp. 252–53) went on in a later paper to discuss how the little girl may also disavow reality—she imagines she has a penis, in part as a way to imagine individuation from the mother—Freud (1927b, pp.152–57) eventually came to relate disavowal of the mother's lack of the phallus and the defense against fears of castration to fetishism. To take the place of the absent phallus, the boy substitutes for it an object, what Freud calls a fetish, for example a shoe or foot. As he grows older he believes only he knows the true value of the object, although he also knows it is just a foot or shoe. As Laplanche and Pontalis (1973) put it, Freud "shows how the fetishist perpetuates an infantile attitude of holding two incompatible positions at the same time: he simultaneously disavows and acknowledges the fact of female castration" (p. 119). Another interpretation is offered by Slavoj Žižek (1994), who reads the disavowal not in terms of castration but in terms of what the fantasy of castration defends against—the fundamental reality of sexual difference. If the boy imagines castration, he must also imagine that his mother initially had a phallus and thus that there was fundamentally no difference between them.

If we read this primary example of disavowal not in terms of perception (how does one perceive absence rather than a presence?) and instead in terms of, for the boy, anguish and terror over the potential and actual loss not only of pleasure and power but also of sexual sameness and oneness with his mother, or, for the girl, anguish over an *imposed* lost power and unachievable sameness with the father and differentiation from her mother, then disavowal is really about defending against difference, pow-erlessness, and incompleteness, or in the girl's case suffocating sameness. Jane Flax (1990) writes, "[T]he dread of castration appears in part a displacement of more primitive and deeply buried anxieties—the fears of annihilation, loss of love, our aggression and rage at the mother for her autonomy and power over us, and our desire to take that power for ourselves" (p. 80). And in fact Freud does not equate disavowal only with knowledge of the absent phallus, although any disavowal may resonate with castration anxiety.

According to Freud disavowals "occur very often and not only with fetishists" (1940a, p. 204), but they always constitute and result in a splitting. This splitting gives Freud pause, until he theorizes it in terms of the ego.

> [T]he ego often enough finds itself in the position of fending off some demand from the external world which it feels distressing and [this fending off] is effected by means of a disavowal of the perceptions which bring to knowledge this demand from reality. ... The disavowal is always supple-mented by an acknowledgement; two contrary and independent attitudes arise and result in the situation of there being a splitting of the ego. Once more the issue depends on which of the two can seize hold of the greater [psychical energy]. (p. 204)

Freud did not consider this splitting of the ego unusual. He theorized that in the case of neurosis, and we can remember here Bettelheim's description of the relationship between education and psychoanalysis as neurotic, one of the contradictory attitudes is either repressed or disavowed.

> Let us suppose, then, that the ... ego is under the sway of a powerful instinctual demand which it is accustomed to satisfy and that it is suddenly frightened by an experience which teaches it that the continuation of this satisfaction will result in an almost intolerable danger. It must now decide whether to recognize the real danger, ... renounce the instinctual satisfaction, or to disavow reality and make itself believe that there is no reason for fear, so that it may be able to retain the satisfaction. (1940b, p. 275)

But, in fact we take neither course because we take both courses simultaneously. "On the one hand, [we] reject reality. ... ; on the other hand ... [we] recognize the danger of reality, ... and try to divest [ourselves] of the fear" (Freud 1940b, p. 275). And is this not exactly what we have done with psychoanalysis, which is both everywhere and nowhere? It is part of the culture yet remains unrecognized. It is acknowledged yet denied. And in the academy and teacher education it is disavowed.

A Threat to Institutionalized Knowledge

> The experience of wholeness and completeness is an illusion ...
> for it can never become one's own.
>
> (C.Fred Alford, 2003, p. 47)

Why would psychoanalytic knowledge provoke disavowal, and of what would the splitting consist? What is being disavowed, and in what sense does such disavowal echo older castration anxieties? My speculation is that institutionalized knowledge and the aspiration to scientific certainty, control, and prediction on which it is founded cannot bear psychoanalytic knowledge because psychoanalytic knowledge reveals a hole in institutional knowledge, reveals that it cannot ultimately be transparent to itself or one with itself. The knowledge that reveals this hole is knowledge of the unconscious. By that I do not just mean familiarity with how the unconscious works. I also refer to the knowledge that arrives from the unconscious and reveals to us what we do not know, and how we are always already implicated in what we do know and what we resist knowing. The unconscious is not simply an object of knowledge; it is also its subject.

To put this idea another way, we can enlist Shoshanna Felman's (1997) classic essay "Psychoanalysis and Education: Teaching Terminable and Interminable." She writes there that "the unconscious ... is precisely the discovery that human discourse can by definition never be entirely in agreement with itself, entirely identical to its knowledge of itself, since as the vehicle of unconscious knowledge, it is constitutively the material locus of a signifying difference within itself" (p. 24). The point is that the unconscious subverts any "possibility of totalizing what is known or of eradicating one's own ignorance" (p.25), because it reveals the radical otherness within knowledge. In other words, the unconscious not only de-centers us, subverts our sense of ourselves as masters in our own house but also, because it remains outside our rational comprehension of the world and always threatens to disrupt that comprehension, it bores a hole from within that comprehension, exposing its precariousness and incompleteness. For example, we may exalt the edifice of science, but if science can be understood as a defense against our fears of death, then its claim to be the epistemological horizon that keeps expanding but beyond which we cannot go, loses some of its power.

For some time, the academy has blamed postmodernism for the dismantling of grand narratives and for threatening science's status as having the final say, but that maneuver—to blame postmodernism—can be read the way Žižek (1994) reads the boy's fantasy of castration in Freud's explanation. The very idea that his mother had been castrated posited a fundamental sameness that was then taken away. In the same way the attacks on postmodernism can be seen as positing through implication an original fundamental certainty or movement toward certainty that the academy once could claim, when, in fact, there always was a fundamental otherness or difference within the knowledge it produced and laid claim to.

A Threat to the University

Final certainty, of course, may no longer be the aspiration of the corporate university. In its corporate incarnation the university does not aspire to absolute knowledge and mastery but to a constantly receding excellence (Readings, 1996). But even here the unconscious serves as a radical otherness within and threat to the academy. Because *the unconscious is exactly what distinguishes subjectivity from individuality*, psychoanalytic knowledge also threatens an academy or educational system based on neoliberal systems of standards and accountability. Those systems both construct and monitor an individual, who is not only knowable and predictable, but who, with the aim of self-empowerment and growth, endlessly pursues ideals, which are themselves hollow markers, used like the fake rabbit in the greyhound races, to sustain endless progress toward an excellence with no real referent or value.

The individual of the corporate university is transparent to himself or herself, not divided. On the other hand the Freudian subject is not a unified self. "It looks as though his own self were no longer the unity which he had always considered it to be, as though there were something else in him that could confront that self" (Freud, 1926, p. 188). The "something else" is the unconscious. The split and the subjectivity that emerges with it undermine the drive for complete self-control, for the fully administered self, the self measured by defined skills, the self the corporate university puts under surveillance. That is another reason why the corporate university puts an even higher premium on rationality and reasonableness than the Kantian and Humboldtian universities: an individual collapsed into rationality, capable only of thought defined as logical operations, calculation, and reasoning, and pursuing health, defined as adjustment to set norms of beauty and longevity is, like a computer, more easily programmed. When Elizabeth Roudinesco (2001) wrote that "the era of subjectivity has given way to the era of individuality" (p. 3), she was simply gesturing toward the excision or exclusion of the unconscious, and the consequent erasure of a subjectivity torn by moods, dreams, drives, and desires, a subjectivity which resists reduction to social identities or individuality or psychology, a subjectivity threatening to the corporate university.

Psychoanalytic knowledge, therefore, puts into question both the university as a corporation, with its pursuit of content-less excellence, of outcomes, and of transparent communication and with its emphasis on administration, and the university as either Kantian, with its regulatory ideal of reason: "argue as much as you want but obey!" or the Humboldtian, with its regulatory ideal of culture and the unity of knowledge (see Readings, 1996, pp. 54–69, on this distinction). The latter ideal, captured in Arnold's notion of valuing the best that has been thought and said in the world was implicitly one of the subjects of Freud's *Civilization and Its Discontents*. Freud wrote there,

> One thing only do I know for certain, and that is that man's judgments of value … are an attempt to support his illusions with arguments. The fateful question for the human species seems to me to be whether and to what extent their cultural development will succeed in mastering the disturbance of their communal life by the human instinct of aggression and self-destruction. (1930, p. 145)

Even the celebrated *Bildung* so much a part of Humboldt's vision of the university assumes the teleology of cultured de-libidinized rationality within that university, although recent reformations of *Bildung* by Tero Autio (2006), William Pinar (2006a, 2006c), and Sarah Winter (1999) seek to implicate the unconscious in self-formation.

A Threat to Teacher Education

Psychoanalysis also threatens approaches to teacher education and teaching, because it posits an antinomy between the unconscious and the simple induction of students into conventions, culture, and social ideals. Psychoanalytic knowledge renders the meanings of what we are taught or what we study unpredictable and subject to constant revision. Furthermore, psychoanalysis reveals the unconscious drives, like aggression, behind our ideals. "When we read of the atrocities of the past, it sometimes seems as though the idealistic motives served only as an excuse for the destructive appetites" (Freud, 1933b, p. 210). Ideals do not only justify aggression but also can, like our own ego ideals, become voracious task masters, yanking our gaze from the present to focus on the future, and in doing so, keeping us from seeing the present more clearly and more compassionately. And, as if that is not enough, psychoanalytic knowledge, gained from the most trivial, nonsensical, embarrassing, and vulgar sources, gained also, in part, from the domestic sphere so long associated with women, and from family dramas, which it locates everywhere but on which it offers us some perspective, reminds us that subjectivity, understood as an unruly dream-like interplay between an unconscious and an ego, plays havoc with conventions, the right way to be, and the correct answer. Psychoanalysis draws out the un-thought, the otherness in thinking. It keeps thought radically open and phrases rationality, not in terms of linear sequential thinking and experimentally testable hypotheses, but in terms of what Rodinesco described as "thought's ability to invent new explanatory models" (p. 110) and the free associations that bubble up from the unconscious. Knowledge of and from the unconscious disrupts the aspiration to create the smoothly functioning machines with which current educational discourses are so enamored. And it complicates the hope of transforming society through democratic education or teaching social justice.

The Response

This is horrifying knowledge, indeed, and the response of the academy and of teacher education is swift. The only psychology allowed will be a scientific psychology, one whose effects we can test and measure. The only way to understand our mission will be to measure its outcomes. The only approaches to teaching that will be allowed are those that cherish high ideals, appeal to reason, and rely on scientifically based research. And yet ... and yet, the very people who deny its value, participate in their daily lives in and are part of a culture that values therapy and talking about feelings, a culture in which it is natural to point out how someone is unconsciously self-sabotaging or trapped in destructive patterns of behavior. One has to wonder if therapeutic culture, itself, is not a kind of fetish, like the foot or shoe, a reminder of and stand in for what is disavowed. In that case we can read the therapeutic culture outside the university and the airtight administered world of certainty, control, and cure within it, as two forms of defense against the enormous anxiety psychoanalytic knowledge provokes. After all, if, as Freud said, education is impossible, what are we doing?

But perhaps that is the wrong question, although given the century long repetition compulsion trapping teacher educators—the dreary cycle of educational crisis, followed by proffered panaceas, followed by blaming teachers for their failures, followed by new alarms—it may be the right one for schools of education. Perhaps the more interesting question would be how does disavowal work within education and psychoanalysis and how does it split them?

The Split within Education and Psychoanalysis

> This success is achieved at the price of a rift in the ego
> which never heals but increases as time goes on.
>
> (Freud, 1940b, p. 276)

I want to suggest that neither psychoanalysis nor education can tolerate the knowledge of the impossibility of their own respective professions. Psychoanalysis knows that its knowledge is knowledge of the unconscious, and thus it can never be a knowledge that is certain. The analyst who, in Lacan's famous phrase, is the subject presumed to know, can never take him or herself for the subject who actually knows, for the expert. In the relationship between analyst and patient or analyst and analysand, the dynamics of transference and counter-transference interrupt any certainty of what is "really" going on. Furthermore, psychoanalysis knows that analysis is interminable, that the "after education" of which Freud spoke (1916, p. 312; Britzman, 2003), is on-going. Only the analytic perspective of remaining open to the significance of the insignificant, of sustaining as much as possible a free-floating attention as Freud called it, remains un-revised. And finally, psychoanalysis knows that it exists on the border between science and philosophy, that its aim is not the pursuit of truth, but speaking truthfully.

Freud had written Fliess in 1896 the following: "I see how you, through the detour of being a physician, are reaching your first ideal, to understand humans as a physiologist, just as I most secretly nourish the hope of reaching my original goal, philosophy" (quoted in Gay, 2006, p. 118). Thirty-seven years later, in 1933, he would say to the poet H.D. (1974) who was in analysis with him, "My discoveries are not primarily a heal-all. My discoveries are a basis for a very grave philosophy" (p. 18). But such knowledge, that psychoanalysis is not a science in the normal sense, that its material inherently disrupts its own stated goals, such knowledge within psychoanalysis, itself, was threatening. It undermined the desire for cure and for scientific status—for power—and therefore it came to be disavowed. As we shall see in Chapters 3, 4, and 5, the rapid medicalization of psychoanalysis defended against and conspired to disavow the knowledge that psychoanalysis itself couldn't cure or control or predict. It could only offer a particular kind of listening, a particular knowledge, and a particular analytic perspective which could expand meaning, turn misery into existential angst (Britzman, 2003), and cultivate the Eros of thinking.

This split within psychoanalysis hardened, as we shall see, and as it did, psychoanalysis became a stranger to itself, as it disavowed the other at the heart of its endeavor: the Freudian unconscious.

A Split in Education

Education too has always suffered from a fundamental split, caused by its own disavowal of what it knows. What education knows but doesn't want to know it knows is not dissimilar from psychoanalytic knowledge. It knows that there are no foolproof methods, that one can teach exactly the same thing in the same way in two different classes and have totally different results. It knows that the idiosyncratic subjectivities of student and teacher subvert any attempt at controlling outcomes or predicting success. What the teacher considers to have been a fantastic class the students may have found boring, and vice versa. A lecture can hold a class of middle school students enthralled while group work may fall flat. The charisma of the teacher will most often trump the content, but not always. Students interpret, accept, resist, or ignore in a hundred different ways unique to each of them what the teacher says and offers. That which is taught is never synonymous with what is learned, unless what is taught is exactly that which can be reproduced, in which case we have two machines, both transmitting and receiving. Furthermore, on some level teachers know that while they might "touch" that one life, "save" that one mind, or "reach" that one student, the effects they have dissolve into the complicated lives those students lead. The effects exist only as mutable memories, and their visible traces rest in thank you cards filed in a drawer or appear in statements such as: "I wouldn't have been a teacher were it not for you" or "I got out of the neighborhood and into writing because of you." But such sentiments, however genuine, ultimately ignore the fact that all those other students who didn't become teachers, or go into writing, or get out of the neighborhood, also shared that teacher. Those other students seem disinclined to separate out the influence of a particular teacher from the millions of variables shaping their future. And one must wonder if such billiard ball causation is not too simplistic, however comforting it might be to those teachers who enjoy their small victories. Finally, teachers know that for all the talk about their being the most important element in a student's success, or the nation's economic health, or in the solutions to the country's race problems, all these have much more to do with economic and social policies, and with the students themselves than they to do with "my favorite teacher."

Such knowledge is, of course, profoundly unsettling. It can seem to drain the meaning out of one's work. If we are not curing ignorance—ignorance of injustice, of the best that has been thought and said, of disciplinary knowledge, of one's body, of right conduct—then what are we doing? One way to approach such a question is to ask another one: can we teach about these or create conditions to study them without the desire or drive to cure or control? I'll put that question aside for now and return to it in Chapter 6. My point here is that education disavows the knowledge it knows, knowledge of the vicissitudes and effects of the unconscious, and in so doing splits.

The movement toward standards and accountability in the last thirty years is symptomatic of that disavowal and split. The pursuit of scientific certainty has served as a way not to know what education knows. And one might even argue that the social justice agenda, which originally, in its theoretical work, tried to point out how the other lived in us, and how the social penetrated our psyche (see Cho, 2009; Edgerton, 1996; Todd, 1997, 2003), now serves as a kind of fetish for education, much as humanistic therapy has for psychoanalysis. Originally meant to expose and loosen oppressive structures and systems of privilege and inequality, and to reveal the psychic effects of these, the social justice agenda seems to have collapsed into a sociological, psychological, and political gaze that renders subjectivity epiphenomenal to power relations and articulates it in terms of socio/cultural identities and group psychology (Pinar, 2009).

The Therapeutic and Emancipatory Projects

Having suggested these splits within psychoanalysis and education, I now want to give them names. I want to suggest that both psychoanalysis and education have come to be torn between two projects, what I will call the *therapeutic project* and the *emancipatory project*.

Clearly these projects are intertwined as is evident by the fact that both education and psychoanalysis consist of many theories and clinical practices. The difference, I shall argue, is that while both have clinical dimensions, only one project seeks to cure illness or ignorance—the therapeutic project. Furthermore, it is the emancipatory project that is often disavowed because it provokes too much anxiety. The emancipatory project, in its acknowledgment of and respect for the unconscious, reminds education and psychoanalysis of their impossibility and reminds us of our own incompleteness and the inherent messiness of our endeavors. It points out how we can terrorize ourselves and others when we believe we finally know or could finally know who we are and that what we know is beyond doubt. To face such troubling knowledge is to risk annihilation, the loss of love and power, and the confrontation with our own complicated hates, desires, and terrors.

The Therapeutic Project

American analysis became a method of cure and
a form of self-improvement rather than a critical stance.

(Zaretsky, 2004, p. 67)

Reforming the public schools has long been a
favorite way of improving not just education but society.

(Tyack and Cuban, 1995, p. 1)

There are systematic … aspects of effective teaching,
and there is a base of verifiable evidence … that supports
that work. In that sense it is like medicine or engineering.

(Bransford, Darling-Hammond, and LePage, 2005, p. 12)

The therapeutic project focuses on the practical or clinical and aspires either to scientific certainty, so that it can control if not predict its effect, or to truth, so that it can rightfully persuade others of its ideals of health, normalcy, or political rectitude. The goals of the therapeutic project are *caritas*—a presupposed knowledge of what is good for the soul coupled with a love for humankind, and *logos*—a belief in the power and superiority of rationality and logic and that the real *is* rational and the rational *is* real. The therapeutic project places the student or patient at the center of all its efforts, and sets as its sole criterion for success the positive change in both. It therefore subjects all of its theories and methods, including self-exploration, to the criterion of use value in the clinical setting, be it the psychoanalytic session or the classroom. Teacher and analyst are intent, with or without the patient's or the student's full agreement, on moving the patient or student toward health, academic achievement, or a social conscience. The analyst or teacher in such a project may or may not refuse the role of master, at times may present him or herself as an equal to the patient or student, but always assumes the role of a person of care and, more often than not, the one who knows. Such a project culls its language from the sciences and the social sciences, and while it aims for interdisciplinarity, it finds its intellectual roots in psychology, social work, and/or medicine. The therapeutic project offers itself as the solution to many of society's ills—economic decline, mental illness, social injustices—and as a way to cure suffering or ignorance. It promises empowerment, utilitarian problem-solving, and the possibility of social and psychic transformation and mobility. It moves in the direction of progress.

Certainly the therapeutic project has dominated both education and psychoanalysis for most of the twentieth century and is now hegemonic in the beginning of the twenty-first century. The exclusive focus on the therapeutic project, paradoxically, results in a programmed existence—our subjectivities and relationships can be bypassed in our pursuit of fool-proof methods we use to cure, control, and predict. The desires to love and be loved and to know and be known, however, cannot simply or only be reduced to instrumental rationality, although such a reduction always threatens to become a goal of the therapeutic project. But the therapeutic project also reflects our need to point the world out to students, to contradict, without denigrating, the familiar and familial knowledge we learn in our homes and neighborhoods, and to risk knowing what might be better for someone. In that sense the therapeutic project is both necessary and dangerous.

The Emancipatory Project

Any analyst who out of the fullness of his heart, ...
and his readiness to help, extends to the patient all that one human
being may hope to receive from another commits [an] ... error.

(Freud, 1919a, p. 164)

[T]here is no true teaching other than the teaching which succeeds
in provoking in those who listen [the] desire to know which can only
emerge when they themselves have taken measure of ignorance as such—of
ignorance in as much as it is, as such, fertile—in the one who teaches as well.

(Lacan, quoted in Felman, 1982, p. 27)

Analysis is first and foremost a method of deconstruction ...
with the aim of clearing the way for a new construction.

(Laplanche, 1999, p. 165)

The emancipatory project, on the other hand, focuses on all the ways we make sense of or try to understand our experiences, no matter how trivial or traumatic, and brings to bear on that experience and those meanings a particular theoretical orientation that continually puts itself and all else into question. Such a project aspires to free us from our taken-for-granted views of ourselves and others, to loosen the psychic knots and intellectual ruts we find we are stuck in, and to broaden and deepen the meanings we make of our experiences. To that end it opens itself to and values speculation, questioning, tentative understandings, a restless curiosity, and most of all talking freely and truthfully. The emancipatory project places the teacher and analyst at the center of its efforts, because, it argues, both know the student or patient only through the teacher's and analyst's own idiosyncratic subjectivities and through a relationship fraught with unconscious desires and shadows from the past. The analyst or teacher in such a project rejects the role of expert but is willing to assume temporarily but explicitly the position of the one supposed to know, the one who possesses a knowledge rendered vulnerable by its own otherness but for just that reason a knowledge all the more open to encounter.

The emancipatory project culls its language and insights from the humanities, particularly literature and the arts since these carry affective knowledge without assuming to know its meaning in advance (Britzman, 2006). Such a project is inherently interdisciplinary, because it subverts boundaries and reveals the terrors and dreams within disciplinary knowledge. It relies on a critical hermeneutic, but one that attends to its own desires, the unruliness of the body, and both the Eros and aggression of conscious and unconscious thought. At its best such a hermeneutic refuses allegorical readings, assuming that any Ur-text is, itself, contingent and rife with fantasies that defend against fears of loss of control and powerlessness. It offers, as John Rajchman (1991) said of Lacan's teaching, "a form of love that never supposes that it knows what is good for someone else" (p. 43). Finally, and perhaps most important, the emancipatory project asks teacher, analyst, patient, and student to recognize their own psychic complicity in what they claim to know and what they ignore.

The emancipatory project not only raises threatening questions, but also can itself fall into a kind of self-satisfied position of knowing it does not know. Eschewing certainty, the emancipatory project would seem to follow desire wherever it travels and thus to fall into a kind of eternal free association. If a child's interest consists only of watching television or reading Harry Potter, do we as teachers seek to move that child somewhere else or do we follow the child's curiosity, asking questions about the matter at hand? Or do we follow our own curiosity about the child? Desire and its articulations constitute the content in analysis, but what then is the content in a classroom? While the therapeutic project errs on the side of cure and control, the emancipatory project can ignore content, unless desire, itself, read as the child's interests, becomes the content. Certainly in the early part of the twentieth century and in the 1960s and 70s some educators sought to transform the child's desire and interests into the curriculum.

Undeniably the therapeutic and emancipatory projects have overlapped; Freud and Lacan both equivocated on whether psychoanalytic theory was a science, philosophy, or a mode of observing and thinking on the boundary between both. Dewey struggled whether to locate his own pedagogical creed as a science, political program, or philosophy. The two projects I have delineated are ideal types, and their boundaries blur, but I offer them as a way to think about not only what happened to psychoanalysis and education in the twentieth and into the twenty-first century, but also about how the relationship between these two impossible professions became, as Bettelheim said, neurotic. If, in fact, education and psychoanalysis are inherently split and disavow what they know, a relationship between them would be difficult unless they shared similar projects. At those moments a relationship might obtain. That is exactly what happened when the mental hygiene movement arose: the therapeutic projects of both psychoanalysis and education joined forces. To a lesser extent, efforts to combine the emancipatory projects of education and psychoanalysis prevailed in the early part of the century and in the 1970s and 80s. But the need to disavow the more troubling aspects of psychoanalysis and education has always led educators and analysts to defend against the emancipatory project and forward the therapeutic project. That refusal to acknowledge the radical knowledge from and of the unconscious, a disavowal that lies at the heart of the split in these professions, has also led to the vicious cycle in which education gets stuck.

Most of us who teach or practice are committed to both the therapeutic and emancipatory projects, shifting back and forth between them. While the professions may be split, we are too. My own desires to control and to cure, to know with certainty are evident in this writing. I hold in tension the knowledge that I want to sum up, change people's minds, and make a difference or have the final say and be recognized for it and the knowledge that what I have to say is partial, incomplete (I unintentionally wrote "complete"), and not only alchemized in the reading but filled with gaps and the slips of my unconscious. On one hand I wish I could write out of my unconscious; on the other hand I want a perfect product; and on the third hand, anything I do write, perfect or not, will reveal that unconscious. I am drawn, as if inexorably, to wanting to care for and cure my students and I am prone to assume that my methods are responsible for their success or failure. Yet, I also know better, and take a much more modest view of the possibility of progress. I realize that what happens in a class or in schools has much more to do with the psycho/social forces that cannot be captured by and are much more powerful than the imagined bounded unities of individuals exchanging knowledge in a seemingly rational and intentional circuit of communication. I know, too, that those students whom I have encountered long after they graduated, and who tell me how influential I was in some aspect of their life are not lying. But I also know they are conveying something else: some feeling of warmth or gratitude or pleasure or nostalgia, some feeling that is about many, many intangibles other than what they imagine as my influence. Those intangibles, including most importantly their own subjectivity and unconscious desires, fears, and defenses informed the relationship we had with one another and shaped the learning they then, in retrospect, attribute to my teaching. This knowledge, of course, does not prevent me from feeling proud when students do express appreciation or plummeting when they don't, but these swings have more to do with my own needs and desires, conscious and unconscious, than with the students' memories or lack of them.

Such splits go deeper, however, than just the professional schizophrenia that Bettelheim suggested. Perhaps one reason I have been drawn to reconstructing the history of this neurotic relationship between Dr. Freud and teachers has had to do with another relationship between a doctor and teacher—my father and mother or between them as they live in me.

Psychoanalysis tells us that when we talk, we never really know who is talking or for that matter, to whom we are talking. Freud himself suggested as much in a letter to Fleiss (Masson, 1985), when in discussing bisexuality, he claimed that "every sexual act [is] a process in which four individuals are involved" (p. 364). I suspect he underestimated the number, but his comment gestures toward the fact that an analyst may discover he or she is a different gender when the patient starts talking and even that gender may change during the session or over time. I wonder which of my parents these two projects—the emancipatory and therapeutic—are as I write and how that shifts. Both were at times intent on curing and controlling although in different ways. My father controlled by removing himself, through a kind of distance—I suspect he was controlling his own anxiety at times. My mother controlled by being helpful, another way to handle anxious feelings. But both also seemed to use humor to put into question any certainty. Nothing was always and forever *that* serious. Was that, too, a defense or was it rather the recognition that the unconscious, as Lacan said, "always fails, laughs, and dreams" (2008, p. 81)? Certainly in thinking back about my family in light of these projects, splits, and disavowal, there are no easy causal narratives.

Whether she was comforting me or teaching me, my mother would frequently begin her sentences with, "Let me ask you this," and there followed an open ended question, one to which she already had settled on an answer. My father would offer homilies as advice "Everyone puts their pants on the same way—one leg at a time," and test me on homework with some impatience, wanting me to get the right answer. Who was the analyst here, who the teacher? Which was the emancipatory project, which the thereapeutic? While I identified and felt closer to, enamored of, my mother, I found as I wrote the following chapters that the figures to whom I devoted the most space were men. Initially I justified this on the grounds that women analysts were few, but I believe my exclusion also had to do with my own identification with my mother and my aggression toward, fear of, and guilt about my father. At times I longed for him to break up the intense dyadic relationship with my mother, to offer the warmth of a large hand in which he'd held mine when I was very young, and I hated him at times for doing neither. But I also felt guilty that he seemed so vulnerable at times—I recall my mother telling me how his feelings had been hurt when I called him "baldy." I suspect too that her way of expressing love was often in terms of feeling sorry for oneself and others, a mode not unfamiliar to me, and one that can bury more aggressive feelings. And I am sure I was unconsciously terrified of losing my father's love and being punished for my perhaps semi-realized fantasy of taking or being his wife and rejecting him. And so the, men that appear in these chapters and my critiques of them may reproduce those familial dramas. But they also have some attachment to a history that cannot be absorbed into or fully explained by personal dramas.

Reconstructing the Past

> [I]t is, I am suggesting, a matter of ... constructing an
> alternative legacy out of the archive of symptoms and
> parapraxes that bear witness to what could have been
> but was not.
>
> (Santner, 1990, pp. 152–53)

The history of the relationship between psychoanalysis and education that I have tried to recover is in fact a particular kind of reconstruction, not unlike the reconstruction that patients do during analysis. In "Constructions in Psychoanalysis," Freud (1937a, p. 259) stated that the task of the analyst is to "construct" the past based on traces in the present, and he compares such work to archeological excavation. The work of construction, Freud writes, "or, if it is preferred, reconstruction, resembles to a great extent an archeologist's excavation and reconstruction of some dwelling place that has been destroyed or buried" (p. 259). Just as the archeologist proceeds with his work of building a house from the ruins of the past "so does the analyst proceed when he draws inferences from the fragments of memories, from associations and from the behavior of the subject in analysis" (p. 259). Now the first question one might ask is how can one determine the truth of such a "reconstruction"? Freud (1918) raised this question in terms of the primal scene described in the Wolfman's case history. Was the primal scene real or was it a fantasy? In asking that question Freud was raising another question, one which disturbs taken for granted assumptions about psychoanalysis.

Psychoanalysis is frequently interpreted as a process whereby repressed content is brought into the patient's awareness. In other words the content, like the buried house in Freud's analogy, is waiting to be revealed. Such a view, I would argue is implicit in the therapeutic project, which seeks to bring the past into consciousness so the patient will be cured. Were I to follow such logic, I would argue that by reconstructing the past of psychoanalysis's relationship with education, I would cure it of its neurosis; the two impossible professions could get along. The split would be fused. But this I think misses one of the radical points in Freud's work, which is that no narrative can capture what "actually happened" or can establish a cause and effect relationship between the past and present. This was the radical move Freud made when he decided that even if his patients had been molested or seduced as children, their Oedipal fantasies would still be important to consider as central to their construction of reality.

Only in their passionate but defensive attachment to ideals and cure do those who take up the therapeutic project rejoice when the patient says, "Ah yes, I see now, I have problems with sustaining relationships because my mother was too intrusive." We come to understand why, to take this example, we have problems sustaining relationships, not by locating and fixing the truth of a determinant historical event or generalization which is then assumed to explain all the minute comings-and-goings and the impossible complexity of a life lived. We come to some deeper or more complicated sense by gradually allowing these causal narratives to emerge as reconstructed and then to dissipate under further analysis, as we come closer and closer to taking responsibility for not only their construction but their inadequacy. The narratives we at first produce, so often causal and so often drenched in tears, function not to reveal the origin of our sickness, but to puncture or rupture or revive anaesthetized or numb psychic areas, after which the narratives lose their force. We come to understand that all we see, including our reconstructed past, is always from a certain perspective, our own. We are invited by analysis to take responsibility for that perspective.

The work of history then is always "shot through," as Walter Benjamin (1969) said, "with explanation" (p. 89). An emancipatory project would aim at analyzing those explanations as fantasies that may be defensive, perhaps, but are always libidinzed, always bear traces of the unconscious, and always are implicated in the social. They are our own subjective but never individual creations.

But there is another element in the reconstruction of all these histories—the history of the relationships among psychoanalysis, education, between my parents, and me. Melancholia lingers beneath the surface of the writing. The extended passages reproducing other people's words, which assume such an important place in this book, constitute a refusal to let go of a history that I kept looking for but was unable to find. Melancholia haunts all histories, but in this particular project, I have yearned for something that may never have actually been—a moment when education took seriously the profoundly disturbing knowledge of the unconscious and its implications. Such a moment may never have occurred, but is it possible to reconstruct another history, one hidden in the one that was, one which might offer the potentiality for such moments?

In *Stranded Objects: Mourning, Memory, and Film in Postwar Germany*, Eric Santner (1990), discussing ways to reconstitute a cultural identity in post World War II Germany out of the psychic wreckage from that period, suggests such reconstruction of alternative legacies requires careful attention to the "signs of a history-that-might-have been" (p. 153) and to the archive of symptoms contorting the under-surface of everyday family and private life. He writes:

> It might be possible to discover in the lives, in the words, in the faces and bodies of the parents traces of another history, another past that might have

been but was not. The 'oppressed past' that Benjamin speaks of is, in other words, one that never took place but that nevertheless might become available to future generations. This past would be … a construction. It would be pieced together out of a different sort of stranded object. … These stranded objects would be composed of symptoms. (p. 152)

Let us add to "parents" in this quote educators and psychoanalysts. But from what symptoms would we piece together an alternative history? Freud taught us that symptoms were another way the unconscious remembers. Santner describes them as "traces of another, unconscious reality that haunts one's conscious reality like a revenant being" (pp. 152–53). They are "traces of knowledge denied, of deeds left undone, of eyes averted from pain, of shades drawn, of moments when it might have been possible to ask a question or to resist, but one didn't ask and one didn't resist" (pp. 152–53). It seems to me, given Santner's interesting approach to constructing a past, that one approach to the history of the relationship between education and psychoanalysis is to call attention to the symptoms from its past. Such symptoms may be the repetition compulsions, the failed experiments, the dis-avowals, the anxieties, and the mechanically repeated hopes that seem to haunt education and psychoanalysis. These need to be reconstructed for us to rethink or to think through their relationship. And, I would add, we need to reconstruct the fantasies harbored by both education and psychoanalysis, including the one about the beginning of their relationship.

Primal Scenes

According to Laplanche and Pontalis (1973) the primal scene, one of three primal fantasies, the others being of castration and seduction, "provide[s] a representation of and a solution to" a fundamental enigma "which confront[s] the child" and "pictures the origin of the subject" in the child's fantasy surrounding the parents' having sexual intercourse (p. 332). But this fantasy of the primal scene is itself formed within the history of the family and within the culture transported and transmuted by the family. The primal scene then is always part of the history of the social, the history of the family, and the history of the subject. With the under-standing, then, that the primal scene may in fact be a fantasy but one grounded in the real of history and one which may open up areas that have been disavowed, let me turn now to the primal scene of the meeting between education and psychoanalysis in the United States—the Clark Conference in 1909.

3

BEGINNINGS: 1909 TO WORLD WAR II

The Clark Conference

> In a sense [psychoanalysis] owed most of its initial momentum
> in this country to this meeting.
>
> (Hall, 1923, p. 333)

Background

The fall of 2009 marked the one hundredth anniversary of Sigmund Freud's one and only visit to the United States. In September of 1909 Freud and Carl Jung traveled to Clark University to receive honorary degrees in, respectively, psychology and pedagogy and to present a series of lectures. They had been invited to the twentieth anniversary celebration of Clark by its president, G. Stanley Hall, one of America's preeminent child psychologists and educators and considered by many to be the father of child development and adolescent psychology. He not only had established at John Hopkins the United States' "first systematic research laboratory" in psychology and been recognized by Wilhelm Wundt as "the first to introduce experimental psychology into America, [and] recognize its influence for pedagogy" (Rosenzweig, 1994, p. 82), but, as president of Clark, he also had overseen the creation of a department of psychology and pedagogy.

Such a combination of disciplines was unusual at the time, since at many colleges and universities, such as Harvard, psychology was part of the philosophy department (Rosenzweig, 1994, pp. 83, 92). Pedagogy or teacher training was housed in normal schools or a few scattered departments of teacher education, where it consisted most often of coursework in philosophy, rhetoric, history, and law (Lucas, 1999). In fact, thirty years previous to the visit most academic "psychologists were professors of philosophy and saw their psychological work as intimately related to their philosophic commitments" (Koch and Leary, 1985, p. 16). The separation of philosophy and psychology proceeded in the other direction as well. In 1901 philosophers founded the American Philosophical Association "as a splinter group from the American Psychological Association, which, since its founding by Hall in 1892, had served as the professional organization for both psychologists and philosophers" (Toulmin and Leary, 1985, p. 599). Hall was not only carving out a new department in psychology and tying it to education but in bringing Freud to the university was recognizing the importance and centrality of psychoanalysis to both psychology and education at the very moment when both were separating from philosophy and finding a home in the social sciences.

The honorary degree bestowed on Freud would be the only one he received, and he was fifty-three when it was awarded. To provide support for Jung and Freud, particularly for Freud, who suffered on the trip from colitis and fainting spells, their colleagues, A.A. Brill, Sandor Ferenczi, and Ernest Jones, accompanied them to Clark. While Freud had been dubious about traveling to the States and worried about the American receptivity to psychoanalysis, he apparently viewed the invitation as a kind of arrival. "As I stepped onto the platform at Worcester" he wrote in his autobiographical study, "it seemed like the realization of some incredible day-dream: psychoanalysis was no longer a product of delusion, it had become a valuable part of reality" (Freud, 1925c, p. 52). While Freud was ambivalent about bringing psychoanalysis to the States—he is often erroneously quoted as saying he was bringing the plague—he understood he had indeed arrived in both senses and that those he was about to address represented some of the best minds in America.

The Attendees

It was by all accounts a successful conference. Certainly it was well attended. According to Saul Rosenzweig's (1994) exhaustive account, of the twenty-nine "distinguished lecturers" in disciplines that ranged from history and mathematics to psychology and pedagogy, twenty-one received honorary degrees (p. 119). George Prochnik (2006) describes the conference as "a kind of middle-aged, intellectual Woodstock" (p. 99), and argues that it "embodied that American faith in the possibility of gathering the fruits of the globe, transmogrifying them and then re-exporting them to universal, salvational effect" (p. 99). Indeed, in addition to the highly respected international academics honored, several other well-known intellectuals attended, among them the anarchist, Emma Goldman.

Emma Goldman

Goldman had heard Freud lecture thirteen years earlier in Vienna, where his talk, according to her autobiography, helped her grasp "the full significance of sex repression and its effect on human thought and action" and to "understand myself and my own needs" (quoted in Rosenzweig, 1994, p. 133). Her presence at Clark was documented by the *Boston Evening Transcript,* which was covering the events. They reported that she asked Freud several questions about education at the end of one of his lectures. "Is not pedagoguery today filling the minds of the child with predigested food, instead of aiming to bring out his individuality? ... Does not successful teaching depend on individuality rather than method?" she asked (quoted in Rosenzweig, 1994, p. 132). Goldman's interest in education was at a high point, and a year after the conference, she would be instrumental in the opening of New York's Ferrer School, one of the many schools in the Modern School Movement (Avrich, 1980, p. 69). The commitment of that movement to anti-authoritarianism not only had roots in anarchism but also in Freudian psychoanalysis.

According to Rosenzweig, Freud was pleased with Goldman's questions about education, which is not surprising given that over his lifetime Freud at times turned his attention to education, swinging between a therapeutic project and an emancipatory one. Toward the end of his life he wrote that the "application of psychoanalysis to education, to the upbringing of the next generation" is "exceedingly important, [and] rich in hopes for the future, perhaps the most important of all the activities of analysis" (1933a, p. 146), but four years later, as he had before, he would refer to education as an impossible profession capable only of achieving "unsatisfying results" (1937b, p. 248).

It is also not surprising that Goldman raised questions about education, given that the conference in many ways addressed Hall's view "that education had become 'the chief problem of the world, its one holy cause'" (Hall, quoted in Prochnik, 2006, p. 99). That view was, according to Prochnik, shared by several of the conference attendees.

> The whole concept of the Clark Conference was conceived in a spirit of educational idealism stamped with American self-improvement mania ... [T]he entire first week ... was devoted not to experimental science but to a discussion of the current state and future needs of child welfare operations in the U.S. (p. 98)

This optimistic sense, shared by Americans like John Dewey, William James, Theodore Roosevelt, and Woodrow Wilson, the latter two students of Hall, that education held the key to national progress and social uplift, was, as C.A. Bowers (1967) suggests, a hallmark of progressive education, although given its centrality to the current neoliberal reforms imposed on U.S. education, it may simply reflect a strain of corporate boosterism and the faith that the United States' future is hers alone to shape. Such views would come in conflict with what would be Freud's growing pessimism about human perfectibility.

Franz Boas, William James, Adolf Meyer, Edward Titchener, William Stern

Luminaries in psychology and anthropology, disciplines increasingly connected to education, attended the lectures over the course of the four days. We know Franz Boas, who received an honorary degree, was there and that he along with Edward Sapir would be central in introducing psychoanalysis to anthropology. William James, who had written *Talks to Teachers* (1958) fifteen years earlier, and would remember Freud as being closed-minded, was present. So was the physician Adolf Meyer, a prominent psychopathologist, who was influenced by Edward Thorndike. Meyer would go on to chair the department of psychiatry at Johns Hopkins, and, when he was in New York, dine frequently with John Dewey. Around the time of the conference Meyer was becoming interested in the mental hygiene movement to which he would supply the name and some of its ideas. Eventually he would come to describe the Freudian unconscious as "an imagined cesspool" (quoted in Zaretsky, 2004, p. 83), a description perhaps influenced by his mentor, Thorndike, who had gone so far as to describe Hall's work as "chock full of errors, masturbation and Jesus" (quoted in Lagemann, 2000, p. 57). One can only imagine what Thorndike thought of Freud. According to Ruth Leys (Leys and Evans, 1990), the contrast between Meyer and Freud "could hardly have been greater" (p. 99). "Everything of interest to Freud … was omitted by Meyer in the positivist belief that the truth of the patient's biography could be known objectively to both patient and physician by a process of direct observation" (p. 99). Meyer's ambivalence about psychoanalysis was not lost on Freud (Hale, 1995a).

Edward Titchener, who received an honorary doctorate and whom Hall described as easily the first among experimental psychologists (Rosenzweig, 1994, p. 200) was also in attendance. Titchener would conduct a correspondence with Meyer over several years, although the two men would never agree, the former being an experimentalist and the latter a psychobiologist. In one of his letters to Meyer, Titchener would recall his meeting with Freud at Clark. He wrote, "I think his psychology is antediluvian and his constructions largely precarious" and his "psychology is a very outworn travesty of psychology" (quoted in Leys and Evans, 1990, p. 95). Titchener and Meyer were not the only ones at Clark in 1909 to pursue a different path than that articulated by Freud. William Stern, who had been on board the ship that brought Jung, Ferenczi and Freud to the States, was also present.

Stern had reviewed Freud's *The Interpretation of Dreams* in 1901 and had expressed doubts about its scientific validity. According to Rosenzweig (1994), "[h]e believed that Freud's uncritical treatment of the topic would lead readers 'to end up in complete mysticism and chaotic arbitrariness'" (p. 55). Clearly Stern's review bothered Freud because on the trip over, Freud referred to him as "a shabby Jew" (quoted in Rosenzweig, 1994, p. 57), suggesting, according to Rosenzweig, that not only did Freud see Stern as a rival but he also projected onto him his own self-loathing. Stern, praised by Titchener at the conference, would go on to make a name for himself in academic psychology. In 1911 he introduced the concept of the "Mental Quotient," which Lewis Terman, another of Hall's students, would then transform into the intelligence quotient or I.Q.

Given the skeptical reaction of some of the more prestigious personages at the Clark Conference, it would not be surprising if Freud quickly surmised the obstacles that lay ahead for psychoanalysis's reception in the United States. Certainly it was clear the criterion of scientific validity would be used to keep psychoanalysis out of the academy and perhaps out of the country. Were it not for the efforts of one man, psychoanalysis might have remained a European phenomenon.

James Jackson Putnam

Perhaps most important for Freud and the future of psychoanalysis was the presence at the conference of Dr. James Jackson Putnam, the celebrated Boston neurologist, who, along with A.A. Brill, would found the American Psychoanalytic Association and be its first president. According to Nathan Hale (1995a), Saul Rosenzweig (1994), Clarence Oberndorf (1953), and George Prochnik (2006), who is Putnam's great-grandson, Putnam deserves credit for the initial spread of psychoanalysis among neurologists and psychiatrists. It was to Putnam's camp in the Adirondack Mountains that Freud, Ferenczi, and Jung traveled after the conference, and it was Putnam, whom Freud would later describe as "not only the first American to interest himself in psycho-analysis, but [its] most decided supporter and its most influential representative in America" (1921b, p. 269).

Particularly noteworthy is Putnam's interest in the philosophical and ethical applications of psychoanalysis. Prochnik argues that for Putnam, "psychoanalysis could not stand alone ... [but] had to be supplemented with philosophy and attentiveness to the complex needs of the human spirit" (Prochnik, 2006, p. 9). While Putnam, unlike many of his other colleagues in neurology and psychiatry, did not draw back from Freud's claims about Oedipal desires—he himself confessed to Freud and tried to work through the "repressed devils" (Prochnik, 2006, p. 275) of his erotic love for one of his daughters—he did struggle with what he perceived to be the absence in psychoanalysis of a spiritual and socially ameliorative dimension. Deeply committed to social causes—he had crusaded against the "effects of lead in water pipes" (Prochnik, 2006, p. 52)—he also had exerted a strong influence on Susan Blow, serving as her informal analyst during her bouts of depression, while she served in part as his spiritual advisor. Susan Blow founded America's first public school kindergarten (Cremin, 1988, p. 547), and, mentored by and in collaboration with William Torry Harris, she "became a leading advocate for early childhood education in the Midwest" (Prochnik, 2006, p. 66). Blow, in turn, pushed Putnam to temper the darker aspects of psychoanalysis and its radical skepticism with an idealism and a belief in the power of education, albeit one informed by particular insights of psychoanalysis, to transform human beings. In the last paragraph of his concluding opus, *Human Motives*, which sought to synthesize all his beliefs, Putnam wrote,

The choice of motives, whether voluntary or instinctively made, must depend in the final analysis on the standards arrived at through education, the true function of which consists in leading to the discovery of deeper and deeper relationships between the outside and the inner life. (quoted in Prochnik, 2006, p. 347)

"The system of education Putnam was championing was in fact identical to the one supported by ... William T. Harris" (Prochnik, 2006, p. 347), who, according to Cremin (1988), saw education as inculcating transcendent ideals, adaption to society, and self-restraint (pp. 161–62).

In his *An Autobiographical Study*, Freud (1925c) would write about Putnam that "the only thing in him that was disquieting was his inclination ... to make [psychoanalysis] the servant of moral aims" (pp. 51–52). This tension between morality and psychoanalysis would quickly seep into the relationship between education and psychoanalysis. In it we see the tension between the therapeutic and emancipatory projects, and, in part, we can read Putnam's advocacy of the former as a result of his own disavowal of the radical nature of the unconscious, which he saw as leading to an overwhelmingly pessimistic view of human development.

Educators would seek to build character based on a variety of ideals ranging, for example, from social adaptation to social transformation, or from creative individuality to collective solidarity, while psychoanalysis put into question the very notion of ideals and exposed their potentially deadly aspects. The intent to place psychoanalysis in the service of morality, or the regulation, restriction, and policing of desires in the name of an unquestioned higher social purpose and social adjustment was antithetical to psychoanalysis's radical skepticism. And yet that intent would inform most of the attempted applications of psychoanalytic theory to education, finding its clearest manifestation in the mental hygiene movement that would play such a major role in progressive education. As psychoanalytic theory eventually splintered, transformed, and assimilated to medicine, and, as it accommodated itself to the optimism and faith in progress so prevalent in the United States, it was pressed into the service of creating what Putnam called "the best self and the best selves of other men" (quoted in Prochnik, 2006, p. 346). It began to lose the very aspect to which Freud alluded when he stated that psychoanalysis "stands in opposition to everything that is conventionally restricted, well-established and generally accepted ... [including the] obscurantism of educated opinion" (1941, p. 178). But such transmutation of its emancipatory project was yet to come.

As I read about Putnam, I found myself drawn to this complicated man, who followed psychoanalysis into the dark corners of his own desires but also held fast to a higher power and a belief in progress although not necessarily perfection. I think teachers and teacher educators find the lure of the transcendent—the belief that we can change lives for the better—compelling. Like Putnam I feel torn between wanting to hold to ideals and hope—do these not inspire?—and the knowledge that those very ideals and hopes may harbor and serve our most aggressive impulses and most brutal politics, may in fact compensate for other life losses, which then filter back into our practice. We know the sadism that can be committed in the name of ideals and how hope can keep us from taking action in the present, and yet, Putnam's struggle is not unfamiliar to those of us who teach and who think psychoanalytically.

Often, when I teach at the high school I helped start some years ago in an impoverished area in Brooklyn, or even when I teach some education students at the urban college where I am a professor, I find that students respond to slogans almost more than they do to complicated ideas. I wonder if it is the chaotic conditions in their neighborhoods, families, or lives that make them grasp at twelve stop aphorisms or slogans meant to capture ideals and hopes. Or, given that the allure of sound bites and slogans seems widespread, perhaps it is the impatience with and fear of chaos and complexity that make such slogans attractive. I certainly have taken comfort in them at times. But I question whether such slogans, not unlike Putnam's and Blos's religious quotations and proverbs, shut down thinking. I wonder whether in their apotropaic function they defend against ideas worth exploring, and whether they accompany the kind of obsessional neurosis Freud called religion (1927a, p. 43). What terrors do such talismans guard against? What messiness or recognition of human imperfection do they ward off? Certainly it was the belief in the transcendent, as a way to direct and order our personal affairs, over which Freud and Putnam disagreed.

The Clark visit, according to Nathan Hale, (1995a) "was a decisive event in the history of psychoanalysis in America for several reasons—the moment at which it occurred, the personal relationships it established, the impression Freud's visit created in a few strategically placed Americans" (p. 4). Most historians agree that after the conference, attention to psychoanalysis grew in discussions in the press, among avant-garde intellectuals, and in the academy (see Hale,1995a and 1995b; Oberndorf 1953; Prochnik 2006; Rosenzweig 1994; Zaretsky 2004), so much so that "[b]y 1910 psychoanalysis had become one of the most fiercely debated subjects in American neurology and psychiatry" (Hale, 1995a, p. 274). The Clark visit, Freud would often say, was the first official recognition of psychoanalysis and, in his view, was a great success. Freud's enthusiasm and appreciation of Hall's efforts might have been tempered if he knew that he was not Hall's first choice to be the star speaker at the conference.

Wilhelm Wundt

Hall had initially asked his own teacher, Wilhelm Wundt, the father of experimental psychology and a mentor to William James, to come to Clark, but Wundt had declined the invitation for reasons of health (Rosenzweig, 1994, p. 24). While the invitation had been sent to Freud on the same day as the one to Wundt, Hall offered Freud less money and the dates were inconvenient for Freud. For those reasons Freud declined. It was only after Wundt's declination, owing to health, that

Hall offered Freud more money and a change of dates (see the Freud-Hall correspondence in Rosenzweig, 1994, pp. 339–44).

The fact that Freud may be seen to have been a second choice, and that the inability of Wundt's student to attend opened a place for Jung is interesting in retrospect, in that it portends the respective places psychoanalysis and experimental psychology would come to play in the academy. It is important to remember that for psychologists, particularly academic psychologists, Wundt was and is considered the father of scientific psychology, so much so that the American Psychological Association used the founding of Wundt's Leipzig laboratory for the centennial celebration in 1979 of the hundredth anniversary of scientific psychology (Koch and Leary, 1985, p. 1). In *A Century of Psychology as Science*, Koch and Leary write:

> What Wundt effectuated by his 'founding' was a semantic change: one of a very curious character. … It was the stabilization of *a* meaning of a word that had been invited and worked toward over several prior centuries and an arrogation of that 'new' meaning to sovereign status relative to all prior usages in the history of thought. Henceforward the core meaning of 'psychology' would be dominated by the adjectives *scientific* and *experimental* (italics in original). (1985, p. 8)

Not unlike the theory of the man who replaced him at Clark, Wundt's experimental psychology, however, in its transatlantic migration "was divorced from the philosophical context that had originally nurtured its existence. … [and] was transplanted into a pragmatic soil that … abided overt philosophical nurturance less and less" (Toulmin and Leary, 1985, p. 594). Wundt, himself, had warned against separating psychology from departments of philosophy and opposed the "creation of a separate discipline of psychology" (Winter, 1999, p. 162). In America Edward Titchener, who was at Clark, completed the positivistic rendering of Wundt's psychology and "did much to instigate the movement toward reductionist … empiricism in American psychology" (Toulmin and Leary, 1985, p. 599). Increasingly in the United States, Freud's "hope of reaching [his] original goal, philosophy" (Freud, quoted in Gay, 2006, p. 118) would be dashed against the rocks of pragmatism and scientism.

It is interesting to pause here and wonder if on some level Freud knew that he had not been Hall's first choice and whether such knowledge rumbled his own insecurities about being recognized. Certainly his enormous ambitions were causing him problems. He himself interpreted his urinary incontinence on the trip in terms of his professional status and acceptance in the United States (see Rosenzweig, 1994, p. 65 and Prochnik, 2006, p. 95). It would not be surprising then if certain insecurities crept into the initial founding of the relationship between education and psychoanalysis, insecurities about professional and scientific status. Certainly if we read the views about Freud expressed by James, Meyer, Stern, and Titchener, we can fathom how Freud may well have sensed, at the very least, their skepticism about his work. We have to wonder what effect the doubts about his work had on him. It is not surprising perhaps that at the conclusion of his third lecture at Clark—he was there after all to educate—he would say that resistance to his ideas "finds it easy to cloak itself as an intellectual rejection" and that "our opponents" reveal "a very marked affective influence upon their judgmental capacity which tends to diminish it" (quoted in Rosenzweig, 1994, p. 424). One can certainly hear in such a claim Freud's insistence that affect and cognition were inseparable. But perhaps more important, one can also hear in such a preemptive defense the anxiety that would creep into the relationship between education and psychoanalysis—anxiety around both fields' relationship to science.

The issue here is not the old complaint that psychoanalysis rejects any criticism or disagreement by labeling it resistance. Sometimes the complaints or criticism may be resistance. And sometimes they may be an understandable defense against psychoanalytic interpretations wielded as weapons or veiled moral judgments. Rather, the issue is that the emancipatory project of psychoanalysis requires a suspension of certitudes and taken-for-granted common sense so that one can be attentive in a different way, so that one can notice the affective shocks, the odd mishaps, and the strange dreams that emerge from the trivia of daily life and that can be formed into new and interesting meanings. It was only when psychoanalysis labeled as resistance the rejection of *a priori* interpretations or disguised moralizing, only when it labeled as resistance the challenge to its dogma, that it could rightfully be called totalitarian. But it would take an alliance with medicine and the muting of its emancipatory project for that to happen. Freud's preemptive move in the Clark lectures can be read, then, in terms of his unwillingness to cede the horizon of value and meaning to science as it was understood by men such at Meyer, Stern, and Titchner.

While psychoanalysis would in the years ahead certainly enter popular culture and gain professional recognition, particularly through its alliance with the field of medicine, it would always stand on precarious ground in the academy, never achieving the status held by experimental psychology, the related testing and measurement movement associated with Edward Thorndike (see Hale 1995b; Hunt, 1994; Winter, 1999), behaviorism, or cognitive psychology. It was the work of Wundt, Thorndike, and Watson and their descendents, particularly the behavioral and cognitive psychologists, as opposed to psychoanalysis, that would exert the greatest influence on the way educational institutions in the United States came to understand their mission, the organization of knowledge and teaching (see Lagemann, 2000).

I have dwelled at some length on the Clark Conference because I have found it interesting that at the place where psychoanalysis would begin its future in the United States, one can already see in the various personages attending the conference, or in Wundt's case, noticeably absent, the forces that would shape psychoanalysis over the next century and in particular its relationship with education. In Titchener and Wundt we see the drive toward a positivist psychology; in Hall the interest in establishing a child centered educational psychology; in Meyer, the emergence of the mental hygiene movement; in James the pragmatism that would influence progressive education; in Putnam the liberal hopes for harmonious relations among individuals and the seeds of what would become a humanistic psychology seeking to realize human potential; and in Goldman the interest in psychoanalysis as a way to throw off the shackles of a repressive society and build a new social order. Each of these strands: academic psychology, child-centeredness, the mental hygiene movement, pragmatism, the focus on individual self-realization and social efficiency, and the drive for social transformation would constitute the therapeutic projects of psychoanalysis and education, and would in varying degrees denounce, appeal to, claim allegiance with, integrate, react to, and, when it came to its more radical aspects, disavow the emancipatory project of psychoanalytic theory that Freud offered at Clark. And each of these strands would influence approaches to pedagogy and how education was understood for much of the twentieth century.

Primal Scene

I referred earlier to the Clark Conference as a primal scene and I want now to explain why. Freud used the term to specify the child's first sight or sensation of the parents' sexual intercourse, but Freud never concluded to his own satisfaction whether the scene was a retroactively constructed fantasy, a primal fantasy that partook of some pre-subjective mythopoeiac structure, or whether its basis lay in empirical reality. Freud did maintain that the scene influenced how the child would form identifications and desires. In such a scene, which is not unlike a dream, the child is both in it and out of it, participant and observer. The complexity of the scene, therefore, makes it difficult to know from where and whom the child desires and with whom he or she identifies. I wonder if part of my reason for referring to the Clark Conference as a primal scene had to do with the fact that my own identifications were ambiguous. Drawn to Freud, I also identify with Putnam, and know that the other strands that were represented in Worcester also shape my relations to teaching and my own pedagogical desires. Furthermore, as my own parental figures became identified with the psychoanalyst and the teacher, the medical and the pedagogic, the therapeutic and the emancipatory, although at times changing places, I wondered if I was trying to reconstruct some primal scene between my parents and between education and psychoanalysis. Did I need to assure myself I was the psychic offspring of both? And finally, my setting the conference up as a primal scene speaks to Freud's own ambivalences. He referred to the event as the realization of a day-dream, but he detested America and resented that his fame might lie in "Dollaria", as he referred to the country (Danto, 2005, p. 147).

Let us now turn to the lectures themselves presented extemporaneously at Clark that warm September of 1909. Freud's (1910a) five lectures given at Clark appear in revised form in the *Standard Edition*, and they reflect the revisions Freud made over the three months between delivering and writing them. I have, therefore relied on Rosenzweig's publication of the lectures as they were originally presented. Quotes below are taken primarily from the lectures, as given and recorded by Rosenzweig. Other quotes, as specified, are taken from the *Standard Edition* of Freud's works.

The Lectures

The First Lecture: The Unconscious

While Freud delivered his five lectures in German (the audience members were all fluent, many of them having studied in Germany), they were geared to the lay public. The first lecture focused on Breuer's treatment of Anna O. and presented several points, four of which are important for our purposes. The first point was that "hysterical patients suffer from reminiscences" (quoted in Rosenzweig, 1994, p. 402). In other words, Freud argued that symptoms result from memories that are remembered in ways other than by conscious memory. They are remembered or revealed somatically or emotionally in altered form: in the symptom, in dreams, in bungled actions or slips of the pen or tongue, what he called parapraxes, or in jokes, but they are not consciously remembered. The second point was that the repressed material lives on in the unconscious, exerting a silent but effective influence on how we experience our lives. Not only do patients experience, read, and react to present events through these forgotten memory traces, but we all do. The third point was that the unconscious is structured in conflict. It comes into being and persists because of conflicts between drives and one's own internalized version of socio/cultural conventions and laws and familial "do's" and "don'ts." And, finally, Freud told his audience that only through a reliving or re-symbolization of the repressed material accompanied by an emotional discharge, called by Freud "abreaction," might the patient be freed of the symptom and over-determined ways of feeling, thinking, and perceiving.

The points Freud raised here, some of which he revised later but all of which were fundamental to his theory, posed problems for his listeners and would pose problems for educators. If the unconscious was structured in conflict and could sabotage conscious projects, wouldn't it threaten education as a conscious project of progressive development? How could we ever trust what we or others said, if we couldn't be sure of what we or they really meant? Even though the concept of the unconscious and the various paths to it would be defanged in an American context and transformed almost beyond recognition by the strands noted above, they raised and continue to raise several interesting but troubling questions for educators. For example, how does the unconscious affect our curiosity, what we are drawn to, how we form relations with others, and what and how we learn, study, and teach? How does the unconscious interfere with learning, and what does learning mean if there are two agencies always at work in the psyche? Are misbehaving, not knowing, and wrong answers types of parapraxes and thus as meaningful and interesting as appropriate conduct, mastery, and right answers? How would we interpret them? How might we, and should we, create conditions such that teachers and students have opportunities to explore and re-symbolize dreams, the nonsensical, and inchoate or repressed emotions and ideas?

Freud's consideration of everyday events that otherwise had appeared trivial also had implications for education. If the minor occurrences of everyday life were worth attending to, perhaps a curriculum might include them. Furthermore, the realm of the domestic, traditionally a woman's domain, and one that was cast as epistemologically insignificant, might, in fact, deserve intellectual attention in its own right.

Freud used the case history of Anna O.—her condition and treatment—to exemplify the points he raised in his first lecture. It is interesting to note that when Freud gave this lecture, Bertha Pappenheim, the actual Anna O., was lecturing in Chicago on the evils of "prostitution and white slavery among Jews" (Rosenzweig, 1994, p. 108). According to Rosenzweig, "Pappenheim attributed neurotic adjustments and social evils involving sexuality ... to conflicts ... between classes of citizens who tolerate poverty, inferior education and economic exploitation" and those who suffer from these (p. 109). Pappenheim was a socialist committed to educating the masses, particularly about sexual issues and the plight of women. Freud considered Pappenheim's analysis unsuccessful, not because of her politics but because of her subsequent addiction to morphine (Roazen, 2001, pp. 237–38). And yet, she went on to great achievements in social work. Her case raises three questions that will haunt psychoanalysis and its relation to education: Can we ever determine a successful analysis or teaching, and if so, how? Will not such determinations always be tied to social and political values and thus contestable? What are the relationships between social forces and psychic forces in psychoanalysis and education?

In that first lecture Freud told his audience that Pappenheim had referred to the treatment as the "talking cure" (quoted in Rosenzweig, 1994, p. 400). Freud used the term again in his second lecture, but never afterward, and yet it has become a familiar descriptor for psychoanalysis. It is interesting to consider how much teaching, too, presents itself as a kind of talking cure for ignorance. Educators have often reversed the analytic relationship, though, since they do most of the talking and the student listens. The question does stick, however, of why Freud abandoned the term "talking cure." Was it that he grew increasingly skeptical of psychoanalysis as cure? Or was it that he worried such a label would diminish his work in the eyes of those who placed a preeminent value on science? The question lingers of how words do transform or shape our consciousness. How did they shape Freud's consciousness? And how do they shape our unconscious? This latter would be a question Jacques Lacan would address. The focus on language, which the "talking cure" implies, whether one understands it in terms of Freudian or Lancanian psychoanalysis, requires a certain sensitivity or attention to language. Perhaps if we educators took the talking cure more seriously, we might address the words spoken or written rather than leaping solely at the content they supposedly signify.

Finally, perhaps the talking cure has other implications for teaching. What, for example, would it mean, given that we teachers work with groups of students, to reframe our thinking about teaching, curriculum, and teacher education in terms of a conversation or as a complicated conversation (see Pinar, 2004), one in which the unconscious, paradoxically, occupied a more explicit focus, but one which was not directed toward cure? Such conversations require the teacher to follow associations, to attend to seemingly insignificant material, to cast everything as interpretable, and to follow the threads of an idea into the loam of psychic/social life and weave it through the disciplinary knowledge offered.

The Second Lecture: Repression and Resistance

Freud's second lecture focused on repression and resistance. According to Freud, the very forces that led someone to deny or repress specific ideas in consciousness acted to keep those ideas out of consciousness. But why would ideas be repressed and what was meant by "ideas"? An idea would be repressed because an unacceptable wish had been "aroused which [stood] in sharp opposition to the individual's other wishes and ... [could] not be reconciled with the [individual's] ethical and esthetic standards" (quoted in Rosenzweig, 1994, p. 409). Freud argued that we unconsciously repress that which we cannot tolerate in consciousness, because it offends our sense of morality or taste. The "incompatibility of the idea in question with the ego of the patient was thus the motive of the repression; the ethical and other demands of the individual were the repressing forces" (quoted in Rosenzweig, 1994, p. 410). Exiled to the unconscious, the repressed material and the unacceptable, even inconceivable wish clinging to it, continued to exist "waiting for the opportunity to become activated, and when this happens to send into consciousness a distorted and unrecognizable substitute for the repressed idea" (quoted in Rosenzweig, 1994, p. 412). The substitute or symptom carried with it the same unpleasantness which the "repression had been intended to prevent" (quoted in Rosenzweig, 1994, p. 413). In other words, that which is repressed returns, often in painful ways.

While Freud talked of repressing ideas, he was neither explicitly or consciously referring to linguistic formations—Lacan would re-read them this way—nor was he talking about ideas as fully formed logical conceptual structures or plans, such as democracy or an outline for a book. Rather he was referring to a more nebulous constellation of wishes, images, words, and impulses that, because the constellation, or parts of it, was unacceptable to the psyche, was repressed but could be read—re-constructed—in the patient's symptoms, dreams, and parapraxes.

Unlike neurologists and psychiatrists at the time, who believed that psychological problems were caused by disturbances in the brain or nervous system and/or were a result of hereditary degeneracy, Freud argued that repression was not a result of "congenital incapacities in the mental apparatus to synthesize experiences" but rather a result of a dynamic "conflict of opposing mental forces" (quoted in Rosenzweig, 1994, p. 411). Only by following back through analysis the chain of events and by surfacing the repressed material could the patient have a choice of either giving up the desire or wish at the nucleus of the repressed material, accepting it, or re-channeling it. The latter choice Freud called sublimation, a concept whose complexity would become apparent over time. In 1909 Freud still believed in "happy terminations" (quoted in Rosenzweig, 1994, p. 413).

Perhaps no concept in Freud's theorizing prior to 1909 would have as much traction among educators as that of repression. While a good many academic psychologists rejected the idea that repression occurs unconsciously, they were more than willing to accept the idea that we consciously push some thoughts and desires out of mind, often, they claimed, for good reasons. They definitely were drawn, as we saw in Putnam's case, to the idea of sublimation, since they saw this as offering a way for dangerous feelings or ideas to be re-channeled into positive endeavors. Cultural conservatives liked the idea, for example, of re-channeling lascivious thoughts or desires into, say, a hobby or a sport. Boys could put off their sexual impulses and re-channel them into tackling their football opponents. Radical political activists, on the other hand, saw in the concept of repression proof that unjust and oppressive social and class structures crippled individuals' very souls.

More important for our purposes, progressive educators came to use the concept of repression to argue for more permissive approaches in the classroom, but in doing so they often misinterpreted the material that was repressed solely in terms of emotion rather than ideas. Freud had made it clear that ideas are repressed and that the emotions that accompany them are displaced into other objects, people, or events. By ideas he meant a mixture of images, impulses, and words, and he often assumed that what was repressed was an entire constellation of these accompanied by emotion. Thus, for example, if, as a child, I repressed the pain of beatings and yelling, the experience of which was dispersed over and attached to memories of smells, sensations, and fantasies, I might reconstitute those experiences in any number of ways, some of which would be available to consciousness, but all of which would influence my emotional life. Or, if in my childlike thinking, I equated such treatment with love or with libidinal satisfaction, such an "idea" would be repressed but come to influence how, as an adult, I related to others.

Progressive educators often focused on the releasing of emotions or on refraining from discipline so the child's feelings or needs could be freed. Fred Kerlinger (1956) argues in "The Origins of the Doctrine of Permissiveness in Higher Education" that "Freudian psychology and thinking resulted in a strong trend toward emphasizing the basic needs of children and the necessity of meeting or 'permitting' these needs" (p. 162). As it emerged in pedagogical approaches in Vienna and Berlin in the early part of the twentieth century and made its way into U.S. education, the concept of repression and its negative results led educators to focus on a kind of Rousseau-like pedagogy, but one which posited the natural man as a sexual child.

Articles in *Progressive Education* between 1926 and 1932 suggest the integration of Freud's concept of repression into the "new education" (see for example Bode, 1931; Dell, 1932; and Wittels, 1931). Educators and psychoanalysts warned that current education was "literally a forcing house for various neuroses" (Ferenczi, 1949a, p. 220) and that "repressions and resistances ... present the greatest problem to the task of education: (Coriat, 1926, p. 26). Responding to these claims were educators such as Margaret Naumburg, founder of the Walden School, who viewed art education for children as a way to release that repressed material.

The second lecture certainly posed questions for educators. How far should we go in releasing repressed material? Should educators cultivate the exploration and expression of memories or ideas that might be seen as potentially dangerous? Is the ideation that is repressed more natural than the social conventions responsible for the repression or is the ideation in fact shaped by those very forces? Are teachers meant to address, articulate, and bring understanding to emotions displaced from the repressed ideas? Perhaps most important, however, was the seemingly irresolvable tension between, on the one hand, enculturating students by developing their tastes and their character and, on the other hand, acknowledging and integrating their unconscious, which challenged that enculturation.

The Third Lecture: Dreams, Slips, Free Association, Psychic Determinism, and Scientific Status

The third lecture presented at Clark focused on dreams, the *"via regia* to the knowledge of the unconscious" (quoted in Rosenzweig, 1994, p. 418). Freud presented his theory that dreams were the disguised fulfillment of repressed wishes (Freud, 1900a, p. 121). Through the process of free association or saying whatever comes to mind, one could follow the road back from the actual dream, the manifest content, to the repressed wishes, which, emerging in and through the processes of metaphoric substitution and affective displacement, constituted the latent content or dream thoughts that were condensed and disguised in the reported dream.

Free association was for Freud the cardinal principle of psychoanalysis: say whatever comes to mind, no matter how embarrassing, seemingly trivial, inappropriate, or worthy of dismissal. It sounds easy, but it was not, and the very places where free association dried up or stumbled or negated itself or left gaps or diverged from our inner monologue, the very place from which we judged it, there, according to Freud, the unconscious showed itself. Only in its traces could the unconscious be glimpsed. But while the patient was freely associating, so was the analyst. Allowing him or herself to be in unconscious communication with the patient through what Freud termed "evenly-suspended attention" (1912b, p. 111) and his or her own free association, the analyst would at some point suggest an idea, raise a question, proffer a tentative interpretation. If it hit the mark, more associations would flow out from the patient, often including furious denials or mis-understandings.

For educators the idea of free association, of course, raises questions of coherence, making sense, and getting back on track so we can reach the right outcome. We worry that if we allow students to free associate, we or they will never get to the point or take a position. But perhaps, following Freud, the drive to make sense may be a defense against the unknown, although he might also have suggested that the commitment to open-endedness, to free association, is a defense against the particular intimacy made possible by bounded difference as opposed to the sense of oceanic oneness that can be engendered by free association but can dissolve difference into the soupy flow of sameness.

It is interesting, in thinking about free association and its place in the classroom, to recall Jerome Bruner's (1996, p. 181) suggestion that we apply in the classroom what, following Sperber and Wilson (1986), he termed the 'principle of relevance,' a principle that suggests all the meanings we make, make sense somewhere. Perhaps then if we allow students to freely associate, they will not only make sense but also reveal the very places where they resist knowing. They may also suspend particular identities, for example social identities, that constrain as well as enable thinking.

The concept of free association, the centrality to self-understanding of dreams or illogical and irrational thinking, which appears to be what a dream is, and the view that an entirely different kind of thinking, one that shapes who we are, goes on outside our consciousness, somewhere else—all these began to burrow holes in the edifice of rationality that reigned supreme in the extant academic disciplines and approaches to education. They offered opportunities to explore other modes of knowing, and, indeed, much of the focus on arts education in the early progressive movement would implicitly or explicitly draw on psychoanalytic theory to validate less rational ways of understanding and expressing one's pre-verbal and affective experiences (see in particular the work of Margaret Naumberg, 1928, 1947, 1950, 1966). Of course, the challenge to rational thinking provoked an aggressive resistance from those who saw the real and the rational as synonymous. That resistance partially accounts for what might be understood as psychoanalysis's defensive embrace of medicine and its own ambivalence about its status as a science.

Toward the end of the third lecture Freud raised the issue of psychic determinism, claiming that "the psychoanalyst is committed to a very strong belief in the determination of mental life" and arguing that unlike the single causes sought in extant approaches to psychology, psychoanalysis found "several motives for the same mental effect" (quoted in Rosenzweig, 1994, p. 423). Freud's initial belief in psychic determination as opposed to environmental or hereditary determinism altered over the course of his work, and became more nuanced and complicated than what he presented at Clark, but it would be this simplistic picture of the individual as a puppet of internal unconscious forces *in the psyche* that would provoke serious challenges from those focused on the chemical or neuronal causes of human suffering. It would also be misinterpreted by those who accused Freud of being politically reactionary, since he seemed to be saying that our suffering was the result only of inner forces as opposed to external social or political ones. Putting the lie to these latter accusations was Freud's commitment to free psychoanalytic and medical treatment for those who couldn't afford it, to the eradication of poverty, and to cooperative mental health clinics. Furthermore, and perhaps most important, his theory radically undermined sexual, religious, and social conventions (in particular see Danto, 2005, Jacoby, 1986, 1997; Lasch, 1997; Zaretsky, 2004). In terms of education, however, Freud's claim that our mental life is multiply determined by unconscious internal forces added to the move away from blaming people's problems on their lack of will or on their moral depravity. This change led educators, such as August Aichhorn (1939), to focus on *understanding* a child's or adolescent's misbehavior rather than on simply punishing it. It also contributed to what would be the intensifying interest in the inner life of the child, and thus to positioning children of all ages as objects of study and the focus of educational interventions.

There was one point about determinism, however, that came to be overlooked or ignored as psychoanalysis made its way in American culture and into education. Perhaps because it undermined the drive for certainty, Freud's claim that an individual's actions or mental states were *multiply* determined, and thus no one cause could ever be posited with certainty, let alone generalized to others, suggested that we could never know for sure the origin or cause of psychic phenomena and thus we could never predict with certainty its occurrence. Although there was no reference to Freud, we can see the tension such a view might provoke in the exchange between educator William Bagley and psychologist Lewis Terman. According to Ravitch, Bagley denied "any possibility of a science of education, [since] of course the essence of science is that it enables us to predict" (Bagley, quoted in Ravitch, (2000) p. 148). Terman accused him of sentimental naïveté. Ruling out the possibility of prediction was Freud's suggestion that only in retrospect, for example while looking back on and interpreting one's childhood and its relationship to the present, could one attribute a cause. That cause, however, was not understood as an empirical historical fact nor was it understood in terms of a billiard-ball causality. The cause could not be predicted in advance. Most disturbing to a science of prediction, such retrospectively attributed cause was not necessarily the definitive cause, only one among many. Sounding almost like a pragmatist, Freud would argue that the truth value of the causal narrative, whose objective origins we could never know, consisted of the effect it had on the patient's shift in perspective, rather than in its historical accuracy. As the century progressed and the therapeutic project of psychoanalysis came to the fore, psychoanalysts and educators came to disavow such troubling knowledge, but it might be helpful here to pause and consider the implications for teaching such a view of cause and effect might hold.

In eschewing the logics of a billiard-ball causality, education administrators might focus less on mandating specific techniques or interventions or bringing particular school reforms to scale, and instead consider the conditions, always multiple, that might provoke or encourage or support students' engagement with curriculum or in conversations in the classroom. For example, smaller classes, better libraries, a richer extra-curriculum, well-educated teachers, and more extensive community support services, in other words all the resources the children of the wealthy have, might be the goals of educators, even though there is no direct causal relationship between these and academic achievement. Zip codes, families, desire, and, of course, the unconscious disrupt such easy causal narratives. The acceptance of multiple and even unknowable causation might push teachers to focus more on appreciating and engaging the idiosyncratic ways students make meaning in classrooms. Certainly such acceptance subverts any claim that a particular teaching method produces a particular result with the guaranteed consistency that say antibiotics have on bacterial infections. Denied the surety of fixed protocols, i.e. the cause and effect logic psychoanalysis challenged, teaching must attend to each student's ways of making or resisting meaning and knowledge. But at Clark several members in the audience who seemed bent on viewing psychology in terms of control and prediction remained skeptical of Freud's claims.

It was in this third lecture that Freud's anxiety about the status of psychoanalysis and its claim to scientific validity emerged. "It seemed almost scandalous," he said, "that in a country so devoted to practical goals I should present myself to you as a 'dream interpreter'" (quoted in Rosenzweig, 1994, p. 418), and yet, that is exactly what he did, later on going even further to assert that one becomes a psychoanalyst "by studying one's own dreams" (1910a, p. 33). Sensing that his listeners might be scornful of or reluctant to accept the centrality of dreams in understanding the human psyche, he suggested that such judgments revealed a resistance disguised as "intellectual rejection," the same kind of resistance that patients would show when confronted with painful knowledge. Positioning criticism of his theory as an emotional response occasioned by repressed affect-laden ideas, Freud tried to preempt any derogatory critique.

As we shall see, the dismissal of psychoanalysis on the grounds that it was not scientific would doom it to a marginal status in the academy and lead, a century after the Clark Conference, to its almost complete absence from discussions of teaching and education. The paradox is that the very fear of losing scientific status drove psychoanalysts to downplay, if not disavow, its own radical knowledge. As that disavowal deepened, the emancipatory project of psychoanalysis gave way to the therapeutic project, and tied that project to medicine. It would seem that the inherent split within psychoanalysis, occasioned by its own ambivalence and anxiety about its truth claims, contributed to its medical mimicry, the resulting short term bursts of glory and attention in the 1950s, and then the demise of psychoanalysis itself and its relationship to education.

The Fourth Lecture: Sexuality

Freud saved his ideas about sex, the Oedipal drama, the sexuality of children and their sexual researches, the distorting influence of civilized morality, and the strange workings of transference for the last two lectures. These topics would, of course, help define the popular sense of psychoanalysis and provoke the greatest resistance to his theories, initially voiced by conservatives who were outraged at the claims, and then later, in the second half of the twentieth century, by feminists and gay rights activists who condemned his views on sexuality as harmful to women, gays, and lesbians. While Freud would alter his conceptualization of each of the concepts he introduced in the last two lectures, evolving a darker and more pessimistic view as he aged, his own ambiguous, at times contradictory, elaboration of them, does allow for multiple interpretations of his work.

At Clark, Freud presented a picture of the human infant vulnerable to and exuberant in the impulses and sensations arising from the sensitive areas of the anus, mouth, urethra, genitalia, skin, and "other sensory surfaces" (quoted in Rosenzweig, 1994, p. 428). In childhood, autoerotic stimulation, such as masturbation, playing with one's own feces, and thumb sucking, is accompanied by erotic activities involving others, such as voyeurism, sadism, masochism, and exhibitionism. The polymorphously perverse infant, who enjoys erotic contact with others regardless of their gender, eventually must pass through a series of sexualized phases, ending with the Oedipal drama where the dynamics of renunciation of and identification with parental love objects, who according to Freud, unconsciously elicit their children's erotic fantasies, culminate in a particular gender identity and the vicissitudes of sexual life.

For Freud, childhood experiences, suffused with libidinal ecstasies, longings, questions, impulses, traumas, and wounds would not only provoke and inform the wishes that we come to repress and that, more generally, shape the way adults relate to one another and their symptoms, but also influence the curiosity with which we approach the world. The sensed but not articulated, haunting questions of who am I to my parents, what do they really want of me, and who are they to one another shape how we come to know and feel the world. But the elusive answers to these questions are already caught in invisible networks of communication within the family, networks that carry parental losses, secrets, and our parents' own conscious and unconscious questions. There are no final answers to these questions, although certainly children can learn where babies come from, the most fundamental research question. In fact, Freud urged a matter-of-fact approach to answering the child's questions about sex so that the child will continue to sustain curiosity in the face of family enigmas, but he had little faith such answers would or could dissolve or replace the child's own theories, which were often formed in the service of answering ineluctable and enigmatic questions about familial desires, loves, and fears.

It would seem we could draw an important lesson about teaching from Freud's discussion of childhood sexual researches and the theories children spin to answer their questions. If the questioning child is "not intimidated or oppressed with a sense of guilt, he gives expression quite ingenuously to what he thinks" (Freud, 1907, p. 135). If the child's questions are answered forthrightly and his or her curiosity about these fundamental questions encouraged, he or she will keep alive a "genuine instinct of research" (p. 136). For educators influenced by Freud, the implication was clear: introduce sex education and encourage children's questions about sex.

But in one of his last works, "Analysis Terminable and Interminable" (1937b, p. 234), Freud argued that children, even when given the correct information about sex, do not abandon their theories. Here the implication is not that the educator should focus on sex education or creating conditions such that the students can discover on their own the answers to their sexual questions, although Freud did recommend these. Rather the implication is that the theories, the *words*, and the *ideas* of children and students, need to be respected and worked with. This is a different approach than one centered on simply providing the correct information or eliciting the expression of affect around these topics. Such an approach shifts ever so slightly the focus from personal expression to intellectual engagement with ideas, ideas that are, however, suffused with affect. So, for example, rather than ask students how they feel about a particular piece of literature, or an incident under discussion, we might ask them what they think of it or what they think or make of their feelings about it. A further implication of Freud's claim that children do not abandon their original theories concerns the lingering, unspoken questions for which their questions and theories about how babies are born serve as a substitute. In other words, if we assume that children do not give up their theories in part because the questions their theories purportedly address—questions about where babies come from and the mysteries of sex—are not the only or real questions troubling them—questions about their place in the family and what their parents really want from them—then teachers, when they listen to students' questions or responses, might consider or gently raise the more pressing existential questions behind these and relate them back to the curriculum. Who am I to others? What do they want from me or of me? These might be some of the questions around which an academically rich curriculum could be shaped, one which does not silence the unconscious.

Freud worried that the introduction of infantile and childhood sexuality to an American audience, no matter how educated, would land psychoanalysis, as he put it, "up shit's creek" (quoted in Zaretsky, 2004, p. 81). He was, at least partially, right. Those educators and psychologists who turned to psychoanalysis for applications to teaching often domesticated, neutralized, or marginalized Freud's more unsettling observations about childhood and adult sexuality. Most often educators translated his insights into calls to re-direct or sublimate sexuality—the content of which was quickly passed over—into socially acceptable or morally sound activities. American psychiatrists also soft-peddled Freud's more radical insights. In doing so, they created lucrative practices for themselves, suggesting that Freud's scatalogical outburst, given his association of money and feces, was prescient.

Over time, the primal sexual components of drives and desires would be acknowledged by physicians, psychiatrists, and psychologists who would use them for diagnostic purposes and translate them in terms of the normal and abnormal, a division Freud viewed as porous if not useless. On the other hand, the conjoining of exhibitionism, sadism, and masochism with childhood development and the positing of homosexual dimensions to our desiring, while initially shocking, may have led to their acceptance as part of our psyche, further weakening boundaries between the normal and abnormal. Certainly his introduction of the sexual life of children was in part responsible for later efforts at sex education. If "the purpose of educators [is] to stifle the child's power of independent thought as early as possible, in favor of the 'goodness' which they think so much of," he wrote, "they cannot set about this better than deceiving him in sexual matters" (1907, pp. 136–37). Many of the early educational efforts influenced by psychoanalysis were, in fact, directed toward sex education. Some were motivated by a desire to respond to the horrors and cruelties that resulted from sexual ignorance, such as those depicted in the Viennese playwright Frank Wedekind's 1891 *Spring Awakening*. Others were based on Freud's theory that responding candidly to children's sexual questions kept their appetite for knowledge alive.

Perhaps most important though, Freud's introduction of the sexual life of children and the focus on the child as the "father of man" reemerged as, or at least contributed to, the child-centeredness of the progressive education movement and the focus on sex education in the mental hygiene movement. The child around whom the curriculum came to be centered was not, however, the polymorphously perverse infant Freud theorized but rather as Boyd Bode (1938) would point out in his *Progressive Education at the Crossroads,* Rousseau's child with needs mired in the present. Bode criticized progressives who appealed to Freud in support of catering to the needs of children and building a curriculum around those needs. "The purpose of sound education," Bode wrote, "is precisely to emancipate the pupil from dependence on immediate interests" (quoted in Ravitch, 2000, p. 310). What Bode and the progressives he was criticizing missed was Freud's insistence that interests were not neutral, not simply good in and of themselves, but always a result of the complicated dynamic between culture, the unconscious, and the family.

Freud's early theorization about sex and his belief that moderating the demands of the superego and easing repression would make people healthier made sense at a time of enormous sexual and gender oppression. Certainly, his theorization continues to be relevant. We might, for example, ask not only how early libidinal forces and the child's sexual researches affect curiosity (see, for example, Freud, 1910b) but also how the keeping of secrets in a family, the averted looks and palpable silences around what cannot be mentioned, come to arrest the child's curiosity or provoke the defensive strategy of compulsive questioning. On the other hand, for educators who currently face students deeply involved in the so-called "hook-up" culture, Freud's admonition to ease repression seems out of date and raises complicated questions. One has to wonder whether sexual liberation constitutes another form of superegoic demand in a consumer society and what the balance is between erotic emancipation and the commodification and instrumental deployment of the body in its name (see McGowan, 2004, on this point). And, too, one might ask, following the work of Michel Foucault (1978), whether the sex that is liberated is already one deformed by extant discursive grids of gender and sexuality? Or are such concerns simply the most recent, albeit theoretically sophisticated, incarnation of a conservative appeal to sexual prohibitions and restrictions? What does it mean to lead or enjoy an erotic life and what values, if any, should we promote in ensuring or guiding such a life? These are questions into which psychoanalysis, itself, might still offer insight, particularly if we interpret Freud's theory of drive not as biologically based and transparent but as inherently fused with internalized cultural demands formed by language and family.

Fifth Lecture: Transference, Sublimation, and Culture

In his fifth lecture, Freud assured his audience that he knew that human relationships were shaped by earlier libidinal experiences because of his discovery of transference. Reminding his audience that people were rarely, if ever, candid about sex, he turned for corroboration of his theories to what he described as the phenomenon of transference. "I know that all my adherents became convinced about the correctness of my views on the pathogenesis of the neuroses through their experiences with the phenomenon of transference" (quoted in Rosenzweig, 1994, p. 435) Transference, according to Freud, reproduces in the present older, often unconscious, emotional patterns or what he would later call "stereotype plates," or "anticipatory ideas" (1912a, p. 100) that have been shaped by libidinal relations with and fantasies about siblings and parents. Transference would allow the analyst and patient to encounter the non-rational or un-reason, to meet the unconscious at work.

For Freud, transference opened the door to exploring the patient's unconscious history as it unfolded in the love/hate relationship with the analyst. "It is only through this reliving in the 'transference' that the patient becomes convinced of the existence, as well as the power, of the unconscious sexual impulses" (quoted in Rosenzweig, 1994, p. 435). But Freud also told the audience at Clark that transference "arises spontaneously in all human relationships" (p. 435) although it is disclosed to conscious treatment in analysis. This unsettling claim, which Freud seems to have passed over rapidly during the fifth lecture, suggested that all our relationships, particularly those of love and hate, reproduce older patterns of relating, suggesting that how we see the world and how we react to it do not simply result from rational observation, character, upbringing, and logical cause and effect, but are rather the result of long forgotten fantasies, wishes, impulses, and emotional patterns we had experienced in our families but repressed.

Interest in how transference affects teaching peeked in the 1920s when writers such as Alexander Coriat (1926) and G.H. Green (1922) urged teachers to pay attention to their transferential relations with students. In later decades those educators who talked about transference did so in passing, gently reminding teachers that their feelings for and views of students might have more to do with their own personalities than with those of their students. It would not be until the 1980s that transference among students and teachers would again be a focus of curriculum theorists, literary critics, and composition theorists. And the questions still linger. If all our relationships are haunted by ghosts of older ones, how do we know what our real feelings toward someone are and on what basis do we build relationships? Is the classroom a transferential and counter-transferential hall of mirrors reflecting only the past? If how we see others is to a large extent based on transference, is transference central to our knowledge of others or to knowing anything and what can we know beyond our own projections? Does transference suggest that the messages we receive back from others are in fact the materializations of our own transferences, as for example, when Bertha Pappenheim's hysterical pregnancy was, as suggested by

Freud, simply the realization of Breuer's own wish for a child? Breuer's wife conceived, according to Freud, soon after Pappenheim left treatment, although there is some controversy over this claim (Malcolm, 1981, p. 165).

The attention psychoanalytically informed educators initially paid to transference tended to be along the lines Freud had spelled out, i.e., focus on the patient's transference, but as psychoanalytic theory evolved, psychoanalysts and psychoanalytically informed educators did urge teachers to pay more attention to their countertransference, that is to their own feelings and ideation aroused by their students, and to bring these into the pedagogical relationship. Sandor Ferenzci suggested as much in his article "Confusion of Tongues between the Adult and the Child" written in 1932. There he urged the analyst to "make the source of the disturbances in us fully conscious and to discuss it with the patient, admitting it perhaps not only as a possibility but as a fact" (p. 226). And teachers did begin to discuss how their students' behaviors made them feel, although most didn't go so far as to explore with their students the origin of those feelings. The implications for teaching here are interesting. Does one announce one's boredom in class? Do we say we are angry but make clear such anger has to do with our own expectations and psychic determinants rather than the behavior of the class? Are such questions manipulative, and can pedagogy be anything other than manipulation? For Freud, suggestion in analysis was "used ... to induce the patient to perform a piece of psychical work" (1925c, pp. 42–43), but such work could only be undertaken if the analyst was aware of his or her own counter-transference. Otherwise such power of suggestion was, as Freud pointed out, simply too horrifying (1915a, pp. 165–66). We might wonder here about those educators who, neglectful of their own counter-transferences, punish, seduce, manipulate, and mold students in the name of some higher ideal but in actuality may be reproducing archaic emotional patterns.

Finally, Freud in the fifth lecture raised the issue of the complex relationship between the individual's desires and society's rules, norms, and morals. In his lectures at Clark, Freud argued that our puritanical mores were literally making us, particularly women, ill, and that we would be better off if we "did not aim so high that we completely neglect the original animality of our nature" (quoted in Rosenzweig, 1994, p. 438). He understood the prison of domesticity and idealized love in which both men and women, particularly white, middle class women, were imprisoned and the horrors of disease contracted by men who turned to prostitution for sex. He rebelled at the silence and disgust surrounding homosexuality, the grim pictures presented to him of marriages drained of life due to ignorance about sex, and the cost of limiting sexual delight to a side effect of reproduction. Such observations led Freud to tell Putnam that it was not "moral estimates that were needed for solving the problems of human life and motives, but more knowledge" (quoted in Hale, 1995a, p. 15).

Freud's insights that the repression of sexuality led to neurosis and that the impossible standards of civilization forced people to turn away from reality (quoted in Rosenzweig, 1994, p. 437) and to flee into the "cloister of neurosis" (quoted in

Rosenzweig, 1994, p. 434) would shape the initial relationship between psycho-analysis and education. If children, parents, and teachers could be exposed to a psychoanalytic pedagogy, if they could be educated about sex and sexuality, as these were understood by psychoanalysts, then neurosis might diminish. So thought many of Freud's colleagues and followers, although, as we shall see, their optimism soon faded. At the same time, Freud's theories about childhood sexuality, the separation of sexual pleasure from procreation, and the relationship between sexual repression and civilization prompted several educators to call for a sex education that would inculcate conservative attitudes toward sexuality, promoting chastity, and proclaiming the dangers of sexual behavior (Strong, 1972).

Freud's lectures and their influence on his listeners had a profound effect. Clarence Oberndorf, in his first hand account of the history of psychoanalysis, writes, "By 1919 psychoanalytic principles had permeated psychiatric thinking in America to an extent unknown anywhere else" (Oberndorf, 1953, p. 128). Nathan Hale writes that a year after the Clark lectures "psychoanalysis had become the most fiercely debated subject in American neurology and psychiatry" (Hale, 1995a, p. 274), and, he continues, "[w]ithin six years of the Clark Conference psychoanalysis had eclipsed all other psychotherapies in the nation's magazines" (p. 397). According to Eli Zaretsky, by World War I, "the United States had the largest number of analysts in the world" (p. 83). George Makari writes in *Revolution in the Mind: The Creation of Psychoanalysis* that "[b]etween 1908 and 1911 the Freudians consolidated into an international movement" and that by 1909 "allies were arriving in greater numbers than adversaries" (2008, p. 234). Many of them were arriving with ideas about teaching and education.

The Initial Influence of Psychoanalysis on Education: 1909 to World War II

Radical Possibility

> Free thinkers and lovers, disparate in their creeds, goals
> and degrees of radicalism, they were united by their fight
> against those tendencies in American life that were driving
> their fellow citizens in the direction of increasing standardization,
> mechanization, and materialism: the Taylorites and their worship
> of efficiency and cost-effectiveness based on principles of
> scientific management that were turning men and women into
> machines; the specialization of work that further segregated the
> class system and divided the educated and uneducated; the
> manipulations of the mass media ... They have been called a 'Lyrical Left,'
> whose cultural politics sought to undermine the property-oriented,
> regimented, guilt-ridden bourgeois civilization that had spawned most of them.
> (Rudnick, 1984, pp. 62–63)

Lois Palken Rudnik describes in the above quote the sense of radical possibility that existed among avant-garde intellectuals, socialists, political radicals, and some progressives in America before World War I. In Europe too there was a sense of possibility. Psychoanalysis contributed to that sense. On the most superficial level psychoanalysis put into question the conventional morality of the day. On a deeper level it put into question the basis of the social contract and the unspoken compact underlying familial and erotic relationships. As an emancipatory project, it also challenged the privileged position of rationality and agency. In opening up questions about what was most taken for granted and what was most cherished, it unsettled people and occasioned from both critics and defenders an anxious rush to answer and solve the questions raised. The new space psychoanalysis opened for thought allowed in the irrational, the unconscious, desire, and the body, and freed people to think a little differently. But its very openness proved threatening and provoked a rapid drive to fill that space up, to domesticate it, and thus to bury it in a blizzard of categories, certainties, methods, and solutions.

Because education, so often wedded to its own therapeutic project, is the repository for the hopes of a nation and its individual members, and because teachers feel such a sense of responsibility for realizing those hopes, educators often want to "do something now." They rush to turn any theory into practice and measure theory by its use value in the classroom. As Siegfried Bernfeld (1973) argued in his little studied but quite brilliant discussion of education and psychoanalysis, *Sisyphus or the Limits of Education*, educators confuse the noble ideals of education with instruction. Wanting to find methods to achieve the former they continually fail, since "no theory of education can resolve the antinomy between the justified will of the child and the justified will of the teacher; on the contrary education consists of this antinomy" (p. xxvii). Anna Freud would echo these sentiments in 1935, when she wrote:

> Education wants to substitute for love of dirt a disgust for dirt, for shamelessness a feeling of shame, for cruelty sympathy, and in place of a rage for destructiveness a desire to cherish things. Curiosity and the desire to handle one's own body must be eliminated by prohibitions, lack of consideration for others must be replaced by consideration, egotism by altruism. Step by step education aims at the exact opposite of the child's instinctive desires. (pp. 57–58)

If leading children into culture and, more idealistically, leading them to become democratic, socially just, healthy, successful citizens goes against their desires, then we teachers are engaged in a Sisypean struggle. But teachers are resistant to relinquishing the grander educational aspirations—who of us wants only to instruct students in the basics or resign ourselves to conveying information that can be measured on a test, particularly when even these goals are undermined by the child's own desires. Unwilling to allow theory to shape understanding, and insisting on subjecting it to the criterion of use value, we seek ever more desperately for the best application. Theory, therefore, is quickly reduced to practices that can be implemented, as we try to convert our aspirations to educate into methods of instruction, which themselves often fail to realize their promise of sure-fire success. As Bernfeld wrote:

> [Methods of instruction] have run the gamut from love to harsh discipline, from verbal instruction to teaching by personal example. They have recommended that teachers play an active part, and that they practice patient restraint. They have demanded free expression for the child's impulses, and their repression. This whole scale has been tried ever since parents and teachers existed. ... And the result? Humanity as it is today, and always was. The distance between empirical man and ideal man remains essentially unchanged. (1973, p. 27)

While Bernfeld saw socialism as a possible solution to this deadlock in education, his understanding of the impossibility of knowing "exactly how a child will behave in a planned educational situation, what its effect and the duration of the effect will be" (p. 111) and therefore how impossible it is to predict, countered any belief that solutions lay in better methods or a better application of theory. But in fact it was in terms of its application that psychoanalysis entered schools.

Other than Freud himself, who made a few stabs at exploring what appeared to him as the impossibility of education, the early analysts interested in education and those educators influenced by psychoanalytic theory did not analyze the wishes and dreams education and teachers were meant to satisfy. Nor did they speculate about the anxieties and aggression the public and critics so often directed against teachers. While Anna Freud, like Bernfeld, would write about the antinomy between education and instinct, few analysts or educators considered what it might mean to think psychoanalytically about this profound public institution. In their focus on psychoanalysis as cure, educators concentrated their attention on applying psychoanalysis to students' and, in some cases, teachers' emotional lives. They did not see psychoanalytic theory as a way to understand or gain insight into curriculum in terms of the relationship between the psyche and *academic* content or to integrate the former into the latter, as Freud had done with the humanities in his explorations.

While psychoanalysts analyzed almost every other social institution and employed their practice to address the psychic costs of those institutions, education, itself, escaped analysis. It was, rather, a domain where psychoanalytic theory would only be *applied*. Freud and his followers subjected, for example, religion, the family, and civilization to intense, often scandalous, and always thought provoking analysis. But education, the nervousness it provoked, its function as a scapegoat or screen for social anxieties, remained a largely unexplored area. Rather it was the area for intervention.

Initially as teachers imported psychoanalysis into schools and classrooms, where chaos, lack of resources, large classes, and the tumultuous life of students were apparent, they focused on the most easily adapted psychoanalytic concepts. It was easier, in the name of lifting repression, to encourage little children to follow their instincts or express their feelings than it was to encourage teachers to think about the impossibility of their profession and what that might mean or to introduce psychoanalytic theory as a way to make sense of both the academic curriculum and, for example, the child's sexual researches and curiosity. As a result teachers gave precedence to concepts which they could seemingly more easily apply, such as repression, but, of course, something was lost in the translation and application of these concepts. The initial utopian fervor and ambitions of psychoanalysis contributed to the drive for quick translations, which often came at the expense of nuance and complexity. And the rush to apply psychoanalysis to classroom practice—the foregrounding of the therapeutic project—eclipsed psychoanalytic theory's own radical questioning and skepticism—the emancipatory project.

The United States—Initial Applications of Psychoanalysis to Education

> Freudian theory has made a slight entrance into
> nearly all the teaching of educational ideas now being
> carried out in colleges, in training colleges, and in the
> more modern schools. ... The theory of the unconscious
> is colouring their whole outlook in relation to personality
> in its various aspects.
>
> (Low, 1929, pp. 315–16)

> It seems to me that the popularity of ... psycho-analysis
> in America signifies neither a friendly attitude to the thing
> itself nor any specially wide or deep knowledge of it.
>
> (Freud, 1930b, p. 254)

In the years immediately following the Clark Conference, psychoanalysis was making its presence felt in education, both in the United States and abroad. Its entrance into the American conversation was, however, much slower than its spread in urban centers in Germany and Austria. We can gain a sense of the kind of contributions psychoanalysis was making to education in the early part of the twentieth century in the United States, in terms of what was being applied and how it was being applied, if we consider a few of the articles appearing in the *Journal of Progressive Education* by William Boyd (1931), Floyd Dell (1932), Isador Coriat (1926), Frankwood Williams (1926), and Fritz Wittels (1931), and in articles written by Ernest Jones (1910a, 1910b, and1912) and Sandor Ferenczi (1949a and 1949b).

Lifting Repression

The articles depict education as "burdening the mind with still more compulsions than even the already sufficiently pressing external circumstances demand, and [it] does so by strengthening repression" to the point of illness (Ferenczi, 1949a, p. 220). Ferenczi argued that "the excessive anxiety of most civilized people, their fear of death, and their hypochondriasis" are a result of "the libido being repressed during the process of education" (p. 221). Fritz Wittels (1931) maintained "the worst reproach against our educational system [is that] it produces an artificial sense of guilt in our children" (p. 239). He argued that parents and teachers were to blame for the problems of children "*who are the innocent victims of ignorance and sadism*" (p. 239, italics in original), and Ernest Jones (1910b) suggested that the mother in particular held "ignorant, shameful, or lewd" (p. 515) views of sex and thus was to blame for later problems in childhood. In his 1912 paper Jones argued that schooling forced children "through the same intellectual mill" and ignored individual differences (p. 252).

The answer to the problems of a repressive school system were the following: do away with grading, focus on the interests of the child, and institute an interdisciplinary curriculum (Dell, 1932, pp. 473–81); urge teachers to "begin with themselves" by turning to the analytic psychologies and look to themselves to understand their own negative views of the student rather than to assume the problem lies with the student (Boyd, 1931, p. 237); educate teachers to "understand their own unconscious" and their transferential relationships with students (Coriat, 1926, p. 21); organize activities to allow for the fullest development of the child's interests and "make education a more individual matter" so as "to draw out the [student's] potentialities" (Jones, E. 1910b, p. 506); address the emotional life of the child and institute sex education (Jones, E. 1910b, p. 515); "spare the child's mind the burden of unnecessary repression" (Ferenczi, 1949a, p. 221); and banish examinations, punishment, and discouragement of students (Wittels, 1932, p. 232). Many of these ideas were part of the progressive education movement. What differentiated the psychoanalytically informed practices from those of progressives was, of course, the underlying theory—pragmatism was not interested in the foundational topics Freud had raised in his lectures—and, more important, psychoanalysis's focus on the inner emotional life of the student and the intricate, emotional texture or tenor of relationships among students and between student and teacher.

At the Walden School, for example, Margaret Naumburg, who had herself been analyzed by Beatrice Hill, a Jungian, and then by A.A. Brill, sought to create conditions she believed would free the child's repressed emotional life and put into practice her belief, as her son, Thomas Frank, stated, that "the emotional development of children … should take precedence over the traditional intellectual approach to teaching of a standardized curriculum" (Detre, Thomas-Frank, Refsnes-Kniazzeh, Robinson, Rubin, and Ulman, 1983, p. 113). Not only was she sensitive to developing conversations with students that admitted variegated emotional responses, but Naumburg also urged her faculty to go into analysis. Naumburg's commitment to psychoanalysis as a liberation from the repressive strictures of conventional morality with its tethering of sexual pleasure to reproduction was shared by her husband, novelist, Waldo Frank, who, along with Jean Toomer, one of Naumburg's lovers, would weave psychoanalysis into the literary conversations circulating within the Harlem Renaissance (see Douglas, 1995, p. 79 and Zarestsky, 2004, pp. 152–53).

Freud's view prior to World War I that repression and the exaggerated, often punitive, moral conventions of the day led to illness had by the 1920s clearly led some progressive educators in the United States to believe that if schools simply became more permissive, students would develop into not just a healthy, but a new kind of individual. While Freud would come to a more complicated and darkened view than the one expressed early on, and while the disillusionment that trailed such utopian aspirations would come across the Atlantic with the arrival of Jewish analysts escaping Hitler, the initial emphasis on repression and its detrimental effects continued to shape or align with progressive education policies after the Great War. As Sol Cohen (1979) writes, "[I]n the 20s … permissiveness emerge[d] as the major theme of the new psychoanalytic pedagogy" (p. 188), and in attempts to apply psychoanalytic findings to education "the priority went to sex education" (p. 188).

Sex and Education: Toward a Higher Purpose

But it was a particular kind of sex education, one that emptied Freud's conceptualization of sex of all unpredictability, intractability, and drive. To take one example of such domestication, we can look at Wilfrid Lay's *Man's Unconscious Conflict: A Popular Exposition of Psychoanalysis*, published in 1917. Lay, who had been a teacher in Flushing, New York and had earned a doctorate at Columbia University saw the conflict between the unconscious and conscious as a moral struggle (Hale, 1995a). Perhaps even more than Putnam, Lay neutered Freud's sexual theories, combining a very broad definition of sex with "animadversions against prudery" (Hale, 1995a, p. 425). Lay saw the unconscious as harboring immoral thoughts and one of the purposes of education as ensuring that students will put their "thoughts … in order to make [them] as much use to society as [they] could be" (1917, p. 293). Clearly Lay wished to transform psychoanalysis into a program of moral development for children. But even with such moralizing, Lay's points drew from much of the emancipatory project in psychoanalysis. For example, he quotes approvingly the Swiss pastor Oskar Pfister, who had written "If we wish to reform education, I know of no better means to that end than in instructing the teachers in psychanalysis" (sic) (quoted in Lay, 1917, p. 277). Lay believed that "the prerequisite to knowledge is knowing oneself" (p. 303), that "all education is a kind of re-symbolization" (p. 298), and that the unconscious disrupts any attempts at predicting or controlling what happens in the classroom (p. 316), but he also held that psychoanalysis should be directed to higher spiritual ends.

Hale (1995a) suggests that Lay presented a picture of a malleable unconscious, one whose primal urges could be redirected by parents and educators, whose role it was to help the child use the psychosexual energy for healthier and socially beneficial pursuits (see Hale, 1995a, pp. 424–25). In *The International Journal of Psycho-analysis* the British psychoanalyst Barbara Low (1920) praised Lay's book for its moral clarity and its more soothingly acceptable interpretations of Freud. In many ways Lay's work continued the struggle Putnam had waged to enlist psychoanalysis in the service of character building and social improvement. It was not unreflective of books that tried to understand education and teaching in terms of the therapeutic project of psychoanalytic theory. There was, however, one noteworthy exception.

A Notable Exception: George H. Green

George H. Green's *Psychanalysis in the Classroom*, with its odd spelling of 'psychoanalysis,' was published in 1922. It presents a version of psychoanalysis much closer to the emancipatory project of Freud's thought, although a version still sterilized for popular audiences, particularly teachers, to whom it is addressed. While Green proposes that the chief aim of education is to "train children from egotistic levels of expression to altruistic levels" (p. 77), and believes education should lead to heterosexual marriage with gender specific roles, many of his suggestions echo Freud's more radical thoughts about analysis and education. Certainly the views he expresses run counter to the then dominant influence on education of experimental and behavioral psychology. William McDougall, a professor of psychology at Harvard, wrote in the introduction to the book that he hoped it would "serve in some measure as a corrective to the exaggerated 'behaviorism' which is rampant in this country and which threatens to be a serious bar to progress" (p. v).

In the preface, written in 1920 or 1921, Green states outright that psychoanalysis is "probably the most discussed subject before the public" (p. vii). The book aims, Green states, "to present as clearly and as simply as possible, such parts of the psychanalytic theory as were likely to be of use to parents and teachers, and to other people who were connected with and interested in children" (p. 4).

Remarkable about Green's work is not so much his presentation of Freud's ideas, which, like much of the interpretive work at that time, domesticates the more disturbing aspects of the theory, but what he says about their application to teaching. "What then is the value of any study of psychanalysis to a teacher?" he asks (p. 262). Certainly not in providing tips or recipes, he states. Those teachers who are looking for "material that shall be immediately 'useful' to them … have no use for [psychanalysis]" (p. 262). Those teachers who look to apply psychoanalysis to practice, Green states "are not educationists in any sense of the word, and one must not look for vital developments in education from them" (p. 262). At best," he writes, "they are no more than … manipulators of pedagogic tricks" (p. 262). Green continues, "What psychanalysis promises to the teacher … is an understanding of many baffling phenomena that are daily occurrences in the life of the classroom" (pp. 262–63). Psychoanalysis offers a way to understand phenomena, not an advice book on what to do in the classroom. "This is why," he states, "so much stress has been laid upon the word 'understanding'" (p. 264).

For Green such understanding involves a good deal of difficult labor. By familiarizing themselves with psychoanalytic theory, teachers might, and only might, begin to experience themselves and their students differently. They might begin to look at how "many of the difficulties that occur in [one's] work are the result of tendencies in [oneself]" (p. 7). Students' and one's own dreams and day-dreams need not be judged but rather considered for the insights they offer into one's teaching and the lives of students and integrated into the curriculum (pp. 40–53). Play, whether physical or intellectual, might occupy a more central place in the curriculum, because it offers students a way to express, think about, and make sense of the nonsensical. Teachers who strive to understand psychoanalysis will create a curriculum that attends to the interests of the child, with the understanding that those interests are not natural but rather have deeper origins which need to be understood. Furthermore, Green continues, Freud's theory teaches us that we should also "devote some consideration to the ... interests of the adult" (p. 57).

In terms of the emotional life of the classroom, Green suggests that an understanding of Freud's theory will allow teachers to think about the fears or anxieties expressed by children not as marginal or deserving of scolding or judgment or as the ephemeral but predictable experiences children at different stages go through. Rather they could be treated as idiosyncratic expressions of what the student is struggling with (p. 155). Furthermore teachers might look at student work not solely in terms of right and wrong answers but in terms of what emotional or inchoate ideas are being expressed (pp. 208–9). In thinking psychoanalytically teachers might begin to "refrain from applying labels" (p. 256), remain open and nonjudgmental, since "it is impossible to set down an absolute standard of what is normal" (p. 274), and provide the correct sexual information when asked. Teachers can also deepen their understanding of emotional life by understanding the role transference plays in the classroom (pp. 158–61). And finally, Freud's theory can lead teachers to understand that all education is a re-education taking place over time (p. 273).

Certainly Green's interpretation of psychoanalysis is much closer to Freud's own views than were the views of so many American educators and analysts who sought to apply psychoanalysis to the classroom and teacher education. However, while the emphasis on understanding rather than application offered a more emancipatory perspective than the dominant one at the time, understanding was, within psychoanalysis, problematic. When one understood something did it mean that the matter was closed? How would understanding accord with an interminable analysis that Freud at the end of his life would theorize? Not until Jacques Lacan arrived would such questions be opened for examination. "To make oneself understood is not the same as teaching," Lacan's son-in-law, Jacques Alain Miller (1990) would state, "it is the opposite. ... [O]ne never understands anything but one's fantasies. And one is never taught by anything other than what one doesn't understand, i.e., by nonsense" (p. xxvi). Or, in other words, by the unconscious. But in the 1920s understanding was an improvement on the drive to apply psychoanalysis and certainly on the academy's focus on behaviorism. George Green's book was well reviewed and went through two printings, but unlike Lay's book, it is sadly out of print.

While American educators often struggled to place psychoanalysis in the service of character development, in Europe in the early part of the century a more radical interpretation of Freud's relevance to education was occurring. What transpired there would affect the relationship between psychoanalysis and education in the United States, and so a brief detour through the early period of what was at times called psychopedagogy in Germany and Austria is in order.

Psychoanalytic Pedagogy in Europe

> What dominated our actions was the spirit of discovery [...]
> and what we strove to do was to turn what had formerly been
> chores into exciting adventures for the child ... We had tried too
> hard to turn all work into play, neglecting the fact that ... work
> [unlike play] is governed by the reality principle, which means
> that it also is pursued in the face of difficulties until an intended aim is reached.
> (A. Freud quoted in Midgley, 2008, p. 40)

Sol Cohen (1979) argues that in Europe the emergence of child analysis after World War I constituted the bridge between psychoanalysis and education and that child analysts were responsible for creating "a psychoanalytic pedagogy" (Cohen, 1979, p. 191).

> The emergence of child psychoanalysis was almost exclusively the work of a small group of women, many of them former school teachers – Hermine von Hug-Hellmuth, Berta Bornstein and Anna Freud in Vienna, Alice Balint in Berlin, then after 1926 in London – aided by a smaller group of men – Siegfried Bernfeld, Willi Hoffer, and August Aichhorn in Vienna, Ferenczi in Budapest, and Karl Abraham in Berlin. (p. 191)

We can add to this list of men Alfred Adler and Eric (Homburger) Erikson, and to the women, of course, Melanie Klein in England. After World War I, Vienna saw the blossoming of progressive education and what was called *Arbeitschule* or Activity School or school reform. Cohen (1979) writes:

> In Vienna the mood among those concerned with education was one of almost Utopian optimism. ... Many of the idealistic, talented Viennese youth of the new generation were swept up in the 1920s in the enthusiasm for 'the school reform' and went into the teaching profession. Anna Freud and Willi Hoffer saw in these school teachers promising material from which to create ... a corps of psychoanalytic pedagogues. (p. 192)

In 1926 the *Journal of Psychoanalytic Pedagogy* appeared, and in 1931, Hoffer established an official "three-year-long training course in psychoanalytic pedagogy ... at the Vienna Psychoanalytic Institute" (Cohen, 1979, p. 193). In 1919 the Kinderheim Baumgarten was opened by Siegried Bernfeld, a socialist and leader in the Jewish youth movement in Red Vienna. There were almost three hundred children in attendance age three–sixteen and they were exposed to what Bernfeld viewed as the new education, one "founded on psychoanalytic principles" (Cohen, 1979, p. 197). "Anna Freud called Kinderheim Baumgarten 'a first experiment to apply psychoanalytic principles to education'" (quoted in Cohen, 1979, p. 197). Bernfeld's approach recalls A.S. Neil's approach at Summerhill which opened in 1921. At Kinderheim Baumgarten, children's psychological problems were dealt with therapeutically in "a permissive milieu rather than" a controlling, punitive, or coercive one (p. 197). "During the first few months of its existence the Kinderheim Baumgarten was characterized by chaos, or, in Bernfeld's term, … 'creative chaos.' There were no rules. The children were free from all restraints; they received no punishment" (p. 198).

At first there was no curriculum, other than the children's interests. Then the teachers put in place a more formal curriculum, although there were no grades or exams, and discipline was intentionally lax. Students engaged in self-government and met in interest groups, small peer groups led by teachers. The experiment ended in 1920 when Bernfeld fell ill. His energy had apparently held the school together. Later, he would question such lofty goals, as is evident from the title of his 1925 work *Sisyphus or the Limits of Education*. One either accepts the impossibility of education or one is doomed to a repetition compulsion.

Another experiment, Anna Freud's 'Matchbox School' was more successful. According to Elizabeth Danto (2005), Bernfeld introduced Anna Freud to Eva Rosenfeld and the two of them along with help from Dorothy Burlingham in 1927 would "found another antiauthoritarian educational experiment, the … Heitzing School in Vienna" or Matchbox School, which would be directed first by Peter Blos, a friend of Erik Erikson, and then by Willi Hoffer" (p. 42). At various times teachers at the school included August Aichhorn and Erik Erikson. Midgley (2008) suggests that the school itself, while inspired by psychoanalysis, also integrated progressive education methods such as Kilpatrick's project method. The school ran for almost five years, until 1932.

By 1920, according to Danto (2005), the Vienna municipal school system was populated with clinics and schools which integrated progressive education methods, encouraged children to express their emotions, used small groups and peer groups for discussion, integrated sex education and psychodrama, and treated children as co-educators, and assistants (p. 76) and problem children as victims of internal conflicts and anxious, overwrought parents. Above all else, the psychopedagogues believed the children needed strong emotional relationships and compassion (pp. 107–8). While students and teachers were not explicitly in psychoanalytic treatment unless there were serious emotional problems, the schools were suffused with applied psychoanalytic theory. What that looked like is hard to tell. There are few first hand accounts of day to day life in those schools. We can, I think get a glimpse, however, if we consider Adolf Aichhorn's account in *Wayward Youth* (1939) of how he handled delinquent children.

Aichhorn's approach is exemplified by stories of his allowing youth to go wild and trash their own things, his sharing cigarettes with students, and his discussing their thieving or plans to run away, all without his scolding, disciplining, or intervention and at times with his complicity, His method consisted essentially of asking questions, refraining from value judgments or punishment, occasionally breaking the institutional rules to form alliances with the kids, blurring boundaries between rigid identities of authority figure and child, understanding that there are several motives behind any action, and expressing a compassionate curiosity about all the child's or adolescent's actions, no matter how trivial. Rather than allow transference to unfold in the educative relationship, Aichhorn worked to establish positive transferential relationships with the young people with whom he worked. He believed that the social worker or teacher, whether working with youth who are "in open conflict with society" (1939, p. 122) or with "the normal child" (p. 122), should strive to bring the child into a positive transference. To achieve the positive transference we must let the adolescent or child know that we have "insight into his difficulties and that [we] will not interpret the behavior in the same way as do the parents" (p. 122). We "will respond to the child's feeling of a need for punishment, but [we] will not satisfy it completely" (p. 122). With particularly asocial adolescents or children we "must take the child's part, be in agreement with his behavior, and in the severest cases even give the child to understand that in his place we would behave just the same way" (p. 123). But such a move, to establish a positive transference, cannot be inauthentic, which meant that teachers or social workers had to understand that "[t]here is nothing remarkable in the behavior of the dissocial; it differs only quantitatively from normal behavior" (p. 125). Radical about this idea is the insistence that the teacher or analyst respect or take seriously the student's or patient's world view, even enter it, no matter how irrational or unconventional or bizarre that view is. Aichhorn's views resonate with the emancipatory project, in that they promote compassionate curiosity, challenge the status quo, and acknowledge the dissocial, if not psychotic, that lives in all of us.

In Vienna and Berlin the progressive schools and clinics influenced by the work of, in particular, Alfred Adler, August Aichhorn, Siegfried Bernfeld, Paul Federn, and Anna Freud, thrived for a period. The rise of National Socialism ended many of the efforts, however, as Jewish analysts were forced to emigrate, and psychoanalysis, the "Jewish science," fell into disfavor, but this was not the only reason for the decline. Many of the schools had been founded on the principle that lifting repression was a good in and of itself. Although there were some positive results (Cohen, 1979), Willi Hoffer's findings that students who had been allowed free rein were more passive than those who had not been, the disappointment of some analysts with the lack of progress in both students and young patients, and the growing sense that children could not be completely raised non-judgmentally led the psychoanalytic pedagogues to reconsider their views (Cohen, 1979, pp. 203–4).

"Finally, there was a belated acknowledgement that the prevention of neurosis could no longer realistically be a goal of pedagogy" (Cohen, 1979, p. 207). By the time Bernfeld and Federn had moved to the United States, they had become much more conservative in their educational philosophy.

The country where they arrived in the late 1930s was very much in the thrall of progressive education and taken with the view that permissiveness, as it had come to be called, was a good thing. We can see the durability of such views if we consider that in 1956, in his article "The Origins of the Doctrine of Permissiveness in Higher Education" appearing in the *Journal of Progressive Education*, Fred Kerlinger, a professor of educational psychology wrote:

> Almost any student-teacher taking a first course in education learns ... that he should be permissive, accepting and warm with pupils, especially with pupils with personal difficulties. Much of this whole idea is embodied in what is now known as mental hygiene in education, and many university schools of education have special courses in mental hygiene for teachers. Many courses in psychology, especially educational psychology, are saturated with the 'mental hygiene complex' as are many guidance courses. (p. 163)

While initially several educational experiments took place in the United States as well as in Germany and Austria, experiments that allowed the students great freedom, sexual and otherwise, that took seriously the emotional lives of children and teachers, that sustained some psychoanalytic perspective, and that, particularly in Europe, integrated radical political views, eventually psychoanalysis was itself transformed as it spread in the United States. Psychoanalytic insights into the complicated relationship between human desires and drives and social restraints and conventions, however they may have been implemented in Vienna and Berlin and whatever their degree of success, mutated in the United States into the mental hygiene movement and expanded the child-centered wing of progressive education. Rather than as a theory of freedom and radical questioning, although initially it did appear that way in some schools, psychoanalytic theory came to emerge in progressive education as a program of diagnosis, cure, and social adjustment. The therapeutic project increasingly came to dominate the more threatening emancipatory project. As Nathan Hale (1995a) puts it:

> The Americans modified psychoanalysis. ... They muted sexuality and aggression, making both more amiable. They emphasized social conformity. They were more didactic, moralistic and popular than Freud. They were also more optimistic and environmentalist. (p. 332)

In order to understand the transformation in psychoanalytic theory as it migrated to the United States we not only have to look at the forces that worked to change psychoanalysis but also to consider psychoanalysis' own blind spots and collusion in its transformation.

Resistance to Psychoanalysis and its Effects

> Society will not hasten to grant us authority.
> It is bound to offer us resistance, for we adopt
> a critical attitude towards it; we point out to it
> that it itself plays a great part in causing neuroses.
>
> (Freud, 1910b, p. 147)

After the Clark Conference, the opposition to psychoanalysis, according to Hale (1995a), soon mobilized into three main attacks that were aimed at "the scientific status of psychoanalysis, the validity of Freud's sexual theories, [and] psychoanalysis's challenges to 'civilized morality, American culture'" (p. 275), and American values. Those values included optimism, individualism, pragmatism, and faith in both religion and science. Combined, the forces profoundly influenced psychoanalysis' reception in the United States, particularly in the academy, and its involvement in education. In responding to the attacks, psychoanalysis also gradually changed, so much so that by the end of his life Freud felt his work had been completely rejected. "Let us make no mistake," he stated in 1934, "this day and age has rejected me and all I had to give" (quoted in Jacoby, 1997, p. 19).

It is safe to say then that the transformation psychoanalysis underwent in the United States resulted from three inter-related factors: its rejection from the academy for not being scientific enough, its alliance with medicine and psychiatry to gain professional status and the veneer of scientific respectability, and its responsiveness to the cultural milieu which demanded a more up-beat, salvific, utilitarian and ultimately conservative approach to understanding the psyche and the human condition. As psychoanalysis mutated into other forms, its more radical and disturbing insights became muffled. As Jacoby (1986) writes, "The translation of psychoanalysis into a professional and scientific enterprise affected its language, spirit, breadth and even those attracted to it; fewer and fewer individuals with humanist, intellectual or political commitments entered the discipline" (p. 141).

Paradoxically, it would be in the humanities that psychoanalytic theory would find new life more than half a century later. It is interesting to note here, that the current situation in education resembles that of psychoanalysis as the latter adapted to the United States. Today it is education that has been transformed into "a professional and scientific enterprise ... and fewer individuals with humanist, intellectual or political commitments" (p. 141) are entering the discipline (see Taubman, 2009). One might even venture that the interest in education manifested in other disciplines reflects the displacement of those commitments.

It is important to understand, however, that psychoanalysis' initial utopianism, its desire to be seen as a science, its quest for professional status, and its belief that lifting repression under the guidance of a knowledgeable analyst would not only lead to mental health but, if applied to education, also could act as a prophylaxis against mental illness and lead to a just society—all these grandiose claims—abetted its eventual demise. Only later, long after the Clark Conference, when Freud had come to see the limitations of his therapy, had experienced World War I and grown disillusioned with prospects for humankind, and had come to understand more about the death drive and people's profound attachment to their own suffering, would he let fall the ambitions, grandiose claims, and muted optimism he had brought to the Clark lectures. Perhaps it was that he had begun to touch human limits—mortality, pain, profound loss, and failure—but he, himself, increasingly relinquished his belief in cure or the benefit of hope. In some ways, as he aged, Freud increasingly allowed the disturbing knowledge provided by psychoanalysis to penetrate his own psyche. Less and less inclined toward the therapeutic project, although never abandoning it completely, Freud, by the end of his life, confronted the impossibility of psychoanalysis and education.

Let us briefly consider some of the forces that reshaped psychoanalysis in the United States and see how they influenced psychoanalysis' reception within the academy and within education.

The Question of Scientific Status

> Our right to assume the existence of something mental that
> is unconscious and to employ that assumption for the purpose
> of scientific work is disputed in some quarters. ... A gain in
> meaning is perfectly justifiable ground for going beyond the
> limits of direct experience.
>
> (Freud, 1915c, pp. 166–67).

Throughout his career, Freud appeared ambivalent about psychoanalysis's stature as a science. In much of his writing he seemed to be arguing that psychoanalysis was a science, but it was never clear how he was defining science, and it often seemed as if he were appealing to the status of science to gain approval for his radical ideas. After all if one is going to call religion an illusion, claim conventional morality causes undue damage, argue that children are sexual beings who have incestuous desires aroused by their parents, and find truth in free associations, dreams, bungled actions, and slips of the tongue, it helps to have the legitimacy of science on one's side. Indeed, Freud more often than not referred to psychoanalysis as a science, albeit one whose claim to such status rested on its talking truthfully, empirical observation, and most important its "gain in meaning" (Freud, 1915c, p. 167)

Furthermore, if one was going to argue that the talking cure was not the work of psychics, mind readers, and faith healers, then the trappings of science would come in handy. And, in fact, as Zaretsky points out, the translators of Freud's German were careful to introduce the Latin words for much of Freud's German, making it sound more medical, e.g. the German *ich* (I) became 'ego' and *Lust* became 'libido,' *Trieb* (drive) became the biologically based 'instinct' and *besetzt* (taken or occupied) became 'cathected' (Zaretsky, 2004, p. 83). Finally, Freud, although he was critical of America, calling it "Dollaria" (Danto, 2005, p. 147), wanted to gain for psycho-analysis professional acceptance in the United States, and that meant gaining a foothold in the academy or in the medically associated fields of neurology and psychiatry. But to do either, his scientific credentials needed to be flashed.

Freud, however, was ambivalent about adhering to the protocols of science. While he would argue, as he did in "Instincts and Their Vicissitudes" (1915b), that science consists of "describing phenomena and then proceeding to group, classify and correlate them" (p. 117), he refused to reduce psychoanalysis to a series of categorizations or interventions whose success could be empirically validated through trial and error experiments or replication—something psychoanalytically inclined psychologists and sociologists would attempt in the second half of the century. Nor was he comfortable with the idea that psychoanalysts could predict phenomena with any nomological certainty. Zaretsky (2004) reports that when Saul Rosenzweig "sent Freud data purporting to confirm his theories, Freud responded that analysis did not lend itself to experimental testing" (p. 185). The problem, of course, was that psychoanalysis was not a philosophy either, since as Freud pointed out in *An Outline of Psychoanalysis*, "the majority of philosophers ... declare that the idea of something psychical being unconscious is self-contradictory" (1940a, p. 158). Furthermore, because Freud claimed that one had to experience psychoanalysis to determine its truth claims, a good many academicians and psychiatrists worried that cultism rather than science more accurately described the epistemological status of psychoanalytic theory.

Mapping the arguments about psychoanalysis's status as a science is beyond the scope of this book. What is clear is that Freud's claim that it was a science was expedient, defensive, and also genuine, although wobbly. It was, however, certainly necessary.

Reception in the Academy

Psychology Departments

> Psychoanalysis did represent an extreme position
> against which more conservative disciplines like
> psychology and psychiatry had to define themselves
>
> (Hornstein, 1992, p. 261)

Establishing the scientific validity of Freud's theories proved particularly difficult with the academic department most likely to have welcomed his research—psychology. Hale (1995a) claims that academic psychologists "were put off by the apparent psychoanalytic disdain for their discipline and for their laborious attempts to be scientific" (p. 286). We have already seen in the correspondence between Titchener and Meyer the barely disguised contempt in which they held psychoanalysis. While it may be true that psychologists reacted defensively to the superciliousness of psychoanalysts, I would argue that a more self-serving motive lay behind the resistance to psychoanalysis: psychology's drive for its own scientific status. Psychology had just begun to separate from its attachment to philosophy departments and psychologists increasingly aspired to the stature of the hard sciences (Winter, 1999, pp. 164–70). As Danziger (1990) points out, this effort "was greatly encouraged by a swelling tide of scientism during the closing years of the nineteenth century" (p. 41).

> There were two major themes in this surge of scientism. The one was technical-utilitarian, involving an assimilation of conceptions of truth to conceptions of usefulness and a consequent emphasis on practically applicable knowledge. ... The second theme derived the superiority of scientific knowledge more from its close grounding in directly observed facts and its avoidance of airy metaphysical fancies that lacked this grounding. (p. 41).

While both were inherent in the therapeutic projects of education and psychoanalysis, psychoanalysis, with its unconventional speculations and a method that Freud at times referred to as not only "impossible" but bound to "achieve unsatisfying results" (1937b, p. 248), did not appear to fit with these themes. It is true that psychoanalysis was not absent from departments of psychology. We can note Dorothy Park's 1931 study of Freudian influence on academic psychology. Reviewing texts published between 1910 and 1930, she concluded that "Freudian influence has been quite steadily increasing since 1910 and is consistently holding its own at the present time despite opposition and controversy" (Park, 1931, p. 85). Nevertheless its hold was at best tenuous, and the more psychology turned to the hard sciences as a model for its own methods, the less of a foothold psychoanalytic theory, as initially elaborated by Freud, had. And that had serious implications for the reception of psychoanalysis in education.

As Danziger (1990) elaborates, and as we know from Callahan's *Education and The Cult of Efficiency* (1962), as well as several other sources (see in particular Cremin, 1988; Kliebard, 1987, 1992; Pinar, Reynolds, Slattery, and Taubman, 1995; Ravitch, 2000; Tyack, 1974), education in the early part of the twentieth century was very much under the influence of the social efficiency movement and Taylorism. According to Danziger, in the beginning of the twentieth century "a new generation of professional educational administrators" not classroom teachers, "took control of a process of educational rationalization that ... emphasized scientific research as a basis for the rationalized educational system of which they were the chief architects" (1990, p. 103). These administrators turned to psychology for research relevant to "managerial concerns" (p. 103). Such research "had to provide data that were useful in making immediate decisions in restricted administrative contexts. This meant research that yielded comparable quantitative data on the performance of large numbers of individuals under restricted conditions" (p. 103).

Academic psychologists responded to the call for this kind of research, seeing in education a market for their services. More and more they offered statistical knowledge, categorized individuals by group characteristics, measured and compared performance on specific tasks, normed groups, and focused less on the individual and more on group comparisons (Danziger, 1990, pp. 109–10). Increasingly academic psychologists, who saw their role in terms of helping educators, positioned themselves as experts.

The leading journal among this group of psychologists was the *Journal of Educational Psychology*. The first edition of the *Journal of Educational Psychology*, appearing the year after Freud's visit to Clark, included in its anonymously authored editorial the following passage:

> The term "Educational Psychology" will, for our purposes, be interpreted ... as including ... the psychology of sensation, instinct, attention, habit, memory, the technique and economy of learning, the conceptual processes ... problems of mental development ... the study of individual differences, of retarded and precocious development, the psychology of the "special class," the nature of mental endowments, the measurement of mental capacity, the psychology of mental tests, the correlation of mental abilities, the psychology of special methods in the several school branches, the important problems of mental hygiene; all these ... are topics and problems which we deem pertinent for consideration. (p. 1)

The journal did not consider psychoanalysis pertinent. As a matter of fact between that founding issue and the most current issue only a handful of articles have appeared in which psychoanalysis is mentioned, two of which were written by Ernest Jones. The lead article in that first issue was written by Edward Thorndike. He described the contributions psychology can make to education in terms of defining aims, measuring the probability of achieving those aims, and developing a "complete science of psychology [that] would tell every fact about every one's intellect and character and behavior, would tell the cause of every change in human nature, [and] would tell the result which every educational force ... would have (Thorndike, 1910, p. 6). Seven years earlier, "Thorndike had summed up his goal as 'quantitative precision,' 'direct observation,' 'experiment,' and the careful use of statistics" (Hale, 1995a, pp. 114–15). For Thorndike classroom practice served as the testing ground for educational psychology's theories that would establish a science of psychology and education.

The strand of academic psychology that formed alliances with mainstream educators was the very strand that rejected psychoanalytic theory. As Zaretsky (2004) points out, all of psychoanalysis's "attempts to gain a foothold in the university failed" (p. 176). Of course, the rise of Watsonian behaviorism in the 1920s, which "reduced personality to reflexology" (Toulmin and Leary, 1985, p. 601) and substituted 'behavior' for 'consciousness,' and the publication of Robert Woodworth's hugely successful undergraduate text which championed stimulus-response psychology (Graumann and Gergen, 1996, pp. 20–21) only made the spread of psychoanalysis in the academy less likely.

According to Ernest Hilgard (1996) books on child study and child development prior to World War II were slow to incorporate psychoanalytic concepts "averaging less than a page of explicit references to psychoanalysis", and an "examination of 44 educational psychology texts gave the same picture of neglect" (pp. 997–98). Braddock and Lacewing (2007) argue that the absence of psychoanalysis from psychology departments can be attributed to "the early critiques and indeed polemics against psychoanalysis' title to be considered a science" (p. 4) and to its purported confusion of "the scientific with the hermeneutic" (p. 7). Psychoanalyst Barbara Low writing in 1929 reported that "as theory, psycho-analysis was rejected by our great educational institutions" (p. 315).

> The universities and colleges gave it no place in their curriculum; the teacher-in-training devoted no time to its study; the teacher engaged in practical work had no systematic knowledge of it, and the central governing body of our educational system … gave no encouragement to the pursuit of the branch of knowledge. The individual teacher, the writer on education, the student of educational development, all these in the main followed the same example … (p. 315)

Ernest Hilgard (1996) suggests Low's claims may have been slightly exaggerated, although only slightly. "Psychoanalysis," he writes, "was already becoming popularized during the 1930s, and it was finding its way into the thinking of educators, but mostly by way of the public press and literary sources" as opposed to professional coursework or exposure in the academy (pp. 997–98). In *Terrible Honesty: Mongrel Manhattan in the 1920s*, Ann Douglas (1995) argues it is impossible to understand the culture of New York in the 1920s without acknowledging the huge impact of psychoanalysis on "New Yorkers' cultural choices and psychological possibilities" (p. 28). Thomas Bender (1987) paints a rather dismal picture, however, of the psychoanalysis that was being popularized, at least in New York City.

> Psychoanalysis was either vulgarized in the sophisticated and fashionable culture of *Vanity Fair* or the *The New Yorker*, or it was medicalized and localized on Central Park West. In contrast to what happened in Vienna and Berlin, … psychoanalysis in New York did not elicit convergence; it did not bring together intellectuals in a variety of humanistic fields. (p. 250)

While Hilgard (1996) argues that psychoanalysis was entering education through public media, he also acknowledges that "books on child study and child development were slow to incorporate psychoanalytic concepts" (p. 998) and cites as an example the omission of any reference to psychoanalysis in the 1939 *Yearbook on*

Child Development and the Curriculum, compiled under the chairmanship of Carleton Washburne. He also cites a study by Suppes and Warren (1978) which found only minimal impact of psychoanalysis on elementary education before World War II.

Sociology and Anthropology

While psychoanalysis received at best a lukewarm reception in psychology departments, its treatment in departments of sociology was little better. According to Ernest Burgess, writing in 1939, there was little evidence of Freudian influence before 1920 (p. 357). Between 1920 and 1939, the influence of psychoanalysis in sociology increased, according to Burgess, partially as a result of the work of social psychologist John Dollard, who advocated "a union of the methods of psychoanalysis and sociology in the study of personality" (p. 368) and of the application of the theories of Karen Horney and Harry Stack Sullivan, both of whom, it must be said, Freud considered to have misunderstood his theory.

In anthropology departments psychoanalysis was introduced through the work of Franz Boas and Edward Sapir and then Margaret Mead. At Columbia Boas, according to Zaretsky (2004), "taught psychoanalysis as a contrast to nineteenth-century racial science" (pp. 154–55), and Sapir used psychoanalytic theory as an invaluable tool to define "culture as an unconscious resource" (p. 155), and to define the unconscious in terms of a series of patterns learned in the family. Suzette Heald (1994) describes anthropology in the 1930s as succumbing just as psychoanalysis did, to "the essential optimism of American culture" (p. 5) and while it included psychoanalytic concepts, it often did so without attribution. For example, Ruth Benedict "rigorously excluded psychoanalytic terms from her own interpretations," but analyzed "cultures as personalities writ large" (p. 6). Years later, Abraham Maslow would praise Benedict as being one of the foremost influences on his humanistic psychology (see Frick, 1971, p. 124).

But while Freud's *Totem and Taboo* (1913b), with its myth of parricide as the founding gesture of civilization, provoked an interest in psychoanalysis, anthropology departments greeted psychoanalysis with mixed reviews. Those that did incorporate its insights into courses may have indirectly influenced teachers, who at least at Columbia University's Teachers College could take courses in the department.

There were in the 1930s academic leaders who did make attempts to create conversations among psychologists, anthropologists, sociologists, and psychoanalysts about the contributions psychoanalysis could make to research. At the University of Chicago, Robert Maynard Hutchins had invited the Hungarian analyst Franz Alexander to be the first professor of psychoanalysis, but Alexander did not find a warm welcome, particularly among the medical faculty with whom he had hoped to form an alliance. Instead he found the professors in the social sciences more inviting (see Hale, 1995b, p. 132). According to Ellen Lagemann (1989), interest at the University of Chicago "in psychoanalysis was not idiosyncratic" (p. 157). John Dollard, William Ogburn, and Edward Sapir, all of whom were working in the department of sociology and anthropology, met regularly to discuss psychoanalytic contributions to their disciplines. In a statement that today must seem bizarre to our scientifically oriented colleagues in education, Ogburn wrote, "psychoanalytic concepts can tell social scientists 'how to be less unscientific' because they could help people understand their desires and 'the way our desires disguise themselves, how they originate, how they are conditioned, and the part they play in forming specific opinions'" (quoted in Lagemann, 1989, p. 157). The interest in psychoanalysis must not have been too broad because, after a year there, Alexander left and went on to focus on adolescent delinquency, and to consult at Pioneer House, Fritz Redl's project in Detroit. By 1960 Alexander had "come to believe that American psychoanalysis was overly conservative" (quoted in Hale, 1995b, p. 133).

When Sapir moved from Chicago to Yale, he not only brought with him the psychoanalytic interests he had in part developed in conversations with Harry Stack Sullivan, from whom according to Lagemann, he had sought bereavement counseling over his wife's death, but he also brought John Dollard. Dollard had been analyzed by a disciple of Freud's, Hans Sachs, who had also analyzed Edwin Boring, the dean of experimental psychology, causing somewhat of a scandal for those academic psychologists dismissive of psychoanalysis (see Hornstein, 1922, pp. 256–57). In that one instance of Boring's analysis we can clearly see the contradictory attitudes held in tension that Freud described in his work on disavowal. On one hand experimental psychology rejected Freud's theory as unscientific; on the other hand, experimental psychologists might turn to that theory as a cure for suffering.

Dollard was intent on applying Freud's insights to sociology, through laboratory testing. *Frustration and Aggression* appearing in 1939, "used experiments on laboratory rats to demonstrate that aggression is always a consequence of frustration" (Zaretsky, 2004, p. 185). In linking frustration to aggression, Dollard's work led educators and policy makers to focus on the internal and external causes of frustration as a way to reduce racial and ethnic intolerance. Freud had complicated any discussions of group antipathies by positing an instinctual aggressiveness, identification, and the "narcissism of minor differences" (Freud, 1930a, p. 114) as central to group cohesion. Dollard's work, on the other hand, suggested that by reducing frustration through economic interventions or confidence building remedies—the latter more often implemented by educators and federal policy makers—aggression would diminish. We can see the traces of this work in the self-esteem and self-knowledge groups utilized by educators after World War II to combat prejudice and increase tolerance (see Weidner, 1954 and Jones, R., 1960 on group work in education and Herman, 1995, on applications in public policy).

At Yale both Dollard and Sapir were involved in developing seminars for the Yale Institute for Human Relations that had been established in 1929. The Institute offered colloquia and interdisciplinary panels. Several of the seminars focused on applying psychoanalysis to the social sciences. Ellen Herman (1995) argues in *The Romance of American Psychology: Political Culture in the Age of Experts* that the Institute in the 30s and during the World War II era tried to "systematize the basic elements of psychoanalysis, in the form of a series of concrete behavioral principles that could be empirically or experimentally validated" (p. 36). *Frustration and Aggression* exemplified such efforts. In the service of such a project, the Yale Institute brought together psychoanalysts such as Erik Erikson, sociologists, and social psychologists such as Dollard, and psychologists such as Clark Hull and Robert Sears. In part the aim of such collaboration was to "dispel the notion that behaviorism and psychoanalysis were conceptually incompatible" (Herman, 1995, p. 36). Robert Sears (1985) would later write that the net effect for psychoanalysis of these efforts to "integrate, verify, translate and absorb [psychoanalysis] was minimal" (p. 217). The attempts in the academy to unite behaviorism and psychoanalysis did, however, have some influence on teacher education.

Stephen Petrina (2004), in his article "Luella Cole, Sidney Pressy, and Educational Psychoanalysis, 1921–1931" argues that schools of education, the example he details is Ohio State University, were much more eclectic than suggested by those writers who pit Thorndike, Watson and educational psychology against Freud and say that the former triumphed. He writes, "Rather than antagonists, psychoanalysis and behaviorism were complementary and consolidated, working in tandem to individualize students within the confines of mass education" (p. 1). As long as we take a very superficial view of psychoanalytic theory, we can accept Petrina's argument, although his claim that the failure to mention Freud in the vast majority of educational psychology textbooks at the time constitutes an historical oversight rather than a reflection of reality seems a bit of a stretch. It is true though that educational psychology by the 1920s was taught in eighty percent of teacher training programs and that educational psychology, while emphasizing testing and measurement, did, in its attention to mental hygiene, integrate a diluted psychoanalysis, one that tended to focus on normality and abnormality.

Were it not for the progressive movement, psychoanalytic theory as initially conceived might well have disappeared from American education altogether. Certainly its presence in departments of psychology, which exerted influence on teacher education, was minimal. Even at Clark, by 1919, the psychology department was split among Titchenerians, genetic psychologists, and gestalt psychologists. The department through the 1920s seemed to have dropped psychoanalysis (Geldard, 1980, p. 226). Psychoanalysis survived, however, in pockets of progressive schools, such as the Walden School and the Ferrer School, in various permutations in progressive education's view of childhood and discipline, and, most important, in a particularly watered down version, strained through the sieve of medicine and psychiatry, that emerged during the first half of the twentieth century in the mental hygiene movement.

Alliance with Medicine

> As long as I live I shall resist that psychoanalysis
> be swallowed up by medicine.
>
> (Freud, in Federn, 1967, p. 270)

In the immediate years preceding Freud's visit to Clark University, neurologists and psychiatrists had felt confident that they would soon discover the answers to the enigmas of mental illness. Belief in the dominant somatic style, new discoveries localizing particular functions in the brain, and the faith that heredity could explain individuals' psychic suffering, led neurologists and psychiatrists to feel they were on the verge of solving, as Hale puts it, "every puzzle" (Hale, 1995a, p. 50). By the time of Freud's visit such optimism had been dampened. Those physicians who blamed mental illness on heredity increasingly found themselves supporting a theory of degeneracy and accused of shoddy science and overextension. Neurologists hopeful of locating in the brain the origin of every character trait and behavior were thrown back by charges of metaphysical psychology and Cartesian anthropomorphism and by the discovery of neurons, which complicated their initial simplistic views of the nervous system (Hale, 1995a p. 91). Nevertheless, these psychiatrists and neurologists only broadened their purview. "Not only the brain, but the 'whole nervous system and the whole man' should become the physician's concern'" (p. 91). With all the shifts and schisms among them, the psychiatrists, neurologists, and psychotherapists found a common identity in their medical stature. In 1910, under pressure from the Flexner Commission, the medical profession was itself forming a professional identity based on scientifically sound research and licensing procedures.

While academic psychologists were finding a market among educational administrators in the early part of the twentieth century, physicians too were offering advice to teachers. Hale (1995a) writes:

> American physicians and educators warned against too much love or too much harshness, and assumed the child's character would be largely formed by the mother. They taught that the hysterical child must be separated from his parents, whose unhealthy training had helped to bring on his illness. (p. 166)

A focus on normality, health and illness, and cure dominated the medical discourse that entered education. While psychoanalysis was finding it difficult to gain a toehold in the academy, and to contribute its insights to education through the academy, it found, thanks in part to the early efforts by Putnam, and in part to the medical profession's "struggle to establish their monopoly against popular forms of healing and self-help" (Zaretsky, 2004, p. 67) a bond with medicine. To accomplish this alliance psychoanalysis increasingly presented itself as "a cure and a form of self-improvement" and as a "scientific alternative to popular forms of mental healing" (p. 67).

The tie to medicine garnered status in the United States for psychoanalysis, and also funding but at a price, which Freud foresaw. Acknowledging the benefits of an association with medicine, he also warned that medicalization was, "the last mask of resistance against psychoanalysis and the most dangerous of all," and he predicted, "a gloomy future [for] analysis if it does not succeed in creating an abode for itself outside of medicine" (Zaretsky, 2004, p. 186). In 1926 in *The Question of Lay Analysis* Freud would write: "For we do not consider it at all desirable for psycho-analysis to be swallowed up by medicine and to find its last resting place in a text-book of psychiatry under the heading 'Methods of Treatment'" (p. 248). Unfortunately, given how most psychiatric and psychology textbooks treated Freud, his premonition was not far from wrong.

The bond between psychoanalysis and medicine became so strong that even though Freud advocated for lay analysts, opposed requiring a medical degree for analysts, and believed the greatest training for an analyst was undergoing a personal analysis and developing "a free human outlook" in part through study in the humanities and social sciences, by 1925 the American Psychoanalytic Society had passed a regulation requiring a medical degree for every analyst (Zaretsky, 2004, p. 186), and by 1927 the New York Psychoanalytic Society followed suit (Hale, 1995b, p. 33). In 1938 the American Psychoanalytic Association required its members to be "physicians who had completed a psychiatric residency at an approved institution" (Hale, 1995b, p. 128). Furthermore, the personal analysis, basically an "informal apprenticeship between analyst and analysand" (Hale, 1995a, p. 323) that Freud considered a requisite to practicing was split off from the training analysis "which aimed specifically at controlled learning of treatment techniques" (Hale, 1995a, p. 323). The separation placed much greater power in the hands of the licensing institutes and associations. It also affected who entered the profession.

Anna Freud described those who were the first generation of psychoanalysts.

> They were the unconventional ones, the doubters, those who were dissatisfied with the limitations imposed by knowledge; also among them were the dreamers, and those who knew neurotic suffering from their own experience. (quoted in Phillips, 2006, p. 34)

The institutionalization of psychoanalysis, however, resulted in psychoanalysts who had "a different type of personality" (Phillips, 2006, p. 34). Excluded were "the mentally endangered, the eccentrics, the self-made, those with excessive flights of imagination [in favor of] the sober, well-prepared ones, who are hard-working enough to wish to better their professional efficiency" (p. 34). These would be the analysts who would come to dominate psychoanalysis and bring it to education through the mental hygiene movement. As psychoanalysis's absorption into the medical profession by way of psychiatry deepened, the power of its original theoretical insights, as Freud had foreseen, decreased. On the other hand, its influence on education expanded.

The Mental Hygiene Movement and an Optimistic Psychoanalysis

> Few intellectual and social movements of this
> century have had so deep and pervasive an influence
> on the theory and practice of American education as
> the mental hygiene movement. ... The mental hygiene movement

provided the inspiration and driving force behind one of
the most far-reaching yet little understood educational innovations
of this century, what I call the "medicalization" of American education.

(Cohen, 1983, p. 124)

The alliance between medicine, psychiatry, and psychoanalysis affected education indirectly but distinctly, and it did so through the rise of the mental hygiene movement, a branch of the progressive education movement (Ravitch, 2000, p. 327), and one which saw its mission as "keeping the mind, brain and nerves of humans healthy," preventing the spread of mental disease, modernizing mental institutions, and training youth for social adjustment (*Time Magazine*, 1930). According to Hale, the mental hygiene movement embodied American optimism, promoting a belief that delinquency, domestic abuse, and social unrest could be cured by addressing mental maladaption. The mental hygiene movement's watchword was:

'[s]cience,' that is, the new 'sciences' of psychiatry and psychology which would replace traditional religion. Mental hygiene would supplant theology as the foundation of the new order. Its priests would be the psychiatrists, the social workers, the psychologists, the experts of the new scientific psychology. (Hale, 1995b, p. 84)

Writing in 1926, Frankwood Williams, an early proponent of progressive education, noted the emergence of the mental hygiene movement in an article in the *Journal of Progressive Education*. "New terms seem to be creeping into the general vocabulary—psychiatry, psychiatric social worker, mental hygiene. Where do they come from?" he wondered (p. 7).

Founded in 1909, the same year as the Clark Conference, by Clifford Whittinghouse Beers, who got the term 'mental hygiene' from the psychiatrist Dr. Adolf Meyers (*Time Magazine*, 1930), who, recall, had labeled the unconscious "a cesspool," the National Committee for Mental Hygiene, the movement's lead organization, grew in size quickly, and by 1930 the first International Congress of Mental Hygiene was bringing together "eminent psychiatrists" and, among other associations, the American Psychiatric Association and the American Psychoanalytic Association (*Time Magazine*, 1930). By the 1920s, according to Hale (1995b), the movement had brought child guidance services within its purview (p. 86), was focused on bringing to the public schools the new therapeutic function of molding healthy personalities (p. 88), and was propounding an "ideology that combined elements of Adolf Meyer's psychobiology and behaviorism," with psychoanalysis (p. 85).

Funded largely by the Rockefeller Foundation, the mental hygiene movement's "aim was to create through scientific child-rearing a personality adjusted to the demands of modern social life" (Hale, 1995b, p. 85). Schools would be one of the targets for such an endeavor. Thus psychoanalytic contributions, particular kinds of psychoanalytic contributions mind you, began to dribble and then flow into the schools. Lawrence Cremin (1988) suggests that the work of the movement, the various organizations associated with it, and in particular the influence of the patron, the Laura Spelman Rockefeller Memorial Foundation, under the leadership of Lawrence K. Frank,

> served increasingly as a conduit for newer Freudian conceptions of child rearing that emphasized the centrality of the emotions in human development, the importance of personality adjustment, and the efficacy of more permissive processes of child rearing in fostering proper adjustment. (p. 290)

Important to note here is that Frank was good friends with Lucy Sprague Mitchell whose influence according to Cremin led Frank to become a "mordant critic of contemporary schooling and a champion of progressive methods that would liberate youngsters" (p. 289). Lucy Sprague Mitchell who had founded the Bureau of Educational Experiments in New York City, later to become Bank Street School of Education, had read widely in psychoanalysis, and with her husband, Wesley, would also influence Frank's efforts to spread psychoanalytic ideas in the mental hygiene movement. But important to note also in the above quote is the emphasis on adjustment.

Recalling Putnam's fervent wish to turn the unconscious to socially ameliorative ends and to improve the human soul, mental hygienists combined psychoanalysis, the child-centered strand of progressive pedagogy and what they considered Dewey's new methods, in the hope of building a better society and a healthier person. "Mental hygienists, psychoanalysts, and progressive educators influenced each other, sometimes profoundly" (Hale, 1995b, p. 89). Interesting to note is that Dewey "accused Freud of reducing social events to psychic causes" (Rieff, 1979, p. 32) and regarded psychoanalytic theory "as so much mythology" (quoted in Hale, 1995b, p. 89) and "the most depressing and pessimistic of all possible doctrines" (quoted in Feuer, 1960, p. 129). Freud, on the other hand, considered Dewey one of the few men he held in high esteem (Hale, 1995b, p. 89). Freud also didn't necessarily reject Dewey's estimate, rhetorically asking Albert Einstein in 1932, "Does not every science come in the end to a kind of mythology ... ?" (1933a, p. 211), and claiming his theory was not for the faint of heart. It was certainly, at least in terms of the emancipatory project, skeptical of the social meliorism trumpeted by Dewey and the mental hygiene movement.

In social work, guidance clinics, and schools Freudian psychoanalysis emerged through the mental hygiene movement in several ways. First, while greater focus was placed on students' and teachers' personal histories, attention was also given to the "baneful psychological influence of parents" (Hale, 1995b, p. 86). In particular, faulty mothering was blamed for abnormal or socially deviant behavior. Second, while mental hygienists advocated for sex education and advised teachers and parents to refrain from punishing masturbation or talk of sex among the young, they promoted a normalizing discourse on sexuality, reinforcing conventional sex roles and heterosexual supremacy. Third, while the movement focused on the individual child and his or her development, often advocating for individualized curriculum rather than a college preparatory curriculum or solely academic curriculum (Zachry, Kotinsky, and Thayer, 1939), it also argued for a curriculum that would promote social adjustment.

Sol Cohen (1983) in "The Mental Hygiene Movement, the Development of Personality and the School: The Medicalization of American Education," argues that the mental hygiene movement promoted three central tenets, each of which was culled from and translated findings from psychoanalysis. "A major thrust of the mental hygiene movement in education," he writes, "was to de-legitimize academic subject matter. … Hygienists condemned the academic subject-matter-centered curriculum as a Procrustean bed, resulting in disaffection, failure, behavior problems, or personality maladjustment" (p. 130). Discipline was a second focus of the movement. Rigid discipline was:

> the other cardinal offense against children's personality development. … What hygienists desired, simply, was that the concepts and techniques that psychiatrists were then applying to the study and rehabilitation of delinquents and criminals be applied by teachers to the misbehavior of children in school. (p. 130)

Hygienists viewed students' misbehavior as symptomatic of deeper problems. They called upon teachers "to adopt a 'scientific approach' toward children's behavior, to adopt 'scientific detachment'" (p. 130). Finally, hygienists held teachers accountable for establishing the therapeutic milieu in the school.

> Hygienists urged teacher-training institutions to screen prospective teachers on the basis of personality adjustment and to shift from a pre-occupation with subject-matter, curriculum, teaching methods and discipline to those subjects which would lead teachers to a scientific understanding of children's personality. (p. 131)

Cohen concludes his overview of the mental hygiene movement by stating that the

> [h]ygienists formulated a medical or therapeutic model of schooling: the school as child psychiatric clinic; every child a "problem;" the teacher as clinician-therapist; the general ambience of the class period that of a therapeutic hour; and the goal—the adjustment of children's personality. (p. 131)

Philip Cushman (1995) concurs with Cohen's assessment. In *Constructing the Self, Constructing America: A Cultural History of Psychotherapy*, he describes the movement as applying "the bourgeois values of quantification, objectification, and cleanliness to the realm of emotional and psychological complaints" (p. 152). He goes on to suggest that the movement appropriated psychoanalytic concepts but betrayed them. For example, hygienists translated Freud's concept of the unconscious as a "container for psychological uncleanliness" (p. 152). Conceiving of emotional life in terms of physical illness and pedagogy in terms of prevention, the mental hygiene movement acted as a conduit into schools for what it understood as psychoanalytic insights, ones translated through a medical discourse.

Stephen Petrina (2006) has complicated Cohen's and Cushman's presentations of the mental hygiene movement by documenting how its influence on schools came through "complex and subtle interrelationships among the likes of janitors, nurses, pediatricians, pathologists, pharmacists, psychologists, psychiatrists, social workers, and teachers during the ... first three decades of the twentieth century" (p. 503). These interrelationships positioned the child as the focal point of a whole series of therapeutic interventions, which were informed by a particular version of psychoanalytic theory that brought into awareness the emotional lives of children. But that version, in its association with medicine, had already been instrumentalized, rendering analysis in terms of protocols, prophylaxis, and cures.

Rather than perpetuate a kind of moral dualism here between the emancipatory and therapeutic projects of psychoanalysis, I want to interject that the mental hygiene movement was, to Petrina (2006) and de Forest (2006, 2007), well-intentioned and not only had health benefits but also ushered more liberal attitudes into the schools. The complication in terms of psychoanalysis is that the mental health movement's version of psychoanalysis stripped it of its more radical insights and questions, and, in sustaining its alliance with medicine, edged it closer to becoming a male profession, which told a predominantly female dominated occupation—teachers and nurses—what to do. As we shall see, psychoanalysis, which had been one of the few professions with a high number of women, became after World War II completely male dominated.

It is interesting that Clarence Oberndorf (1953) saw the mental hygiene movement as being one of the three main reasons he believed psychoanalysis had attained its substantial place in the United States by the end of the 1940s. In addition to what Oberndorf saw as the practical success of psychiatry and the influence of "the liberal-minded physician" (p. 231) in the United States, he attributed the success of psychoanalysis to its embrace by "educators in schools, public and private, elementary and collegiate, [who] were ready to welcome and to understand the psychoanalytic psychiatrist as an aid and co-worker in preparing students for adaptation in a democratic society" (p. 233).

On the other hand, Ferenczi thought that psychoanalysis's popularity in America, particularly as it related to its alliance with medicine, was also its undoing (Danto, 2005, p. 195). Why? Because he believed that in America physicians and educators were translating psychoanalysis into a doctrine of the pursuit of individual mental health understood as adjustment to American values and because they themselves were not going into analysis and thus were misappropriating psychoanalytic concepts.

The view that the school was responsible for determining the underlying reasons for the child's behavior was common in the mental hygiene movement, and it is captured in a comment by Caroline Zachry. "It becomes the duty of the school to discover the causal elements in the child's conduct," she wrote in 1929, "and so to guide him such that his personality and emotional adjustments will be constructive and thus he will be able to be helped to properly face social situations" (p. 3). Influenced by Kilpatrick's project method, Zachry wrote that it could be used to help students follow the "rules of mental hygiene which one must obey if one would maintain, a 'normal' personality" (p. 251). Zachry had studied with Carl Jung during the 1930s and had been a fellow in the Orthopsychiatric Association. She would go on to direct the Mental Hygiene Institute at the New Jersey State Teachers College, where she wrote frequently "about the importance of 'personality adjustment'" (Lagemann, 2000, p. 146). Later she directed "a psychoanalytically oriented training center for child care professionals called the Institute for the Study of Personality Development" (Cremin, 1988, p. 291). There she would work with and mentor Benjamin Spock, who would credit her with having the greatest influence on his ideas (p. 291).

In 1932 Zachry was appointed to the Commission on Secondary School Curriculum, the Thayer Commission, which according to Lagemann (2000, pp. 144–45) was established to balance the more academically oriented curriculum recommendations made by the Eight-Year Study and to promote a secondary curriculum centered on adolescents' interests. While on the committee, Zachry attended in 1934 seminars in Hanover, New Hamsphire, sponsored and influenced by Lawrence Frank, himself a supporter of psychoanalysis. The seminars drew several anthropologists, such as Franz Boas, Margaret Mead, and Edward Sapir, all interested in psychoanalysis. When, in 1936, Zachry was appointed to chair the Thayer Commission's committee on adolescence, she wielded, according to Lagemann, great power over the direction of the commission, pushing for secondary schools to relinquish a curriculum determined by college demands and traditional academic disciplines and to individualize instruction. As her influence grew on the commission, Zachry attracted the psychoanalyst Peter Blos, Erik Erikson's friend, to the commission. Shortly after Zachry became chair of the committee, Boyd Bode who was on the committee, resigned, stating the committee had become dominated by the attitude of the psychiatrist and was "far too sentimentally child-centered" (Lagemann, 2000, p. 146). Bode accused the committee of neglecting the academic curriculum and emphasizing the student's present needs at the cost of independent intellectual development. Zachry (1941) would later state, "Many of the basic principles of progressive education are entirely consistent with Freud's contribution to understanding of psychic development" (p. 432). But were the tenets of the mental hygiene movement really consistent with psychoanalysis as conceived by Freud?

Toward the end of his life Freud refused to inflate the curative power of therapy and even questioned the possibility or at least the meaning of cure. Furthermore, he rejected the idea that psychoanalysis offered a method or practice that could, if applied, once and for all solve humankind's problems. He certainly opposed any idea of adapting oneself to the status quo. "Not in any beyond, but here on earth most men live in hell," he had written. "My knowledge, my theories and my methods have the goal of making men conscious of this hell so that they can free themselves from it" (quoted in Jacoby, 1997, p. 119). Freudian psychoanalysis differed from both the mental hygiene movement and progressive education's translations of it, in two particularly crucial ways. First, the mental hygiene movement and the child-centered wing of progressive education sought to determine and cater to the interests of the child. In so doing they took for granted the naturalness of those interests, and refrained from trying to understand them apart from the consequences of acting on them (Menand, 2001, p. 375). Psychoanalysis, on the other hand, sought to shed light on the desires behind those interests, how they were shaped, and how they might be over-determined by unconscious forces. Freud struggled to explicate the complex relationship among desire, the unconscious, the family, and social rules and regulations, and that struggle led him to conclude that education was always an unsatisfactory balance among these forces, and that its effects could never be anticipated.

Second, the mental hygiene movement and the child centered movement within progressive education held to a liberal belief in progress. On the individual level progress consisted in achieving healthy, normal relationships and developing self-expression, although the latter often came into conflict with a belief in moral perfection, a sense of responsibility, and social adaptation. On the social level, progress consisted in establishing harmonious, equal relations among individuals. Freud's skepticism about human perfectability, his understanding of the unconscious not as a seething cauldron of salacious impulses but as a radically unknowable, conflict ridden, and irruptive kind of thinking that occurs elsewhere than the conscious mind, his insistence on looking at aggression and our attachment to suffering as part of the human condition, his sense of the tragic dimension of virtue, and his conviction that the division between normal and abnormal was at best tenuous and contingent, all these contradicted the sunny belief in progress central to the tenets of the mental hygiene and child-centered movements.

The psychoanalysis that the mental hygiene movement offered was certainly not that of the emancipatory project. As World War II exploded, less and less would the radical insights of psychoanalysis find a place in discussions about education. By the outbreak of the war, the social reconstructionist movement had triumphed over the child-centered wing of progressive education and, for a while, it over-shadowed the mental hygiene movement (Bowers, 1967). Volume I of Harold Rugg's *Readings in the Foundations of Education*, a required graduate text for teacher educators at Teachers College in 1941, is devoted to articles on building democracy and social transformation. There is no mention of psychoanalysis as social or cultural critique. Marginalizing a consideration of the psychic dimensions of social life, social reconstructionists' focus on radical social change coupled with the triumph of behaviorism and experimental psychology in the academy all but assured the more troubling insights of psychoanalysis would be a muffled presence in discussions of curriculum and teacher education.

Paradoxically, as the profoundly disturbing insights and radical questions psychoanalytic theory offered were increasingly disavowed, psychoanalysis would reach its apogee in post war America. It would be a psychoanalysis, however, translated into the social conservatism of ego psychology and psychiatry, reduced by academic psychology to a series of experimentally tested concepts and hypotheses, and turned by clinical psychology into a cure-all, an expedient therapy, and a way to maximize human potential. It would lead, as Philip Rieff (1966) described, to the "triumph of the therapeutic."

Additional Thoughts

As my research took me toward World War II, and as I looked back on the accounts of the early relationship between psychoanalysis and education, I experienced a certain almost visceral sense of loss. I kept imagining the heavy woolen clothing, the laced boots, the skirts sweeping the floor, the rag-tag children, all of whose images no doubt came from old family photos coupled with Jacob Riis's photos of city urchins. I pictured Freud's train and carriage trip to the Adirondack Mountains to visit Putnam, and the conversations the men had around a great stone hearth about sex, incest, and dreams.

I imagined the wooden floors and desks in schools, the silences and uproars and teachers, predominantly women teachers, encouraging students to draw, to express their feelings, to ask questions about sex. I experienced a sense of anxiety that the imagined thick texture of Freud's study, with its oriental carpets, archeological artifacts, book-lined shelves, slow ticking of the clock, the musty odors of his dogs, and smells of cooking could never exist in the smooth, sanitized realm of today, where smells are banished unless perfumed. But such melancholy, not only, as Freud suggested, masks a sense of powerlessness, but also offers the fantasy that such a mourned past, that is a past drenched with the affect mourning attributes to it, actually existed. Such melancholy often assumes or sustains the fantasy that somewhere in time there was someone who really did have the answers, who had the secret to pleasure, who lived in a better time, a time when teachers and students were on the right path and lived in prelapsarian classrooms.

In some instances, the more radical schools might have allowed children to run naked, to masturbate and explore sex, to find their interests. If A.S. Neill's description of the psychoanalytically based Summerhill, founded in 1921, is any example, kids wrote "shit" and "fuck" wherever they liked, bathed naked together, broke windows with teachers, and attended classes, when they liked. Summerhill, of course, was not the norm, may even have been unique, but its Lawrencian flavor stirred a longing in me for a sense of communal letting-go, playful abandon, and intellectual experimentation. The willingness to allow nonsense to eventually make sense somewhere has always appealed to me, but I also pulled myself back, worried that pedagogy cannot be reduced to free-association. I certainly resist the normalizing procedures I read about in the mental hygiene movement, but I am drawn to pointing the world out to students and protecting them from its dangers, and it is a world I think they should know about. How can that impulse be reconciled with relinquishing what A.S. Neill called "the old patriarchal demand for obedience and discipline" (1972, p. 237)? How can the desire for control and cure accommodate a commitment to the emancipatory project of psychoanalysis and education?

As I thought about the tensions between these two projects, I recalled my own attempts as a child to move between what I believe I experienced as my parents' very different sensibilities. I see myself quite happy as a child, but I wonder why around the age of six I began to take a certain pleasure in a sense of nostalgia. I would project myself into the future, and looking back from this imaginary point, weep over the passage of time. In part I may well have been trying to assure myself that there was a time in the past when I was happy—a kind of nostalgia for that which never was. Imagining a loss suggests one once possessed what was lost. But the time I was imagining as lost was the present. I suspect perhaps that I was crying over the loss of my father, who, as the 1950s dawned, spent more and more time at the office, and, as I became a boy, started treating me as a man, with whom he shook hands goodnight well into my teens. It was not, I believe, an uncommon situation in post World War II America.

How can I read this longing for a particular relationship between psychoanalysis and education, such that I do not reduce it to nostalgia for that which never was or to mourning the loss of an unrecoverable past? If we follow Santner (1990), we can look in the symptoms of the relationship for another possible past, one that could have led to a future that may still be possible.

I want to suggest that in the misinterpretations of psychoanalysis, in the rush to apply it, and the consequent failures, and in the denials and secret aspirations, we can locate another possible history of the relationship between psychoanalysis and education. In Freud's fainting spells and urinary incontinence on the way to Clark University, in Hoffer's findings that students, left to explore their own impulses and interests, became passive, in the attention to emotional life as an end in itself, in the assumption that students' interests were transparent, in Zachry's futile search for causal connections, and in the absence within social reconstructionism of any reference to the political projects of psychoanalysts such as those of Federn, Adler, Bernfeld, and Reich, we glimpse another future and history hidden in the past.

That future and history have much more to do with a modest acceptance of psychoanalysis's and education's limits and the balancing of the emancipatory project with the therapeutic project. Such a history and a future may be found in embracing the very impossibility of education, renouncing hope and ideals, and allowing the madness and knowledge of the unconscious to infuse disciplinary knowledge and remind us of its origins in human desires, terrors, and aspirations. But such knowledge and madness must come to us from a psychoanalytic theory grounded in the humanities. As Mark Edmundson (2007) writes in *The Death of Sigmund Freud:*

The Legacy of His Last Days "Freud hoped that humanists would carry forward his legacy, not scientists" (p. 172). It appears his hope has been realized but to the detriment of education, which continues to look to the social sciences and in particular academic psychology for its language and ideas.

As the end of the 1930s approached and the future of a medicalized psychoanalysis and hygienic education dawned, alternative histories and different futures seemed increasingly impossible.

4

PSYCHOANALYSIS AND EDUCATION IN POST WORLD WAR II AMERICA: WORLD WAR II TO 1968

[O]ften we find in American physicians and writers a
very insufficient familiarity with psycho-analysis,
so they know only its terms and a few catch-words ...
Many of the evils which I have mentioned with regret no doubt arise
from the fact that there is a general tendency in America
to shorten study and preparation and to proceed as fast as
possible to practical application.

(Freud, 1930b, p. 254–55).

Freud died in 1939. In his eulogy, "In Memory of Sigmund Freud," W.H. Auden (1940) wrote, "to us he is no more a person/now but a whole climate of opinion." Indeed by the end of the 1930s Freud's psychoanalytic theory had atomized into the cultural air. It had spread everywhere, but in its dispersion, it had become both mist-like and mystified. In some quarters it provided terms—the "unconscious," the "ego," "narcissism," "castration anxiety"—whose roots and elaboration in Freudian theory were either not acknowledged or not understood. In other quarters, it hardened into a medicalized dogma, with its own classifications of the normal and pathological. Freud may have become "a whole climate of opinion" but familiarity with and understanding of the more radical and disturbing aspects of his theory were rapidly fading from memory. Psychoanalysis, in versions that may well have been unrecognizable to Freud, would enter education in the post war years, not as it had in the 1920s and 30s as a plea to ease social repression, moderate the demands of the superego, and allow the child's and teacher's unconscious into the curriculum but as a way to help students adapt to society, solve social problems, and develop mentally healthy personalities.

Education on the Eve of World War II

> When the weather and other conditions are right, a weak or
> insignificant current assumes more force and prominence only
> to decline when conditions particularly conducive to its newfound
> strength no longer prevail.
>
> (Kliebard, 1987, p. 208)

Although the mental hygiene movement served as a conduit for a particular version of psychoanalysis to enter public education, at the end of the 1930s two movements within progressive education had a much greater impact on the schools and teacher education, and neither of these were tied to psychoanalysis. In a speech given in 1928, Dewey had raised the question of what constituted progressive education. While he was critical of the social efficiency movement and its obsession with measurement, he also expressed his concern that teachers were placing too much emphasis on the individual child's needs and not enough on the larger curriculum. "I wonder," he wrote in "Progressive Education and Science," "whether this earlier and more negative phase of progressive education has not upon the whole run its course" (1928, pp. 262–63). Dewey was concerned that the child-centered wing of progressivism focused too much on natural development and, in allowing children and students to follow their own interests, had become sealed off from the larger society and issues relevant to education in a democracy.

Taking Dewey's concerns further than he perhaps intended were the social reconstructionists who, led by George Counts, wanted the schools to help create a new social order. In 1932, in "Dare Progressive Education Be Progressive?" Counts attacked the child-centered wing of progressive education. "The great weakness of progressive education lies in the fact that it has elaborated no theory of social welfare, unless it be that of anarchy or extreme individualism" (quoted in Kliebard, 1987, p. 194). Demanding education turn its attention to curing social evils, Counts seemed oblivious to the questions psychoanalytic theory raised about such a project, particularly as those questions had been articulated by Freud and Bernfeld.

Counts attacked the child-centered progressives, in part, for their elitism (Kliebard, p. 1987, p. 194). It was true that many of the experimental schools, ones where psychoanalytic ideas were being applied, were private and often exclusive. In *Dare the Schools Build a New Social Order?* (1932b), Counts challenged schools to criticize such social inequities. He advocated for a curriculum of social justice and social reform as opposed to a curriculum based on the needs of the individual child. Counts also attacked teacher preparation programs for ignoring the injustices in society and, as he put it, being "merely padded versions of the old" (quoted in Lucas, 1999, p. 67). Faculty at Columbia University's Teachers College, such as John Childs, William Heard Kilpatrick, Bruce Raup, Harold Rugg and Goodwin Watson, were, according to Kliebard (1987) vocal supporters of the movement to radicalize students. Interestingly, Boyd Bode, who had expressed his dismay at

Caroline Zachry's focus on the child's needs, and was generally sympathetic to social reconstructionism, also expressed criticism of the social reconstructionist push to "impose a predetermined social ideal on the child while ignoring 'the vital importance of freedom of thinking'" (Bode, 1934, p. 7; Kliebard, 1987, p. 198).

On the eve of World War II, progressive education was split among the child-centered group, the social reconstructionists, and the social efficiency experts. Among the latter was Charles Bobbitt, who characterized the social resonstructionists as constituting "a smoke-screen for a communist offensive" (Bobbitt, 1934, p. 205; Kliebard, 1987, p. 197). Apparently Bobbitt's comments took, because at least one supporter of social reconstructionism, Goodwin Watson, made it to the FBI/CIA files (see Cooke, 2007). Of importance for our purposes is that on the eve of World War II, not one of the three dominant strands of progressive education was paying much attention to psychoanalytic theory, and the one that was paying some attention, the child-centered wing, integrated few if any of the more radical aspects of psychoanalytic theory. When the war broke, the internal disputes within progressive education fell into the background.

The Effect of World War II on Psychoanalysis and Clinical Psychology

> Man needs orderly knowledge, scientific knowledge,
> a kind of knowledge which permits him to act most of
> the time without the excruciating necessity of choice.
>
> (John Dollard, quoted in Herman, 1995, p. 38)

In 1947 "psychoanalysts across the nation began to experience what one of them described as a gold rush for psychoanalytic training" (Hale, 1995b, p. 211). The war, Nathan Hale, writes, "gave psychiatry an aura of success and scientific status, which also accrued to psychoanalysis as these specialties became more closely identified" (p. 209). According to Hale (1995b), the war had created a demand for psychoanalytic theory. In comparison with other countries, the United States had suffered a disproportionately higher incidence of mental disorder among its troops. The demand for psychiatric help was high, but there were not enough physicians trained to help. Hale (1995b) writes:

> In the dearth of appropriately trained physicians and mounting neuro-psychiatric casualties, psychoanalysis had much to offer: a well developed theory of war neuroses and psychosomatic disorders, methods of therapy, texts, and above all, trained personnel. (p. 189)

The "trained personnel" adhered to a psychoanalytic theory that had evolved in the 1920s and 30s within medicine. For example, the men trained by Adolf Meyer, a Clark Conference attendee, derider of Freud's concept of the unconscious, and leader in the mental hygiene movement, occupied dominant positions in the first wartime appointments, as did those trained by William Menninger, another physician and psychiatrist, who would be instrumental in developing the first *Diagnostic and Statistical Manual*, the *DSM*, for psychiatrists. "The psychoanalysts" Hale (1995b) writes, "not only supplied key personnel ... [but] also developed theories, classification systems, and methods of treatment for war neurosis" (p. 191). Ellen Herman (1995) argues that the war "[b]y normalizing the content and extending the subject of clinical expertise ... redefined psychotherapy in remarkably expansive terms" (p. 118). Psychiatrists and psychoanalysts who had served returned home feeling that they had something unique to offer to the public. Herman quotes William Menninger as saying, "As a result of our experience in the Army, it is vividly apparent that psychiatry can and must play a much more important role in the solution of health problems of the civilian" (p. 119). America was on the road to what Philip Rieff (1966) would refer to as the "triumph of the therapeutic."

But if the war provided psychiatrists and psychoanalysts with the sense that they could treat and cure masses of people, it also transformed psychiatric terms. For example, 'normal neurosis' according to Herman entered the vocabulary as something everyone might suffer from but could avoid. Mental health was the concern of everyone, and psychoanalysts and psychiatrists were there to address that concern. Here, again is Menninger, "The field of medicine must be recognized as inseparably linked to the social sciences and concerned with healthy adjustment of men, both individually and in groups" (quoted in Herman, 1995, p. 119). Medicine, psychiatry, psychoanalysis, the social sciences, and mental health—all that was left out was education, but that was implied.

Zaretsky (2004) points out the complicated, often contradictory results of the war's effects on psychoanalytic theory: the liberalization of attitudes toward race relations, a commitment to improve social services and expand the welfare society, and a strong stance against totalitarianism accompanied the attribution of psychological problems to castrating mothers, the pathologizing of homosexuality, the equation of the healthy woman with being a housewife, and a false scientism (pp. 265–70). Hale (1995b) sees the war as having had overall a salubrious effect on psychoanalysis, because it allowed it to come in from the cold. He, too, argues, however, that the identification with medical psychiatry resulted in psychoanalysis grounding much of the psychic apparatus in biology (p. 214). While the war deepened the identification of psychoanalysis with medical psychiatry, it also gave a tremendous boost to clinical psychology.

World War II and the Rise of Clinical Psychology

Clinical psychology had tried to form professional organizations prior to the war, and had succeeded in 1937 in forming the American Association of Applied Psychology with divisions in clinical, consulting, industrial, educational, and military psychology. Between 1944 and 1945 Carl Rogers was the president of the association. But its successes before the war were compromised by the hegemony psychiatry had on curing mental illness. Prior to World War II, clinical psychologists had depended on the benevolence of psychiatrists (Benjamin, L., 2005). It was literally impossible to attain a Ph.D. in clinical psychology before 1940, and it was not until 1946, after years of being primarily identified with testing, particularly psychological testing of the word association sort, that the American Psychological Association formed Division 12 for clinical psychologists. During the 1940s interpretation of projective tests still remained the bread and butter of clinical psychologists. Ludy Benjamin (2005) suggests that tests like the Rorschach, the Minnesota Multiphasic Personality Inventory, and the Thematic Apperception Test provided clinical psychologists with a sense of expertise—they could interpret the tests as well as psychiatrists if, not better—but the tests also brought psychoanalytic categories into their work.

Just as it had done for psychoanalysts, World War II changed the status of clinical psychologists. The war led to an explosion in clinical psychologists, who were needed to address the psychological demands arising from mobilization, war trauma, and the aftermath of the war. "The federal government called on the VA and the United States Public Health Service," Ludy Benjamin (2005) writes, "to expand the pool of mental health professionals" (p. 12). Medical schools couldn't produce enough psychiatrists, so "the federal directive was translated as a mandate for increasing the pool of clinical psychologists" (p. 12). Psychology departments began to train clinical psychologists and the infusion of funds expanded psychology departments as they included clinical psychology.

Of course psychiatrists were not thrilled with the new addition to the mental health industry. They fought it as best they could, but the exigencies of the war blew away their professional gate-keeping. Neither were psychology departments initially welcoming. But the burgeoning need for clinical psychologists and the rising status of psychoanalytic psychiatry, now associated with medical science, forced open the doors of psychology departments, often dominated by neo-behaviorists (see Hunt, 1994). Clinical psychologists, with their own versions of psychoanalytic theory and their own research interests, rushed in. And that led to some interesting shifts.

If psychiatry had turned Freudian psychoanalysis into a conservative, normalizing, and instrumentalized and medicalized discourse, clinical psychology brought back some of the initial impulses and insights of psychoanalysis but gave them a much more positive spin. For example, Freud had conceived the human psyche as struc- tured in fundamentally irresolvable conflicts between the unconscious and culture or society, conflicts which at best we could become aware of. Clinical psychologists like Rogers and Maslow, on the other hand, saw the unconscious as housing an inherent drive for self-actualization that could be rendered conscious and developed if the environment was right (see interviews with Maslow and Rogers, in Frick, 1971, pp. 33–35 and pp. 88–90). Other clinical psychologists viewed the ego, not as imbued with conflict, aggression, and over-determined fantasies but as housing a conflict free zone with which the analyst could bond in the service of cure. Others followed those, like Erik Erikson, who imagined individuals progressing through various psychosocial stages toward maturity, as opposed to Freud, who other than positing early psychosexual stages, had no illusions about linear growth. Nevertheless these psychologists often advocated, not for adaptation to social norms, but rather for greater personal autonomy. In their approach to analysis, they often incorporated, as in the case with Rogers, a particular type of non-judgmental listening. As clinical psychologists increased in numbers, carved out a more influential place in the academy, and began to practice psychotherapy, they not only transmuted Freudian concepts but they also began to spread them within departments of psychology as well as to sociology and anthropology departments, where they were appropriated and further transformed.

Because clinical psychology sat in academic departments of psychology, and because they drew so many students, their power grew, threatening the experimentalists and behaviorists in those departments. Hornstein (1992) suggests the threat led to the proliferation in the 1950s up to the end of the century of experimentally testing psychoanalytic concepts. We have seen this already in Dollard's and Sears' work at Yale, and in attempts to combine behaviorism and psychoanalysis, attempts that Hornstein argues were really attempts at cooptation. "Every conceivable psychoanalytic concept was put to the test" writes Hornstein (p. 258). For example, experiments on rats apparently produced regression and reaction formation. Children who ate more ice cream than other kids were found to have an oral character. One researcher, Hornstein reports, "found that when children were shown a picture of a father and a child near some stairs more girls than boys fantasized that the father would mount the stairs and enter the room" (p. 258). The increasing power of clinical psychologists may also have led the American Psychological Association to change its constitution. Until 1944 the constitution stated that its foremost objective was "advancing psychology as a science." In 1944 it changed its objective to "advancing psychology as a science *and as a profession, and as a means of promoting human welfare*" (my italics, Carroll, 1964, p. 43).

For our purposes, what is of interest is that the scientific aura provided by such experiments, along with psychoanalytic terminology began to make their way into textbooks used in psychology courses, which in turn were used in teacher education courses. But the texts, as we have seen, failed to mention Freud or psychoanalytic theory itself. "Even as late as 1958, a classic like Hebb's *Textbook of Psychology* barely mentioned the topic" (Hornstein, 1992, p. 260). Paradoxically, when surveyed by the American Psychological Association in 1954 about who had influenced them to enter the field, the majority of members claimed Freud had been the greatest influence (Hornstein, 1992, p. 260). Auden was right, Freud was "no more a person/now but a whole climate of opinion." But that very fact, coupled with the turn to medicine and academic science, suggests the disavowal occurring in the academy and within psychoanalysis itself. The danger and threat of Freud's radical unconscious provoked a splitting—Freud was everywhere and nowhere. At the very moment psychoanalysis was on the verge of becoming famous, its radical insights fell silent.

Popularization of Psychoanalysis after the War

> Popularization ... identified psychoanalysis with the
> established social authorities, and tended to exaggerate
> ... a downplaying of the iconoclastic.
>
> (Hale, 1995b, p. 299)

By the end of World War II psychoanalysts and clinical psychologists were enjoying a new found prestige and acceptance in the academy. Psychoanalysts were benefitting from the scientific and medical respectability that the war and the association with psychiatry had provided. Clinical psychologists were benefitting from their academic legitimacy and the research money that started pouring into the behavioral sciences after the war. And both psychoanalysts and clinical psychologists benefitted from the growing popularization of psychoanalysis.

In the post war era psychoanalysis achieved a level of popular acceptance or at least recognition it had never known previously. Nathan Hale refers to the period after World War II as the "golden age of psychoanalysis" (1995b, p. 276). Newspaper articles, novels, self-help books, and films glamorized and celebrated the successes of psychoanalysts. A typical example of the growing popularization of psychoanalysis was an article in *Time Magazine* published on April 23, 1956, entitled "The Explorer." A drawing of Freud looking old and icy appears on the magazine's cover. The lengthy article inside presents a picture of a man who had affected millions of lives and whose work is to be not simply valued as an historical monument but also appreciated for the enormous help it has offered families, children, adolescents, and troubled adults. Writing in 1958, Philip Reiff would state in the preface to his *Freud: The Mind of a Moralist*, "In America today, Freud's intellectual influence is greater than that of any other modern thinker. He presides over the mass media, the college classroom, the chatter at parties, the playgrounds of the middle classes" (p. xi).

Films portraying the psychoanalyst as hero also appeared. Unlike earlier cinematic versions of psychoanalysis, which—except for G.W. Pabst's 1926 *Secrets of a Soul*, the only film approved by Freud's Vienna Circle—tended to caricature analysts (see Gabbard, 1997, 2002), the post war films presented psychoanalysts as serious, deeply empathic, liberal, and erudite doctors. Recall popular movies such as *Now Voyager* (1943) in which Claude Rains' psychiatrist helps Betty Davis' character achieve the stars rather than the moon, *Spellbound* (1945), with Ingrid Bergman as a knowledgeable psychiatrist, the *Snake Pit* (1948) in which Olivia de Havilland is helped by a psychoanalyst who seeks to reform the horrible conditions in a mental institution, Otto Preminger's *Home of the Brave* (1949), in which only the psychiatrist can get a Black G.I. to walk, *Fear Strikes Out* (1956), which offered a psychoanalytic interpretation of the troubled baseball player Jimmy Piersall, played by Anthons Perkins, *Suddenly*

Last Summer (1959) with Montgomery Clift as the compassionate psychoanalyst trying to release Elizabeth Taylor from her traumatic experience, and *Pressure Point* (1962) in which Sydney Poitier as a psychoanalyst works with a psychopathic racist played by Bobby Darren. John Huston's 1962 *Freud*, with its four hundred plus page script initially written by Jean-Paul Sartre, depicted Freud as a misunderstood genius. All of these films furthered the picture of psychiatrist/psychoanalyst as wise healer.

Or, to take one more example from popular culture, we might consider the lyrics of "Officer Krupke," in *West Side Story* (1957) where the gang members sing:

> Officer Krupke, you're really a square;
> This boy don't need a judge, he needs an analyst's care!
> It's just his neurosis that oughta be curbed.
> He's psychologic'ly disturbed!
>
> (Stephen Sondheim, 1957)

So familiar had analysis become that even juvenile delinquents could make fun of it.

Psychoanalytic concepts and descriptions of psychiatric cases also found their way into public consciousness through best sellers. Benjamin Spock's (1946) *Common Sense Book of Baby and Child Care* relied on Freudian concepts, although Spock disavowed his connection to Freud. Robert Lindner's (1955) *The Fifty Minute Hour* and Ernest Jones' (1953–57) three-volume biography of Freud were widely reviewed and further spread the word about psychoanalysis. And yet, for all its popularization, psychoanalysis continued to be associated with an illness that was shameful. On one hand Freud was shaping the climate of opinion, but on the other, psychoanalysis increased its association with mental illness and pathology and its commitment to the therapeutic project. It would not be until the late 1960s and 70s that young and middle-aged Americans would begin to consider therapy an important path to self-discovery, self-knowledge, and self-fulfillment.

As psychoanalysis came into the living room and the movie house in the post war era, the public's demand for therapy grew. Enrollment in medical psychiatric programs increased, and the numbers of individuals pursing doctorates in psychology swelled. Furthermore, the new national focus on mental health generated enormous federal funding for behavioral research. Given the mental health focus of the projects and the availability of funding, social scientists, among whom were clinical psychologists, sociologists, anthropologists, and psychoanalytic psychiatrists, understandably began to apply psychoanalytic concepts, distilled through their own disciplinary discourses, to a wide variety of problems such as juvenile delinquency, racism, school failure, and community mental health. They also framed policies and programs aimed at educating mentally happy and healthy citizens.

More and more teachers and workers in mental health or human services learned or were exposed to, often without knowing it, some of the terms of psychoanalysis. Clinics, schools and community agencies looked to guidance counselors, social workers, school psychologists for expert advice, and the advice often consisted of a medicalized, popularized, and dispersed psychoanalytic theory, which no longer seemed to know itself. It had in one sense ceased to exist because it had become such a large part of the culture—but at a price. The cure of the soul, one might argue, had lost its soul. Some educators would soon argue that education had also begun to lose its soul.

Education in the late 1940s—the Life Adjustment Movement

> [S]ocial and economic factors point to the failure of our total
> educational system to meet the real need of an efficient life
> adjustment training for America's young people.
> (Charles Prosser, quoted in Kliebard, 1987, p. 249)

Progressive education by the end of the war was in its last stages. The post war era "began with the partial reappearance of social efficiency, this time in the guise of 'life adjustment' education" (Pinar et al., 1995, p. 151). Begun in 1945 (Kliebard, 1987), the life adjustment movement advocated that greater emphasis be given to vocational education and social adjustment. It advanced its program as a response to what it warned was the increasing high school drop-out rate, which it blamed on a too rigorous academic curriculum imposed on all young people. Supporters of the movement argued that schools were nothing but college prep programs that did a disservice to the many not headed to higher education, and that failed to address the needs of students. The movement would very soon come in for widespread criticism and by the 1950s would fall before the scathing attacks of those arguing for a more academically rigorous and science focused curriculum.

Diane Ravitch (2000) describes the life adjustment movement as education run by bureaucrats and social engineers. "Unlike the education movements of the 1930s," she writes, "the life adjustment movement of the postwar era ... aimed to adjust young people to [society]" (p. 327). Life adjustment education included "home and family living education, vocational education, and guidance" (p. 329), and it deemphasized academics. Ravitch paints a picture of schools in the late 1940s and 50s that attended more to the social and personality needs of children and adolescents than to their intellectual needs. Questions about popularity, physical hygiene, how to develop self-confidence, vocational placement, dating, sexual conduct, and relationships between kids and parents replaced questions emanating from the disciplines. It was not as if teachers were urged to use disciplinary knowledge to illuminate these questions. Rather students' social and emotional needs as construed by the social efficiency movement became the curriculum.

Ravitch's depiction of the period is one-sided to be sure, but it also suggests the post war emphasis on social conformity that would be the subject of books such as Riesman, Glazer, and Denney's *The Lonely Crowd* (1955) and Sloan Wilson's *The Man in the Gray Flannel Suit* (1955). In part that concern with adjustment, adaptation, and conformity grew out of a growing sense among Americans that mental health was of prime concern, and that, if not their own, then the nation's mental health should be a top priority. The alarm over mental health was exacerbated by depictions in the media of a nation on the verge of a nervous breakdown.

While the nation turned its attention to mental health, and while psychoanalysts and clinical psychologists were basking in their new prestige, as the 1950s opened and unfolded, teachers received no such recognition. Yet again, teachers were blamed for the failings of society, and yet again, they would rush to prove their competence. Critics tore into the life adjustment curriculum, accusing it of dumbing down the curriculum and preventing Johnny from learning how to read. Teachers it seems were, in ways Freud couldn't have imagined, caught between the Scylla of teaching about mental health and the Charybdis of ensuring academic achievement, between the dangerous seduction of applying psychoanalysis and the whirlpool like repetition compulsions inherent in imagining one could get all students to learn a set academic content. No matter what course they charted, teachers were doomed for blame and depicted as prey to mental illness. As Joseph Shipley (1961) wrote in his book, *The Mentally Disturbed Teacher,* "The sorry fact remains that the incidence of mental disturbance among teachers seems higher than among persons of other occupations" (p. 6). Mental illness, quite literally, seemed to be on everyone's mind.

One does have to wonder how much of the post war concern with mental health stemmed from the unresolved trauma of the war. Eric Santner (1990) reminds us that "it was Freud's thought that the absence of … anxiety … is what leads to traumaticization rather than loss per se. This affect can, however, be recuperated only in the presence of an empathic witness" (p. 25). The need to stave off anxiety during the war and the Great Depression, the shocks internalized, but not fully acknowledged may well have later returned in the form of concerns with mental illness within and communist dangers without. Certainly there were, as William Wyler's film classic, *The Best Years of Our Lives* (1946), makes clear, no empathic witnesses. The film depicts the painful reentry to civilian life of servicemen who find civilians less than willing to hear what they'd been through, but the nation as a whole had been through almost two emotionally wrenching decades. Before the war had been the Great Depression. The suffering of economic disaster, the horrors of war and genocide, and the repression of constant anxiety over whether loved ones would survive must have registered, although even Freud (1921a) had suggested that group cohesion in the face of an enemy could stave off psychic deterioration. But the cost was high. It may well have been that the American attitude of "pick yourself up, dust yourself off, and start all over again," its need to reintegrate millions of men into a labor market largely occupied by women, and the new marketing of consumerism itself, which admonished everyone not to look back, made it impossible to reflect on the pain of the previous years.

In particular the super egoic demand to "think positively and get on with life" rather than dwell in the past, may have exerted a tremendous pressure on the nation not to consider what its citizens had been through, but rather to focus on the present external dangers of communism as a national problem and the internal ones of mental illness as an individual problem. It is almost impossible to find in the mental health literature of the period references to the effects of the war and the Great Depression on mental health. The repression of the emotional effects of these may have been displaced into the general sense that mental health needed attention and that the forward looking mental hygiene movement could provide it. Indeed the failure to acknowledge the trauma of the war may have in fact exacerbated mental disequilibrium in the population. It may also have unleashed a certain amount of rage.

The scathing attacks of the late 1940s and 1950s on teachers and the life adjustment movement (see Bestor, 1953; Fine, 1947; Flesch, 1955; Smith, 1949) accompanied the culturally mandated migration of white, middle class women back into the domestic sphere. Both may have had roots in the unresolved trauma of war. One could well wonder whether all those men returning from combat did not also have some unconscious rage at the mothers and wives who had let them go. Gloria Emerson (1985), in *Some American Men*, described the men coming back from the war as having an "unmistakable, if slight, melancholy[ia]" (p. 14) that suggested the anger lingering under the surface of exuberant triumphalism. Was such anger vented on a predominantly female teaching force? Was it channeled into the domestic revenge of keeping women and children subservient and socially well adjusted? Or was there a silent complicity between men and women after the war that at all costs the previous decades' traumas would be glossed over, we would all take our agreed upon roles and displace our anxieties onto communism, the bomb, those weird neighbors, and rebels without causes? Such questions, of course, have no answer; their purpose rather is to reclaim a bit of the initial curiosity of psychoanalysis at a moment in our history when psychoanalysis was not only avoiding radical cultural critique but, when it did engage in it, blaming bad mothers and frustration for our social ills (see Wylie, 1942).

As psychoanalytic theory became less and less speculative, less and less of a "grave philosophy" with all the metaphorical associations of that term, as it lost its grounding in the humanities, and surrendered its emancipatory project, it para-doxically seemed to lose its libido *and* become sexualized. The familial dramas of love and hate, suffused with erotic and aggressive impulses, and the presence of death and psychosis no longer lived in us to be explored but rather emerged increasingly in terms of sexual illnesses that needed to be cured by fixed protocols and quick inoculations against mental disorder. We apparently were out of control and needed adjustment.

Much has been written about the anxieties that various policies in the 1950s reformulated and then tried to contain (see in particular Salvio, 2007). Those anxieties entered education to be addressed by absurdities such as "duck and cover," but also by the mental hygiene and life adjustment movements that sought to keep us and our children from going to pieces. The psychic tension resulting from but also going into efforts to contain and control so much anxiety appears in the mental health and psychoanalytic literature of the period, now stripped of the affective worlds carried by an earlier psychoanalysis infused with the humanities.

As I read through the mental health texts, the psychiatric textbooks, the commission reports and policy statements that spoke of psychoanalysis as behavioral science, and the psychoanalytically informed articles and books on education written in the 1940s, 50s, and early 60s, I found it increasingly difficult to engage with the material. On one level my own familial history contributed to my increasing boredom with and resistance to the material: my father had been a physician about whom I felt ambivalent for emotionally abandoning me to my mother but about whom I also felt guilty since it seemed to me I had her attention. It could well be that my own repressed aggressive impulses toward him, contributed to my uneasy boredom with the material that read like a medical textbook. It may also have been a consequence of psychoanalysis's own pursuit of and sense that it had attained certainty that rendered it closed and aggressive and thus shielded from my attempts at engagement. And such a thought returned me to what the war had done to my own father who had served. His favorite saying came from the baseball player Satchel Paige. It was, "Don't look back, something might be catching up to you."

The nation's concerns about mental health and the rise of the life adjustment movement did provide a portal through which psychoanalytic concepts would enter education. These concepts had little to do, however, with Freudian psychoanalysis. To understand the forms psychoanalytic theory and approaches to psychoanalysis assumed as they entered education through the portals of the life adjustment movement, social science research, and mental health policies, we need to consider in more detail the complicated nexus of psychoanalysis, psychiatry, and medicine, the emergence of ego psychology, and the influence of a revivified mental hygiene movement in the shaping of mental health policy.

Further Medicalization

The American Psychoanalytic Association in the years after the war, under the leadership of men such as Leo Bartemeier, Ives Hendrick, and William Menninger, moved increasingly to keep the standards for training psychoanalysts high, which in fact meant standardizing them and preserving the requirement of medical training. The American Psychoanalytic Association committed to creating a situation in which psychoanalytically trained psychiatrists would "provide leaders for the medical schools, revivify the mental hospitals, and supervise subordinate, ancillary personnel such as psychologists and social workers" (Hale, 1995b, p. 214) and school personnel involved in the mental health of students. The drive to turn psychoanalysis into an exclusive guild allied with and providing the vision for psychiatry achieved some success. It worked to keep out lay practitioners. In 1954 the American Psychoanalytic Association, the American Psychiatric Association, and the American Medical Association issued a joint statement which clearly specified that "only physicians were qualified to distinguish between physical and mental illness and to prescribe a course of treatment" (Hale, 1995b, p. 215). According to Hale (1995b) it was primarily American born analysts who strove to preserve the M.D. requirement to practice psychoanalysis. He quotes one president of the American Psychoanalytic Association in the early 1950s as arguing that the medical degree offered not only greater prestige but "a better understanding of patients" (p. 214).

> In pursuit of this alliance with medicine, psychoanalysts stressed the medically appealing "biological" nature of psychoanalysis which posited "instinctual forces of bodily origin" as the prime movers of the "mental apparatus" and a "genetic," that is developmental outlook. (Hale, 1995b, p. 214)

As psychiatry and the doctors who practiced it became identified in the public mind with psychoanalysis, psychoanalysis took on an aura of certainty, and the analyst emerged in the popular imagination as a "trained, scientific expert" (Hale, 1995b, p. 276). Popular accounts of analysis portrayed it as the royal road to happiness and normal adjustment, encouraging more and more individuals to seek treatment. After the war, "[t]he terms psychiatrist and psychoanalyst became almost inter-changeable" (Hale, 1995b, p. 289), and by 1954, according to Hale, "a majority of psychiatric residents described their orientation as Freudian or neo-Freudian, and desired psychoanalytic training" (p. 253). Psychoanalytically oriented psychiatrists could diagnose and cure the human soul.

"As analysts conquered psychiatry," Zaretsky (2004) writes, "they increasingly absorbed its values" (p. 289). Those values, according to Zaretsky, included an ahistoricism, a focus on pathology and cure, professional neutrality, including political neutrality, a positivistic approach to science, and a pragmatic focus (pp. 289–91). The psychoanalysis that emerged in alliance with medicine after the war not only pathologized women, gays, and lesbians, not only advocated a normalization of the status quo, but reintroduced a masculinist bias to the profession. As Zaretsky (2004) writes, "the number of female analysts declined dramatically, from 27 percent in the 1930s to 9 percent in the 1950s" (p. 297). That decline, of course, reflected the low numbers of women in medical schools. It also suggests that psychoanalysis had ceased to question the normalcy and foundation of conventional sexual and gender arrangements. All in all it was a medically sanitized version of psychoanalysis.

One of the psychoanalytic psychiatrists who worked hard to identify psychiatry with psychoanalysis was William Menninger. In part he did this by insisting that "psychoanalysis was a veridical, causative, scientific therapy, an argument enhanced by medical rhetoric and analogy" (Hale, 1995b, p. 282). But he also sought to remove from psychoanalysis its more radical or disturbing questions. He argued, for example, that sex without love was abnormal and, sounding like James Putnam, that there were other higher principles more important than sexual freedom to which we should direct our strengthened egos. In 1946 he headed the Group for the Advancement of Psychiatry (GAP), an organization whose platform called upon psychiatrists to help reform society and address issues of mental health, by applying psychoanalytically informed principles to "all those problems which have to do with family welfare, child rearing, child and adult education, … intergroup tensions, civil rights, and personal liberty" (quoted in Herman, 1995, p. 250). Within such a grand goal existed particular conceptions of a healthy and normal society, child, and family, and what the school could do to ensure the health of these.

What those institutions looked like had much to do with what was pathologized in an increasingly medicalized psychoanalytic theory. Happiness and health appeared more and more contingent on a heterosexual nuclear family, in which the mother followed the husband and took care of the children, but did not suffocate them or sissify them, and the husband exerted authority but gently and with understanding. Children were meant to go through normal stages of development, be educated about sex—its healthy aspects and its tie to love not necessarily reproduction—and, as they came to accept reality, achieve maturity and responsibility as adults. If this picture brings to mind the ideal heterosexual family of white, middle class, Christian America at the turn of the century, it is not surprising. Changed was the moral discourse judging individuals' spiritual health and well being. That discourse now defined individuals in terms of their emotional and mental adjustment and normalcy. Homosexuals, for example, were not sinners, but rather victims of a personality disorder which could be rectified by experts.

While psychoanalytic theory's adoption of the medical language and concepts of normalcy and abnormalcy contributed to this picture of what constituted a well adjusted American, a new theoretical movement also helped shape it. The new school of thought called itself ego psychology.

Ego Psychology

> By reformulating psychoanalytic findings into clear-cut
> propositions, work in this area is likely … to facilitate
> scientific discourse.
>
> (Hartmann and Loewenstein, 1964a, p. 12)

> Psychoanalysis is applied social science.
>
> (Hartmann and Loewenstein, 1964a, p. 23)

Heinz Hartmann is the analyst most closely associated with ego psychology, although the names of Bruno Bettelheim, Erik Erikson, Ernst Kris, and Rudolph Loewenstein are also often associated with it. Hartmann "represented the world of academic psychiatry" (Roazen, 1992, p. 518) and when he came to Freud for a training analysis in the mid 1930s, Freud considered his mind too academic (Roazen, 1992, p. 518). It's an odd phrase—"too academic," since given Freud's erudition and passion for study, it could not have referred to being too intellectual or studious. Perhaps it meant that Hartmann was too tied to the academy, to the drive to organize and institutionalize knowledge, or to the drive for mastery. Freud had said that "the psychoanalyst [could] dispense with the University without any loss to himself" (1919b, p. 171), but that the university, particularly medical schools, needed psychoanalysis to offset the inadequacy of academic psychology and experimental psychology (p.172). Regardless of his views about Hartmann's academicism, Freud took him on free of charge, and Hartmann turned out to be the last analyst Freud trained. He was also the analyst whom Anna Freud considered an older brother, because professionally they both had, according to her, the same father (see Buhle, 1998, p. 135) and because they had formed a close relationship.

It is interesting that Hartmann's theories of the ego should have diverged as much as they did from those of his teacher. While Freud's conception of the ego and the topography of which it was a part changed over time, he held to the idea that the ego emerged from the id, that part of it, perhaps much of it, was implicated in unconscious and preconscious conflictual processes, that it was largely determined by libidinal as well as aggressive forces, and that it needed to be strengthened only insofar as such strengthening would allow it to accommodate the surfacing of repressed material. What did surface was a matter of indifference to the analyst other than as material to be interpreted and understood.

Freud (1940a, pp. 178–79) wrote that the work of the analyst was to help the patient overcome the resistance of the ego and release repressed material. The outcome of that struggle, i.e. the overcoming of the resistance and the release of the material, was "a matter of indifference" to the analyst, "whether it results in the ego accepting … an instinctual demand which it had hitherto rejected, or whether it dismisses it once more, this time for good and all" (p. 179). Crucial here is Freud's view that the strengthening of the ego is defined in terms of making the ego less resistant to surfacing unconscious material, more flexible or porous, if you will. He did not advocate making it a muscular organ for social adaptation.

Hartmann's ego psychology, on the other hand, understood strengthening the ego in terms of making it more responsive to the demands of the reality principle, which he interpreted in terms of social normativity. For Hartmann, Kris, and Loewenstein, the ego emerged alongside the id from "inborn givens" (Hale, 1995b, p. 235). It was not shot through with conflict but rather possessed a sphere that was "autonomous from intrapsychic conflict" (Roazen, 1992, p. 518). As Yankelovich and Barrett (1970) state in *Ego and Instinct*, "Just as *conflict* is the central notion in Freud's work, *adaptation* is central in Hartmann's" (p. xi, italics in original). The analyst was to side with the conflict-free space or aspect of the ego, strengthen or expand that part, and lead the patient to maturity, adulthood, and mastery of an external reality.

Not only did such a theory assume the analyst's superior knowledge of health and adjustment, but it also furthered the view of the psychoanalyst as expert, which dovetailed with the identification of the psychoanalyst with the physician and scientist. According to Hale (1995b) Hartmann believed that "psychoanalysis was a science of causes and not merely a psychology of understanding. … The goal of psychoanalysis was the 'explanation of causal relationships' that is the study of the 'laws regulating mental activity'" (p. 232). It is not surprising that Hartmann, Kris, and Loewenstein (1964a) would advocate "reformulating psychoanalytic findings into clear cut propositions" (p. 12), which could be tested, or that they would admire *Frustration and Aggression* for its attempt to "translate some tenets of psychoanalytic theory in terms of behavioristic learning theory" (Hartmann, Kris, and Loewenstein, 1964b, p. 132). Such a science and explanatory approach appealed to young psychologists and researchers trained in the academy. "Now" as Cushman (1995) describes it, they "had a 'thing' to work on in a scientific, technicized way ... and they had a way to discuss not only neurosis but also 'normal' mental functioning, and thus a justification for their profession's involvement in many aspects of everyday life" (pp. 190–91). Sadly, the push to operationalize psychoanalysis would open it at the end of the decade to its absorption in neuroscience and pharmacology. If, as the ego psychologists hoped, tests and treatment modalities could be established, the relational components of psychoanalysis and the analysis of transference diminished in import. Paradoxically, as Zaretesky (2004) points out, "the more the U.S. ego psychologists claimed the mantle of the medical model, the more their critics attacked them as unscientific" (p. 334).

Ego psychology and those who promoted it helped establish a nexus of academic psychology, psychiatry, medicine, and psychoanalysis from which emanated policy statements, approaches to therapeutic practices, and advice to teachers, social workers, and others involved in human services. It is interesting to consider ego psychology's influence in the academy in the post war years, not only in terms of its research findings or its position of influence in psychology departments—only in clinical psychology did it gain traction—but in its usage as a metaphor.

In *American Academic Culture: Fifty Years, Four Disciplines*, Thomas Bender and Carl Schorske (1997) describe disciplines in terms of whether or not they have "strong egos" (p. 5). "For the humanities, philosophy represented an example of a firmly bounded and well-policed discipline, marked after 1950 by high self-confidence ... " (p. 5). Between 1945 and 1960, Bender and Schorske write, "philosophy witnessed the establishment of the analytic method and a quest for epistemological certainty" (p. 8), but so did all the disciplines. "The strongly positivistic, neo-Lockean intellectual foundations ... set the terms for subsequent developments in the disciplines" (p. 8). They quote Talcott Parsons as arguing that sociology is a science and committed to "the advancement and transmission of empirical knowledge" primarily to other sociologists and "secondarily to ... non-members" (quoted in Bender and Schorske, 1997, p. 23). Even in the arts, the work of criticism was to establish "hard and fast cultural distinctions, exclusions, hierarchies" (Bender and Schorske, 1997, p. 36). The university organized itself in terms of a "rigidity of categories that defined not only proper objects of inquiry but also disciplinary terrains" (p. 37). The muscular, contained, and politically neutral ego or at least its conflict free zone resonated with a general sense in the country that containment and a healthy defensive posture went hand in glove with a positive, forward looking, post-ideological present. It is not surprising that the pathologizing of anything different, whether communism, socialism, or the dreaded mental illness, accompanied such a national state. Nor is it surprising that at the end of the 1950s and early 1960s my high school friends and I would associate psychoanalysis with deviancy, homosexuality, and the clinical probing of one's body and life.

Russell Jacoby has described ego psychology as "the most conservative of the mid-century adaptations of Freudian drive theory" (Jacoby, 1997, p. 186) and Nathan Hale (1995b) has written that it "coincided with a period of postwar conservative optimism in American political life, with functionalism in American sociology, and with the unprecedented growth of psychoanalysis" (p. 244). Certainly Hartmann's concept of the ego as a conflict-free zone, holding at bay the unconscious, looks eerily like the doctrine of containment preached during the Cold War. Jacoby (1997) and Zaretsky (2004) argue that Hartmann and his colleagues emptied Freud's theory of its critical edge, reduced psychoanalysis to "a conformist interpretation of the reality principle" (Jacoby, 1997, p. 41), and colluded with the Cold War "project of social control" (Zaretsky, 2004, p. 279). Certainly we can see the rise of ego psychology as exemplary of the high point of the therapeutic project of psycho-analysis. While it didn't coincide with the height of education's near obsession with science and cure—that would come in the 1990s and first decade of the new millennium—it did align with the life adjustment movement, and it did influence social planning.

In varying ways social control, or, as it was more often labeled, social planning, took on a new importance in the post war period. "Because Hartmann's main interest was not the ego's relation to the id but its relations to social norms, mind-sets, and demands," Zaretsky writes, "he became the favorite psychoanalyst for those who sought to harness psychoanalysis to social planning" (2004, p. 279). We can see Harmann's influence in social policy if we consider the study of racial attitudes conducted by Bruno Bettelheim and Morris Janowitz, and published in 1950 as *Dynamics of Prejudice: A Psychological and Sociological Study of Veterans*. The goal of the study was to diagnose and then find a "cure for one of the major disorders in con-temporary American society: ethnic discrimination and aggression" (1950, p. 105). Basically the authors argued that prejudice was the result of childhood deprivations, exacerbated by economic insecurity. These provoked feelings of aggression, which a weak ego allowed to be expressed. While initially calling for economic and social changes to offset the deprivation and insecurity, Bettelheim and Janowitz in the end turned to education as the best way to promote tolerance, build ego strength, and direct aggression into more productive channels.

Bettelheim's "Psychoanalysis and Education"

The appeal to education as the way to properly socialize children is apparent in Bettelheim's 1969 article "Psychoanalysis and Education." This is the article in which he described the relationship between psychoanalysis and education as neurotic. In the article Bettelheim described the child's ego as "feeble" (p. 78). "It was very much the task of education," he wrote, "to see that the sphere of the ego should grow and be strengthened" (p. 75). In order to accomplish this, teachers "must know clearly what is ego correct and what is not" (p. 75). Reversing the psycho-analytically informed progressive education practices of the 1920s and 30s, Bettelheim wrote, "We stunt the child's growth if we view id expressions as creative, instead of being satisfied to recognize their possible value. ... But to dream is hardly an act of creation, nor will it advance intellectual growth" (p. 75).

Urging educators to assess where the student was in terms of their acceptance of the reality principle and their ego development—a bit like Erikson's urging teachers to track which psychosocial stage of identity a student occupies—Bettelheim called for teachers to rely on and bolster the child's superego "on the basis of fear" (p. 78). Eventually, the "mature ego" would "apply reason to these do's and don'ts. ... It takes a mature judgment to be able to do the right thing" (p. 78). According to Bettelheim "what was wrong with old-fashioned (and authoritarian) education was not that it instilled a strong superego" (p. 78) through fear— "that was what was right with it"—but that it failed to gradually replace fear with reason.

Now, to be fair, Bettelheim was not arguing for terrorizing pupils, although he did suggest kids had it too easy, and he blamed parents and "easy street" (p. 84) culture for students' emotional problems. He wanted teachers to create an academic curriculum with "the goal of a well-balanced personality" (p. 83). He advised teachers to steer between the Scylla and Charybdis of superego and id, and learn about the "different developmental tasks ... that dominate our life until mastered" (p. 84). Teachers could strengthen the student's ego by helping the child deal with difficult emotions, such as the impulse toward violence and the anxieties about being a male or female, or about menstruation. The real aim of teachers should be to help students "find their way out of the darkness in which they hide their true selves, to help them toward a rational understanding of themselves and [the] world ... " (pp. 85–86). Such an aim sounds appealing, but on closer inspection it is the psycho-analyst or teacher aided by the analyst who determines the true self and of what a rational understanding consists.

Written during the Vietnam War, which Bettelheim supported, and the height of the youth movement, which he excoriated (Pollak, 1997; Sutton, 1996), Bettelheim's article urged teachers to attend to students' emotional life, and in particular help students develop self-esteem by scaffolding their struggle with the challenges of particular psychosocial stages. Teachers needed to talk to kids about their fears, anxieties, struggles, and "lifelong journey of discovery" in order to help them develop stronger egos or selves or sense of identity. And here is where we can note the effects of ego psychology. Unlike Freud, who urged understanding and an attitude of indifferent, although compassionate curiosity on the part of the analyst toward the material released, Bettelheim urged teachers not just to encourage emotional outpourings or discussions of problems but to help students adjust, to help them mature. How teachers did this was not through using disciplinary knowledge or the insights of the humanities and arts to illuminate the feelings expressed, but through a kind of common sense, therapeutic counsel.

This push to adapt students to social reality, to the reality principle understood in terms of existing social beliefs, does raise questions about educational missions that focus on helping students meet the demands of reality. Today educators, pundits, and politicians articulate reality and academic achievement in terms of tests and job preparation. Teachers understandably wax enthusiastic about methods that raise test scores, but even those who know that test scores measure little, rarely question the reality for which we are so assiduously, almost obsessively, preparing our students—the job market.

It is easy to get swept up in the zeal for best practices that produce results, since test results determine graduation and possible employability. Left unaddressed in the euphoria over quantitative success are questions about the larger purpose of education and assumptions about the labor force, economic conditions, and the politics of class. If we believe our main job is to strengthen a particular kind of student-ego, making the student-ego more muscular, so to speak, better able, for example, to pass the New York Regents, better adapted to the demands of the market place, if we believe that education is about ensuring students know what is on the test—everything else being a by-product—so that they can graduate and get a job, then ego psychology and its emphasis on adaption makes sense. And on one level, who can protest such a goal? It is not hard to position as racist or classist anyone who resists emphasizing pass rates, i.e., You mean you don't want to see these kids have the same opportunities as white kids or rich kids? You mean you don't want to prepare poor kids to compete with their better off peers? These accusatory questions are similar to the charges of elitism and communism that faced those who, at the time, protested against the imperative of social adaptation advanced by ego psychology, and the post World War II life adjustment and mental hygiene movements (see Ravitch, 2000). They were charges that eventually would be reversed by those in the 1960s and 70s who questioned the larger reality to which students and patients were being adapted. Today's response to such questions must be that, of course, we want all children to have equal educational opportunities, which is why they should all have what the daughters and sons of the wealthy have in terms of educational resources. But even then, psychoanalysis teaches us that such equity in educational opportunity is no guarantee of results. Thus our response must be grounded in a belief in the public or collective good over private gain and individual advancement, even though there is no guarantee that its maintenance or expansion will have a direct, positive effect on student learning. The argument for the public or collective good, for equalizing educational resources must be that it is a necessary good in and of itself. But we can only get to this position if we understand education's own inherent impossibility.

Bettelheim's article was one of the few that appeared in post war America on psychoanalysis and education. Ernst Kris, was another ego psychologist who focused on education, but unlike Bettelheim, he drew attention to the interpersonal relations between teacher and student, writing in 1948 that "[p]sychoanalysis has taught us that education rests on interpersonal relationships" (p. 634). Kris more than most psychoanalysts writing about education immediately after the war, urged teachers to consider their own psychic involvement with students. "Any contact with the child tends to mobilize impulses and desires of the parent's [or educator's] own childhood" (p. 630). Furthermore, adults tend to "draw a line between normality and psychological illness in the child at the same point at which it is drawn in the symptomatology of the adult" (p. 631). The implication was clear—how teachers saw their students and how they set up standards reflected their own anxieties and desires more than the purportedly objective needs of students. But Kris's call to attend to transference was not taken up by teacher education programs in any but the most cursory fashion, i.e. "You might not really like all the students, so be careful not to inadvertently take out your own feelings on them" or "We all have favorites, but we shouldn't show it." Such mild advice was not unusual in teacher education texts from the 1950s and early 1960s (see in particular Drayer, 1963; Hansen, 1957; McGrath, 1960), but one professor at Columbia University's Teachers College urged teachers to more seriously face their inner life.

Arthur Jersild

Arthur Jersild was a professor of psychology at Teachers College from 1930 to 1967. His three books, *In Search of Self: An Exploration of the Role of the School in Promoting Self-Understanding* (1952), *When Teachers Face Themselves* (1955), and *The Meaning of Psychotherapy in the Teacher's Life and Work* (1962), and a monograph, *Education for Self-Understanding* (1953) present the results of several studies undertaken to determine the importance for teachers of self-knowledge through psychoanalytic understanding. Jersild found that the curriculum ignored students' and teachers' personal experiences, feelings, and interests, and thus had little meaning for students and teachers, particularly those who "move from childhood into adult years with a burden of emotional stress" (1955, p. 4). Particularly interested in how anxiety inheres in the pedagogical relationship and formal education, Jersild argued that exploring anxiety should be an "essential topic in all teacher-training programs" (1955, p. 7).

Because he believed that self-understanding was central to the mission of formal education and because he believed that teaching required knowing one's students and oneself, he argued that teachers needed to begin with themselves. "The teacher's understanding and acceptance of himself is the most important requirement in any effort he makes to help students to know themselves and to gain healthy attitudes of self-acceptance" (1955, p. 3). "If teachers accept the concept that education should help each child to develop his real or potential self, it will be essential for the teachers to seek the kind of self-understanding which they are trying to help their pupils to achieve" (1952, p. 118). Facing oneself as a teacher meant not only confronting all the dangerous, disturbing, and anxiety provoking feelings that emerge as we teach but that we normally push away—loneliness, rage, hostility, sexual feelings—but also looking at the ways we defend against those feelings, including hiding behind psychological theories (1953, p. 52). Jersild hoped that eventually, teachers, if they went into analysis or were willing to confront their difficult feelings, would come to accept themselves (1962, p. 130).

Jersild relied particularly on the work of Eric Fromm, Karen Horney, and Harry Stack Sullivan in his studies, and he reported his findings as a social scientist. As a social scientist, Jersild followed the profession's discursive rules, and thus, paradoxically, given that he was advocating teachers attend to their inner lives, and that the curriculum integrate the affective with the cognitive, he was, himself, never present in the work. He was the researcher, the social scientist, studying teacher attitudes and feelings. Furthermore, his work seemed to suggest that one could finally know or understand who one was, in some sort of normative life story, and then adjust accordingly. There was in this work a certain Christian ethos. Face the demons within, he seemed to be saying, and one could achieve a healthier, happier life, one where "the finite and infinite are joined" (1955, p. 135). One can't help but hear echoes of James Jackson Putnam, only Jersild had rendered Putnam's views in the discourse of social science. As Hartmann had said, psychoanalysis had become, at least in the academy, applied social science.

While the increasing association between psychoanalysis and medicine lent psychoanalysis an aura of scientific rigor, which then made it more appealing to educators, who in the 1950s and 1960s were themselves once again becoming enamored of scientific approaches to education (see Taubman, 2009, Chapter Seven, and Pinar, 2004, Chapter Three), little of psychoanalytic theory was explicitly informing teacher education, curriculum, or approaches to teaching. Goodwin Watson, an education professor at Teachers College, writing in the 1957, could state, "It is remarkable that the discipline of psychoanalysis, which for over a half century has revealed so much about the dynamics of a child's life, should have so little direct impact upon education" (p. 241). On one hand Watson's comment is accurate, although somewhat odd, given that Jersild was a colleague. Freudian psychoanalytic theory, particularly in its more radical aspect, was all but absent from teacher education and discussions about school. On the other hand, psychoanalytic ideas were entering education during the 1950s and early 1960s from other sources: a more muscular mental hygiene movement and group psychology.

The Mental Hygiene Movement, Again

> One of the curious and ironical aspects of Freud's work
> and its reception is the widespread inability or refusal to
> recognize that in his portrayal of the process of personality
> development in infancy and childhood he has provided the
> most effective support for the ethics of Jesus: to love little children.
>
> (Lawrence Frank, 1948, p. 165)

> The commandment, 'Love thy neighbor as thyself' is
> impossible to fulfill.
>
> (Freud, 1930a, p. 143)

Society is a sick patient, or so suggested Lawrence Frank in his 1948 book *Society as the Patient: Essays on Culture and Personality*. Frank had been instrumental in bringing together educators and psychoanalysts in the 1930s and spearheading the integration of psychoanalytic concepts into the mental hygiene movement. Now, ten years later, he was writing, "There is a growing realization among thoughtful persons that our culture is sick, mentally disordered and in need of treatment" (p. 1). What caused this illness was a crumbling culture and social anomie as opposed to the weaknesses or sinfulness of individuals. Therefore we needed to attend to "cultural patterns" (p. 6), rather than the individual and thus at least relieve some of the anxiety and guilt individuals carry. The individual is not to blame, Frank argued, because his superego "is the culture that has been incorporated into the very personality of the individual" (p. 7). "When the culture no longer provides for a superego that is integrated and wholesome" we must change the culture. Certainly psychiatrists could help do that, Frank suggested. They could "critically examine and assess our cultural traditions and the character structure and personality of individuals which that culture and, more especially, the educational process foster in our society" (p. 153). This is an important task for psychoanalysis, but as Frank understood that task, its focus was not, for example, on America's cultural patterns of psychic repression or the tension between "civilization and its discontents" but on "developing healthy personalities and a healthy social order" (1955, p. 430).

Teachers, especially those knowledgeable about personality, could make the biggest difference in fostering "saner, happier, and more co-operative personalities" (Frank, 1948, p. 239). In 1948, not unlike today, teachers were positioned as the most important figure in achieving whatever educational ends were deemed important. Then the end was a happy, healthy personality. Teachers could achieve this by supporting the child's self-esteem, and "being genuinely concerned about the personalities of children and not merely interested in their mental processes" (p. 242). Given the need for such teachers, teacher preparation programs "should begin ... to scrutinize carefully the personality of ... teachers. ... We will find that many of the ethical, moral, sex and social ideas now being offered represent the projection of the individual's own lifelong anxieties and defenses ... " (p. 243). In this last sentence we can see the way Frank takes interesting psychoanalytic insights, e.g. that we project our own unconscious struggles onto others, and turns them into normative assessments. Nor was Frank advocating that teachers and students "critically examine and assess our cultural traditions and the character structure and personality of individuals which that culture, and more especially the educational process foster in our society" (p. 153). That was for psychiatrists, who could pass on to teachers the models of health that teachers should be striving to teach their students.

Only eight years later, in 1956, Frank would focus on the troubled teenager. In *Your Adolescent at Home and in School*, he wrote, "Why do adolescents often have trouble loving and maturing?" His answer appealed to a version of psychoanalysis that put the emphasis on patterns of culture, the culture of the family. Teens had problems because they repeated patterns of behavior passed on by parents who passed it on from their parents. Those patterns could be changed by psychiatrists, who would help the patient, whether the adolescent or the parent, become aware of those patterns, and by teachers who could "help the young adolescent to use his new emotional energies in positive ways" (p. 204) by drawing out the adolescent's capacities.

Frank's focus on the inter-generational transmission of emotional patterns may recall Abraham and Torok's (1994) concept of encryption, which refers to the way one generation passes on unresolved, emotional issues to the next, but Frank was not talking about unconscious issues. Appealing to a mixture of ecological and cultural terms, which he may have learned from his friends Kurt Lewin and Margaret Mead, he was talking about "environmentally" induced patterns of behavior, such as yelling or hitting, and the system of beliefs that accompany or rationalize these. Furthermore, he was not calling for an articulation of unresolved familial or cultural traumas, but a focus on changing habits of thought in order to interrupt destructive patterns of behavior. "By recognizing the human personality as the latest and most sensitive expression of the plasticity of nature, we may find a new basis for the belief in the value and worth of the individual" (Frank, 1951, p. 143). The implication for education was clear. Teachers should help students reorient negative thinking to "live more wholesomely and effectively" (p. 152). The beliefs that the unconscious was malleable, that teachers should strengthen the student's ego, and that if we just worked on the individual as well as culture, we could achieve a saner, happier world, all resound with many of today's educational aspirations. The difference is that today the psychoanalytic overtones are gone.

In many ways Frank was, in fact, not unlike James Jackson Putnam, a man trying to resolve the darker insights of psychoanalysis with a desire to better society and reduce suffering for the average American. Committed to organizing and wanting to foster social change, he kept trying to apply psychoanalysis as a cure. The result tended to come in the form of social engineering. As I read about Frank, I kept thinking of my mother, who in the late 1930s and early 1940s taught at New York City's Benjamin Franklin high school in what was then called Spanish Harlem. My sense of her is that while she was a successful teacher—lots of those thank you cards were in her drawer—her focus on the other, on the student, on doing something to the student defended against a good deal of anxiety about her own status. She had been divorced before she became a teacher, and even though it had been a "society marriage"—lots of articles in the newspapers—she was deeply ashamed of divorce. I didn't find out about it until I was twenty. Of course my sense of her as a teacher is based more on the mixture of seduction, control, intrusiveness, and comfort I experienced with her—a heady mix indeed, but not unlike what Frank was encouraging teachers to offer to students but at arm's remove. The teacher would befriend the student, enter the student's psyche, offer help, and in some ways, as exemplified by Frank's quote that opens this section, offer to love the child as Jesus would. Whether or not such behavior constitutes a kind of regulatory normalization or a helping hand is not the issue. One of the questions that psychoanalytic theory asks is about the ways such actions act out our own fantasies and defenses. What for example are we looking for in the eyes of our students or our own children? How do we want to be understood and why? And how are those enigmatic questions we read in the student or child reflective of our own elusive desires? Another question psychoanalysis raises concerns how fantasies of loving students and sacrificing for students can defend against very powerful aggressive impulses (see Taubman, 2006). These are the kinds of questions that push us to begin to take responsibility for, paradoxically, our own over-determined destiny. These are questions Frank left unaddressed.

According to William Graebner (1980) Lawrence Frank was "the most influential figure in the child-development movement" (p. 615). His closest circle of friends in the 1940s consisted of Erik Erikson, Kurt Lewin, Margaret Mead, Benjamin Spock and Caroline Zachry. What this group shared was Frank's belief in the way culture can frustrate an individual, make him ill, and that we therefore needed to attend to the environment. "[P]roblems of personality adjustment—that is neurosis—could be explained by reference to basic social patterns" (Graebner, 1980, p. 617), which produced the loss of ego identity. Erikson, Spock, and to a lesser extent Zachry would move to a stage model of development, one closer to the theory of Piaget, who it is interesting to note was a patient of Sabina Speilrein, one of Jung's analysands, patients, and lovers. Spock also took from Zachry and Lewin an interest in groups and group dynamics. I mention this circle of friends because its members, all influencing one another, had an enormous effect on how teachers were taught and the ways teachers came to think about their work in the 1950s. All the members were deeply involved in the mental hygiene movement and subscribed to versions of psychoanalysis that seemed to have little resemblance to Freud's, at least the version I am labeling the emancipatory project. While they may have shared Freud's advocacy of emotional honesty, his understanding of the crippling effects of social norms, his compassion for human folly, and aspects of his clinical method, they subordinated these to a faith in progress, the benefits of a positive outlook and adjusting to society, and a version of what the mentally healthy individual looked like.

When Congress had passed the National Mental Health Act in 1946, it had created the National Institute for Mental Health whose goal was the "prevention of mental illness and the production of positive mental health" (Herman, 1995, p. 248). Members of the mental hygiene movement, emboldened by the legislation, had crusaded "for a larger jurisdiction for psychological expertise" (Herman, 1995, p. 246). Mental hygiene sought to create the kind of personal and social environment which furthered sound mental health (Carroll, 1964, p. 17). The goals provided the justification for the institute to enter all forms of public services, including education. In the 1950s and 1960s the institute poured a huge amount of money into psychological services and the mental health field, as well as research into mental health. The latter lured several academic departments in the social sciences to offer their expertise on how to solve crises, ranging from race relations to containing communism. Psychiatrists were not happy with all the funding being directed to psychologists, researchers in the behavioral and social sciences, and mental health workers. In 1964, for example, "60 percent of NIMH research funds were given to psychologists, sociologists" and anthropologists (Herman, 1995, p. 249), and in part this pushed the psychiatric associations to eventually open the door to a smorgasbord of therapies. It also brought psychoanalytic ideas, or at least ideas that resembled Freudian psychoanalysis into public policy.

In her carefully argued examination of psychology's involvement in the military and civilian policies in post war America, *The Romance of American Psychology: Political Culture in the Age of Experts*, Ellen Herman documents how policies proliferating from government agencies relied on psychological and psychoanalytic approaches that "leaned toward reforming childhood socialization practices, parenting patterns, and family relations of authority" (p. 187). The reports that spewed out from federal commissions and task forces and that were informed by psychoanalytically tinged behavioral science research ranged from Patrick Moynihan's 1965 *Moynihan Report* to the President's Task Force on Manpower Conservation's (1964) *One-Third of a Nation: A Report on Young Men Found Unqualified for Military Service* to Kardiner and Ovesey's *The Mark of Oppression: A Psychological Study of the American Negro*, published in 1964. These reports, as well as the work that prepared the ground for Brown vs. Board of Education, appealed to concepts extracted from psychoanalytic theory, particularly concepts of self-esteem, aggression, repression, and the cultural origins of aggression, deviant behavior, and mental instability.

One aspect of these policies' appropriation of psychoanalytic concepts concerned their focus on personality. In other words, the problem with unequal education or poverty was its crippling impact on the *personalities* of the victims. This approach had three consequences. First, it inadvertently pathologized the victims—their very personalities had been crippled. Second, it implied that if the victims of injustice affirmed their identity and developed self-esteem, one could argue the problems had been solved—thus the focus on esteem building pedagogies. And third, it collapsed subjectivity into personality and individuality. This confusion, antithetical to psychoanalytic theory, which posited a psycho/social subjectivity separate from, split off from, but deeply implicated in one's personality or individuality, would lead to the accusations, sometimes well founded, that psychoanalysis was a theory of personality and that its focus on the individual was politically reactionary.

In 1950 the National Commission for Mental Health merged with the National Mental Health Foundation and the Psychiatric Foundation to form the National Association for Mental Health, which co-sponsored that year the White House Conference on Children and Youth. The slogan of the conference was "A Healthy Personality for Every Child." The conference concluded by affirming the school's responsibility for "the healthy development of the whole personality of each child" (Cohen, S., 1983, p. 139). According to Cohen

> by the early 1950s … the mental hygiene point of view had been incorporated into educational ideology and institutionalized at the center of American

society, a common idiom of educationists, part of the professional lore of all those concerned with children and education. (p. 139)

Teachers were encouraged, as Bettelheim advised, to monitor students' emotional states, attend to their problems, and above all watch for signs of unhappiness or personality maladjustment. Indeed personality took on a whole new meaning, one with overtones of psychological health or abnormality. Textbooks increasingly had titles with the term "Personality Disorders." And increasingly teacher educators looked to define the personality traits of the good teacher.

Laurie Moses Hines, writing in the Hoover Institute's *Education Next*, argues that during the late 1940s and 1950s and even into the 1960s teacher education programs evaluated teachers based on personality traits and looked for well-adjusted candidates. She claims, although she gives no evidence, that some schools used the Minnesota Multiphasic Personality Inventory, a personality test, to assess teachers' personalities. According to Hines, in 1953 education professor Ruth A. Stout "completed a comprehensive study of admission practices in teacher education institutions" and found that nearly half of those institutions surveyed "assessed students' emotional stability, identifying it as the second most important criterion for determining fitness for teaching, behind academic credentials" (2007). Shipley's *The Mentally Disturbed Teacher*, published in 1961, certainly depicts a profession on the brink of a breakdown, and Shipley urges schools of education to ensure teachers are not mentally deranged.

In the 1950s and early 1960s, physicians, psychiatrists, guidance counselors, psychologists, teacher educators, and teachers increasingly used psychoanalytic theory to render internal life itself as pathological. The emancipatory project of psychoanalysis had exposed the midnight of the soul and sought to understand its presence in our daytime lives. The project had started with the idea that one's waking life was a kind of dream and our dreams essentially hieroglyphics of our soul—Lacan would say that we awaken from our dreams to escape the truth of our being. The mental hygiene movement would find not truth but pathology in our inner life. It is not surprising that behaviorism, which Freud had described as "a theory naïve enough to boast that it has put the whole problem of psychology completely out of court" (1925c, p. 52), was in the 1950s dominant in the academy (see Hunt, 1994). The struggle to represent affect and think differently was left to literature departments in the 1950s and in the growing bohemian culture on the edges of the Eisenhower years.

In her brief memoir of life in the 1950s, Barbara Norfleet (2001), the curator of Harvard's photographic archive of American social history, describes life for a middle class, white woman then as a private time.

Friends were told little, and parents absolutely nothing, and they wanted to be told nothing, lest they think this child was not perfect and perfectly adjusted. ... Once [the] babies were born they absorbed every moment of the day. ... Dr. Spock told [mothers they] should feel euphoric ... that ... family would fulfill all [one's] needs. ... Gender functions were rigorously pre-scribed. ... Women spent a lot of time on the analyst's couch ... but ... you didn't tell friends you were being psychoanalyzed. (pp. 9–12)

At the very moment when the mental hygiene movement was at its height, the very moment when psychoanalysis achieved its greatest popularity, the moment when teachers and students were taught to be vigilant about their emotional life, emotional life itself and the emancipatory project of psychoanalysis retreated to the margins.

Two final examples of how the mental hygiene movement appropriated and translated Freudian psychoanalytic theory are Herbert Carroll's (1964) *The Mental Hygiene Movement: The Dynamics of Adjustment* first published in 1951, and a 1958 essay by Louise Tyler, who in the late 1950s and early 1960s was a professor in and chair of the department of curriculum at UCLA.

Carroll's text opens by documenting the extent of mental illness in the country and goes on to argue for the precepts of mental hygiene. I mention the text only because of its use of particular psychoanalytic concepts. For example, Carroll refers to repression as "an undesirable mechanism of adjustment because it is tension producing" (p. 233). Or to take another example, he writes, "Individuals who suffer from obsessions are usually submissive persons who are convinced of their own worthlessness" (p. 257). Or "[a]nxiety, like all of the other learned behavior dis-orders, results from the frustration of one or more of the four major needs" (p. 265), which are the need for mastery, emotional security, physical security, and status. Or, "[i]t is likely that homosexuals as a group are neurotic" (p. 74). Or, finally, "chaotic sexuality ... is probably a manifestation of the neurosis rather than a primary cause" (p. 265). Herbert Carroll was a professor of psychology at the University of New Hampshire, and his book was used for several years in the teacher preparation program there.

Louise Tyler's "Psychoanalysis and Curriculum Theory," reveals, more than Carroll's article, the influence of ego psychology, and exemplifies the tenets of the mental hygiene movement. Although it attempts to bring to curriculum the insights of psychoanalytic theory, it also reveals how far psychoanalytic theory had strayed from the version Freud offered at Clark University in 1909.

Tyler opens her article by proclaiming that "of all the behavioral sciences ... psychoanalysis has made a major breakthrough in our understanding of human nature" (p. 446). Curriculum theory, she states can benefit from it. Arguing that the psychoanalytic concepts of the unconscious, instincts, repression, the structure of the mental apparatus, and the development of personality, all have value for curriculum, Tyler briefly gives her version of each. In her definitions and examples we can hear echoes of the mental hygiene movement, ego psychology, and a medicalized psychoanalytic theory, but we must also acknowledge a desire on her part to bring to curriculum theory an appreciation of inner life that was, if not lacking from extant curriculum theory, often reduced to personality, behaviors, and conscious processes.

Tyler defines the unconscious as including "many contradictory impulses, *many of them neither rational nor moral*" (p. 448, my italics), and repression as a process whereby disturbing thoughts are excluded. She provides an example of teachers who repress their negative feelings toward students and how these feelings return to inform teachers' unrealistically high standards. Such an astute insight might benefit those educators today who are intent on calling for higher standards, but Tyler might, herself, have benefitted from Freud's *Civilization and Its Discontents* and explored the relationship between standards in general and psychic life. Does, for example, the setting of standards, as opposed to goals, reveal our own frustrations or dissatisfactions with ourselves, our own aggressive or sado/masochistic urges disguised as altruism? Tyler's article doesn't pursue such questions.

Following the definition of curriculum established by Ralph Tyler (1949) to whom she was not related, although she was his, as well as Benjamin Bloom's student, Louise Tyler defines the curriculum as limited "to formulat[ing] educational objectives, planning ... learning experiences, and evaluat[ing] the effectiveness of learning experiences" (1958, p. 453). Psychoanalytic theory could, she argues, help us with these. How? First of all, psychoanalytic theory has for its "therapeutic aim the development of rational behavior" (p. 454). Second, psychoanalytic theory helps develop a healthy personality and offers us the insight—here she references Bettelheim—that "thinking strengthens the ego" (p. 454). Further, psychoanalytic theory teaches us that with a strong ego, we can achieve intellectual mastery. In addition to the academic curriculum, she writes, "the adolescent should learn what motivates him," "that there is nothing evil or secret about sex," what the reasons are for his "need for prestige," "that a critical attitude toward parents is ... the problem of an age group," "that all job opportunities are not equally open to everyone," and that "our society is somewhat at fault" for this (p. 455). Subject matter should help students accomplish these objectives.

Psychoanalysis, according to Tyler, teaches teachers they should not take students' views of them personally since students are caught in transferential relationships. If teachers understand transference, they may also be able to detect the underlying motives in troubling student behaviors. Applying the concepts of psychoanalysis further, Tyler suggests that teachers who wish to change student attitudes should be modest in their endeavors, given that the unconscious can hinder such efforts. "Probably, at the very least," she urges, "our instructional efforts should not make learners feel guilty" (p. 458). Lastly, she suggests that free association can help teachers, if, for example, they ask students to talk aloud during tests to determine students abilities and the difficulty of the test.

Reading this article, we sense the tension between the therapeutic and emancipatory projects, between the desire to think psychoanalytically about education and the desire to apply its insights to practice. The language of mental hygiene, ego psychology, and a medicalized psychoanalysis jump out, but so too does the attempt, for example, to understand teachers' focus on standards in terms of their own unconscious feelings about students, teaching, and education. On one hand Tyler's is a curriculum of social conformity in the guise of empathic understanding and attention to adolescents. On the other hand it urges teachers and educators to think more deeply about their own unconscious complicity in the educational reality they find before them. While the radical insights of psychoanalysis have been neutered and become a kind of dredging of what Adolf Meyer referred to as "an imagined cesspool" (quoted in Zaretsky, 2004, p. 83), Tyler also urges us to attend to the influence of the irrational and unconscious in our seemingly logical and transparent decision making. Unfortunately, while there are traces of the emancipatory project in her work, Louise Tyler seemed more interested in using psychoanalytic theory to adjust students to a given curriculum, one based on Ralph Tyler's rationale. Rather than understanding teaching in terms of creating conditions for the re-symbolization within the curriculum of the radical knowledge of the unconscious as it erupts in the classroom, Louise Tyler's turn to psychoanalytic theory appeared to be in the service of more efficient teaching.

Carroll's and Tyler's work give a flavor of how psychoanalysis was applied in education after the war up until the mid-1960s. Misinterpreted and placed in the service of the regnant educational ideologies of the time, it hardened into dogma in psychiatric psychoanalysis, emerged as part of a regulatory apparatus in the mental hygiene movement, and dissipated into trivialities in teacher education. The more radical insights and questions of the emancipatory project of psychoanalysis found shelter in English departments and bohemian culture, where the layers of optimism that had gathered over the years were scraped off, revealing a more tragic but also more human psychoanalysis. There was, however, one other way that psycho-analysis entered the academy and teacher education in the post war period. That was through the introduction of group work.

Group Work in the Academy and Schools

> [A]n individual in a group is subjected through its influence to
> what is often a profound alteration in his mental activity.
>
> (Freud, 1921a, p. 88)

Starting in the early 1950s academic psychologists began to introduce into schools the idea of using groups to increase students' self-knowledge and reduce prejudice. Teachers never fully embraced integrating into academic curriculum what were called training or T-groups or sensitivity training or work groups, although they would eventually use versions in small group work and learning communities. They did, however, incorporate groups into the extra-curriculum. Some teacher education programs, such as those at City University in New York in the early 1960s, used training groups to habituate teachers to the existential dilemma of what to do on Monday (see Miller, 1962), but in general they were used in counseling programs.

Amy Fraher (2004) in *A History of Group Study and Psychodynamic Organizations* traces the emergence of group work in America to the early industrial psychological work of Elton Mayo, to Kurt Lewin's "'*here-and-now*' theories and the human interaction laboratory" (p. 33), to Melanie Klein's work on splitting, and projection, to Wilfred Bion's theorization of different kinds of groups, to the Tavistock Institute's influence, and to the National Training Lab. Of these only the National Training Lab was not initially psychoanalytically oriented, which is perhaps not surprising, given Kurt Lewin's involvement.

To oversimplify, the theory underlying groups was that groups acted in ways that provoked and reproduced certain primitive emotions and defenses, and if the analyst or trainer could point these out in a non-didactic way, individuals would learn something about how groups functioned but also about themselves. Group members, confronted with the existential void, projected onto the leader or the group or various subgroups feelings that they themselves could not contain and were not aware of. So, for example, group members might feel anxious in the unpredictable situation, but unable to hold or come to terms with those feelings might attribute omniscience to the trainer or leader. Anxiety might provoke idealization. Or group members might exhibit counter-dependence by attacking or conspiring against the leader. Anxiety might provoke aggression. A range of reactions was possible. The leader's or trainer's role was to interpret the unacknowledged behavior of the group, rarely of individuals, point out patterns, and reflect back what he or she saw occurring at the group level. The form such interpretations took depended on the trainer's theoretical background. A trainer influenced by Bion's post-Kleinian approach to groups might phrase interventions in terms of splitting, inability to contain anxiety, and group fantasies. A trainer coming out of the National Training Lab might focus on feelings in the here-and-now about, for example, leadership issues.

As the psychoanalytic theory of groups entered the academy and psychiatry, academic scholars, analysts, and therapists not only began to implement group psychotherapy but also to research it. Behavioral scientists involved in the research, particularly sociologists, increasingly saw the attraction in applying group work in school and organizations to change attitudes. In particular the National Training Lab (NTL), established in Bethel, Maine and closely associated with Lewin, influenced psychologists and educators. Many of the first groups for students began in the early 1950s, shortly after a presentation in 1949 by NTL at a national convention of the American Psychological Association, where NTL members demonstrated the use of role playing in the T-groups.

Early uses of groups were often for the purposes of research. In 1954 Gerald S. Weidner, a professor at New York's Brooklyn College, which Abraham Maslow had just left, ran an experiment with college students to study the "relationship between prejudice and certain patterns of emotional development and expression" (Weidner, 1954, p. 332). He designed an experiment to compare group therapy to lecture based instruction. Using psychological pre- and post-tests, he concluded that groups that focused on emotions had a greater impact on prejudice reduction than lectures did, because they created a greater sense of self-confidence among students, thus dissipating prejudice fostered by low self-esteem.

One text in particular captures the use of groups in school settings prior to the late 1960s and 1970s. Like so many groups run in schools at the time, it was meant to increase self-knowledge as a way to reduce ethnic and racial prejudice. Although this group, as well as so many like it, was run for high school and middle school students, none of the students actually studied or were apprised of the theoretical assumptions or concepts underlying the use of groups, nor did any know what the experiment actually was based on or what it was attempting to do. I discuss it here because it reflects not only how psychoanalysis within psychology departments had become the object of experimental testing but also how it had become instrumentalized. If we think back to the Clark Conference for a moment, we might say that psychoanalysis was entering schools in versions that Boas, James, Meyer, Putnam, Titchener, and Wundt would have condoned. It had become a method to increase mental health and achieve a cultural goal, and its worth and success would be measured by experimental tests and outcomes.

Richard Jones' Experiment

In 1960, Richard Jones, a clinical psychologist and member of the Brandeis department of psychology published *An Application of Psychoanalysis to Education* with an introduction by Lawrence Kubie. Jones' book recounts an experimental study of what he called a Self-Knowledge Workshop, which was aimed at increasing students' self-awareness as a way to reduce prejudice. His question was "Does the increase in self-tolerance, demonstrated to have been facilitated by the workshop, result in a simultaneous decrease in attitudes of ethnic prejudice?" (p. 97). His experiment consisted of an experimental group and two control groups, all made up of senior girls from three schools. Two groups were run as a straight lecture, the other as a human relations or training group, in which the leader made only neutral interpretations or raised questions, much as an analyst might. Jones cites Hartmann's ego psychology and Erikson's psychosocial theory as the sources of his own theoretical underpinnings, and Allport's research design as the model on which he based his own. Various psychological tests were administered before and after the group/class met. The results showed that students in the experimental group who had become more aware of their projective tendencies and defensive posturing showed a reduction in prejudiced attitudes relative to members in the other groups as well as an increased sense of self-awareness. But how exactly did the group work? Here is an example from the written narrative of the experimental group. "G" stands for one of the girl students, "L" for the leader, who was Jones.

L: The rule of the group is as long as you put it in words, anything goes.
G: Mr. J., do you think we're accomplishing anything?
L: What do you think?

Or elsewhere, when the girls have put a table between them and Mr. Jones.

L: Why have you put a barrier between us?
G: Oh, you and that table! I'd like to put a bomb under it and blow it to pieces!
G: I've opened up since we moved the table. Now I'd be curious to see how it felt back in the circle. (The group votes in affirmation)
L: That doesn't tell us why we moved the table in the first place.

The narration goes on, but we can get a sense of how the interventions resemble analytic interventions. At the end of the group, the student who Jones considered to have benefitted the most is quoted as saying, "To sum all this up, I have changed. Whether I like it or not, I can't say. ... I did learn more about myself" (p. 83). A girl who Jones believed learned the least also said she had learned a good deal, but because she objects that she might have learned more had the leader "led"' the class more and because she states she learned a good deal from the "psychology class" (p. 83), Jones concludes "this girl had hardly been reached by the workshop" (p. 83). Given a young man in the ambiguous role of group leader with senior high school girls, given that there is no mention of counter-transference in the report, and given that Jones' summation of what happens focuses on "reaching the girls," one can wonder about the unconscious desires and perhaps losses that influenced Jones' experiment.

Again, the issue is not the sexual politics of this scene nor is it Jones' inner life, although as Freud pointed out, any such denial reveals the reverse. The point I want to emphasize is that the application of psychoanalytic theory in the 1950s and early 1960s was already marked by the language and methods of academic psychology, medicine, and the mental hygiene movement. As a therapeutic project during this time period, psychoanalysis disavowed its own radical knowledge, leaving it vulnerable to eruptions from the unconscious.

Also evident in Jones' study is the experimental frame. According to Hale (1995b), controlled comparative studies, using rating scales and experimental designs, of psychotherapeutic methods, including group treatment, increased, in part because of the influence of clinical psychologists in the academy coupled with the behavioral and learning orientation of psychology departments. As those studies proliferated and behaviorists like H.J. Eysenck (1952) and Joseph Wolpe (1958) claimed patients undergoing psychoanalysis and psychotherapy had no greater success rate than those who didn't, psychoanalysis began to lose its status in departments of psychology.

Kubie's Introduction

As I mentioned Lawrence Kubie wrote the introduction to Jones' book. Kubie, who would later be remembered for his attempts (unsuccessful) to cure Tennessee Williams, Moss Hart, and Vladimire Horowitz of their homosexuality (Farber and Green, 1993, pp. 58–62), had been involved in psychoanalysis since the 1930s and had held high offices in leading psychoanalytic associations. Kubie had long advocated for a greater emphasis on testing the scientific validity of psychoanalysis (Hale, 1995b, p. 306) as well as extending its purview. "Psychotherapy," he claimed, "embraces any effort to influence human thought or feeling or conduct ... by charity or social service, by education or by the contagion of another's spirit" (quoted in Herman, 1995, p. 118). Clearly education fell within the purview of psychoanalysis. Since psychoanalysis or psychotherapy, however, focused on one to one relationships, it was difficult to see how schools could apply psychoanalytic theory and methods. One way that they could be applied was through groups.

In the introduction to Jones' book Kubie wrote that educators needed to realize that "both intellectual development and creativity will continue to be seriously hampered unless we find out how to make emotional maturation a part of education" (p. vii). Educators had to start in kindergarten and continue throughout all the years of schooling to address the "interaction between universal but subtly masked neurotic mechanisms and the educational process" (p. vii) which blocks and distorts education. Teachers needed to encourage children

> to talk about their hidden thoughts, and to put them into words, i.e., to talk out loud about love and hate and jealousy and fear, about curiosity over the body, its products and its apertures; about what goes in and what comes out; about what happens inside and what happens outside; about their dim and confused feelings about sex itself; about the strained and stressful relationships within families that are transplanted into schools. (p. viii)

Such talk sounds fascinating and central to education, if it informs a substantive curriculum, if it is not coerced from the student, and if it is not pressed into the service of some higher good. But Kubie wanted students to disclose so that teachers could help the students develop more mature and emotionally balanced views of themselves and their world. In particular teachers could help students become more aware of and readjust their attitudes.

Such a version of psychoanalysis seems intrusive and voyeuristic. Now, psychoanalysis suggests that we are all voyeurs or what Freud called scopophiliacs, in our own idiosyncratic ways, as well as exhibitionists. Today's reality T.V. and the media's tracking of female body sizes, for example, suggest as much. But psychoanalysis also argues that scopophilia and exhibitionism are defenses and compensatory for unfulfilled unconscious erotic desires. In particular, according to Freud, scopophilia could have a sadistic component, where the scopophiliac longs to control and dominate the object of vision as a way to achieve the right distance from it. I would speculate that what such longings compensate for and defend against are the desire for and fear of emotional intimacy. In other words, intimacy, for the scopophiliac is already phrased in terms of pre-Oedipal oceanic oneness or horrifying engulfment. The promise of oceanic oneness offers a soothing defense against anxiety; the horror of engulfment provokes the desire to master and control through looking at or observing the object. Extreme fantasies or fantasies of extremes predominate. Examples of such thinking abound in schools, where teachers, particularly new ones, ricochet between imagining themselves draped with loving students or eaten alive by the kids. As a defense the teachers turn the students into object of research and diagnosis or objects of pleasurable fantasy and the teacher's loving gaze.

Of course voyeurism and exhibitionism have for some time been a part of classroom practice that has appropriated a particular version of psychoanalysis, particularly ego psychology, in which the analyst is positioned as the observer, the one who knows. Teachers will ask students to disclose their innermost thoughts and desires, and many students do so with little prodding. Teachers will then read or listen to the material, themselves remaining neutral, and at times even use the material to bring students' views more in line with their own. It is in part the recoil from what appear to be voyeuristic practices of demanding student self-disclosure that has led teachers to be suspicious of psychoanalysis, with which such practices are associated. In large part teachers equate psychoanalysis with the intrusive demand for unregulated or heavily surveyed expression of feelings, because teachers have overlooked the possibility that thinking about teaching and curriculum through psychoanalysis may, in fact, have nothing to do with the demand for students to express their feelings or divulge what they are thinking. It may have much more to do with acknowledging that the student, as other, has an unconscious, as does the teacher, and that one way we can understand teaching is in terms of playing with and re-articulating or re-symbolizing seemingly odd, peripheral, irrational material that surfaces in classrooms and schools. Material might include, for example, student responses that may appear to make no sense, but read from a psychoanalytic point of view, and offered for re-symbolization, may illuminate the curriculum. From this perspective teaching involves a respect for such material and an acknowledgment of the presence and disruptive potential of the unconscious. Eric Santner (2006) suggests that

> the only way to truly understand the concept of love of neighbor is to grasp what it means that he or she has an unconscious. … The being whose proximity we are enjoined to inhabit and open to according to the imperative of neighborly love is always a subject at odds with itself, split by thoughts, desires, fantasies, and pleasures it can never fully claim as its own and that in some sense both do and do not belong to it. (p. xii)

Santner's comment asks teachers to remain open not only to modes of understanding what occurs in classrooms but also to the irruptions of the unconscious that disturb taken-for-granted causal narratives of learning and teaching or categories of students and teachers. Such awareness is not the same as the emotional expression that group work in the 1950s and early 1960s demanded and examined.

It may be then that while the abreaction Freud initially saw as essential to his patients' recovery can play a part in how we teach or think through and within the emancipatory project, it is peripheral to the shift in perspective that attends to or listens to the unconscious as it moves through our classrooms. While T-groups were, to some extent, meant to conjure the unconscious, they came to be employed as a way to study students as those students divulged their feelings. They were also a way to bring affect into the curriculum. Jones would go on to write *Fantasy and Feeling in Education* (1968) which called for an integration of affective education with the cognitive focus educators such as Jerome Bruner were bringing to education. Groups themselves would rarely if ever come to be used within the classroom, other than as small group work.

End of an Era

> Human creations are easily destroyed, and science
> and technology, which have built them up, can also
> be used for their annihilation.
>
> (Freud, 1927a, p. 6)

According to Hale (1995b) and Zaretsky (2004), psychoanalysis's prestige began to wane in the early 1960s. By the end of the century, it would disappear from departments of psychology and school psychology, although, in large part thanks to the introduction of object relations theory by feminist theorists and to the arrival of Jacques Lacan's teachings, it reemerged in humanities departments and in curriculum theory. Zaretsky (2004) attributes the demise of psychoanalysis to its aspiration to be treated as a medical science. The alliance turned the humanistic and existential bent of psychoanalysis into psychoanalytic dogma, rigid protocols, and categorizations of pathologies that could be experimentally tested. The emancipatory project with its position as a "grave philosophy" and radical hermeneutic that put into question the very possibility of institutionalized knowledge had never really achieved prominence, but in the 1940s, 1950s, and early and mid-1960s, it all but disappeared from psychoanalysis. As a result psychoanalytic theory lost its critical and speculative edge (see Jacoby 1997, 1986; Lasch, 1977; Zaretsky, 2004).

For education, the demise was barely registered. Psychoanalytic theory continued to find a place in departments of guidance and school psychology but not in teacher preparation programs or departments of curriculum and instruction. When teacher education textbooks written in the late 1950s and early 1960s talked about the emotional life of teachers and students, they did so in terms of personality and cultivating health. Even the mental hygiene movement's appropriation of Freudian psychoanalysis faded. In courses on the history of education there were scant references to the psychoanalytic influence in the early days of progressivism. Other than the lone voice of Paul Goodman (1960, 1964), who registered his scorn for bureaucratized schooling and urged teachers and students to release their libidinal energies and find in Freud, Reich, and Gestalt therapy an antidote to conformity and the lonely crowd, there was no voice in education to remind us of psychoanalysis's emancipatory project and its challenge to a normalized individuality. Even at Teachers College (T.C.), where there had been cross fertilization between psychoanalysis, anthropology, and sociology, psychoanalysis faded. Goodwin Watson, a psychologist who had taught at T.C. for several decades, who was close friends with Kurt Lewin and with him had been monitored by the F.B.I and C.I.A. for his radical political involvements (Cooke, 2007), and who had himself been involved in psychoanalysis, would in 1957 bemoan the absence of psychoanalysis from education (Watson, p. 241).

As it became more medicalized, psychoanalysis ignored its own and education's emancipatory project. It lost interest in education, education understood that is in the capacious sense of using the cultural heritage to explore daily existence, with its pain, violence, and boredom, its frustration and terrors, its dreams, desires and illogic, and its repetitions and obsessions. Was that not what Freud had done, except he had located his exploration at the crossroads of love and aggression, Eros and Thanatos, as they warred for possession of the body and psyche? The emancipatory project offered not just the possibility of attending to the fantasies, irrationalities, desires, dreams, and various slips of the tongue, pen, and memory all of which suffuse but remain unacknowledged in classrooms and the curriculum. Solely bringing these to awareness would equate to the demand for student expression of the inner life so much a part of group work and the therapeutic project. Rather the emancipatory project would take such material and offer students opportunities to explore it and re-symbolize it using the vast disciplinary knowledge Freud himself brought to his analytic endeavors. Thus could the disciplines be animated by the life and questions pressing in the psyche and the body just as those questions and life could be re-articulated within such disciplinary knowledge. The emancipatory project, however, did not prevail in those years in post World War II America.

Sexuality and post World War II Psychoanalysis

It was in the post World War II years that I would form my initial views about psychoanalysis. My friends and I associated psychoanalysis with deviancy, sickness, and the sterility of metal instruments and white lab coats. There was something about it that suggested a particular kind of sex that was off limits or simply scary. Certainly in that period sexuality and deviancy seemed closely related, particularly in the medicalized psychoanalysis of the period.

I remember one fall evening in 1961. I was fourteen, and I had just come out of the subway at Grand Army Plaza in Park Slope, Brooklyn. It was dark. A youngish man started walking next to me. He asked me a question about directions and then before I knew it he was asking me if I wanted a blow job. I walked faster and then ran away. I am not sure what I was running from—homosexual sex, the aggression in the invitation, sex mentioned in such a public way—but I thought to myself that this man was sick. He needed help. Paradoxically, at this age and for a few years prior, I had been experimenting with homosexual sex with friends, and can't remember any feelings of shame about this, or rather, I was as free of shame about that as I was of feeling ashamed about masturbation. So the question is why did I react with such terror to that young man's proposition and what does my reaction have to do with the post war relationship between psychoanalysis and education? I suspect on one level it was easier for me to ignore my experiments as passing pleasures with peers, particularly given that there were no words to capture those encounters and my own heterosexual experiments and crushes swamped the less frequent, but more genital homosexual ones. Would I have been equally as frightened had a relatively older woman propositioned me? If so, was it the transgression of age appropriate sexual contact that upset me? Perhaps. But on another level, I think my reactions spoke to the radical otherness of sexuality in the human psyche.

In *The Freudian Body: Psychoanalysis and Art* Leo Bersani (1986) writes that psychoanalysis "defines the sexual itself as that which profoundly disorients any effort whatsoever to constitute the human subject" (p. 101). For all Freud's attempts to deny the revolutionary character of sexuality, he also acknowledged it, not only in his comments about, for example, homosexuals making the best teachers (see Chapter 1), not only in his theorization of polymorphous perversity and bi-sexuality, but also in his own body, which was sexually drawn to Jung and Fliess (see Gay, 2006, p. 276; Prochnik, 2006, p. 75; Rosenzweig, 1994, p. 54). "[E]veryone, even the most normal person," Freud wrote, "is capable of making a homosexual object-choice, and has done so at some time in his life, and either still adheres to it in his unconscious or else protects himself against it by vigorous counter-attitudes" (1910b, p. 99 fn. 3). It is not sex, per se, that is so troubling; it is its radical otherness. And it was, I think, that otherness of sexuality that sprang out of the darkness that night, as I walked home. I couldn't domesticate it into either youthful peer group dalliances or normalizing narratives. Labeling it sick didn't lessen the disquiet. I remember the episode now almost fifty years later. It was the otherness of sexuality that troubled me, and troubled psychoanalysis.

It troubled psychoanalysis so much that in the post war era, homosexuality was both the unspoken and the pathological. Sex—normative heterosexual sex—was the repressed that psychoanalysis was meant to liberate and adapt us to. For example, in his discussion of sex and the teacher, Jersild (1955, 1962), while encouraging individuals to accept their various feelings about sex and feel freer about the spectrum of what he refers to as "sexual attitudes," sustains a normalizing discourse on heterosexuality in the name of openness. That very liberation, as Bersani suggests, placed the otherness of sexuality within a normalized field (Bersani, 1986, pp. 101–2) such that its dangerous pleasures and aggression posed no threat to our stability or social adaptation or within a field of pathologies such that its dangers were coded as illness.

My argument here, more a speculation really, is that the currents of intense somatic pleasures and pains, longings and hates that course through one's body can become open to question at particular moments through a particular psychoanalytic theory that re-articulates the sexuality one develops within families and cultures as questions the world answers. The emancipatory project of psychoanalysis reveals a sexuality that is not a purely linguistic construction, for example the kind Foucault deconstructed and genealogically reconstructed. Rather it is the sexuality that can shatter our hearts and sometimes our bodies. It can tear open, disrupt, slip out of these constructions and our normalized sexualities. It is not, and I need to emphasize this, it is not some natural, pre-discursive force, whose meaning is already written over it. While not synonymous with them, it is always, necessarily, caught up in the socio/cultural discursive networks that carry parental and social desires and questions. As such it *can* set in motion a "quasi-mechanical automaticity of the compulsion to repeat" (Santner, 2006, p. 191), what I would call a prosthetic sexuality, *as well as* disrupt any sense of sexual continuity.

For our purposes, what this means is that we might, in thinking back through the symptoms of the neurotic relationship between psychoanalysis and education, glimpse another future, one that did not get caught in the circuit of repression/ liberation that Foucault would deconstruct. To think through psychoanalysis about education might well mean that just as we might, as an ethical act, appreciate or recognize the unconscious in the other, as Santner (2006) suggests, we might also listen to, without looking for, the otherness of sexuality that erupts within or alongside the normalized and pathologized sexualities that the therapeutic project of psychoanalysis maps and engages. We would acknowledge the otherness within our own sexuality and acknowledge it in others. Education then might occur at those moments of acknowledgment.

There is a story that Donna Foote (2008) tells in her book about Teach for America, entitled *Restless Pursuit: A Year in the Trenches with Teach for America*. She recounts how a female teacher, trapped and sheltered with her students in her darkened classroom during a school riot, witnesses a boy, egged on by his peers, urinate on the floor. It's a shocking anecdote, but there are ways to think about it—homosexual yearning, desire for orgiastic oneness, group psychology—as well as about one's own reactions, in any number of ways that psychoanalysis offers, without criminalizing or pathologizing the act or freezing one's reactions. The emancipatory project of psychoanalysis offers such a perspective to think through or work through such events and one's reactions to them. But what is more important is that in thinking about the curriculum in these terms, one could, using the above example, envision developing a curriculum that would allow students to explore and re-articulate such marginal, transgressive experiences, transforming them into something other than shocking anecdotes told by teachers or into criminalized, pathologized behaviors.

I am not suggesting we revel in some Utopian polymorphous perversity. That call would come at the end of the 1960s and in its symptoms, dreams, and failures we can read another future for the relationship between psychoanalysis and education yet to be written. Rather I am arguing that in acknowledging the very radical otherness of sexuality, in suspending the normalizing grids into which it is pressed, in allowing the disciplines to explore that otherness as a question not an answer, we might expand the curriculum and even further open up, in a modest way, our teaching. But such an exploration was a long way from the ways psychoanalysis came into the classrooms in post World War II America, when the therapeutic project all but silenced the emancipatory project.

There would be one last irruption of psychoanalysis's emancipatory project and then it would all but disappear from the field of education. Its return in the 1960s and 1970s would startle educators and hold out to them the possibility of an ecstatic education. But those educators who sought such ecstasy would, because they had forgotten or not learned of the previous relationship between education and psychoanalysis, repeat, yet again, many of the experiments that had been tried a half century earlier.

5

PSYCHOANALYSIS AND EDUCATION: 1968 TO THE PRESENT

> I bow before their reproach that I do not know how to
> bring them consolation – for that is fundamentally what
> they all demand, the wildest revolutionaries no less than
> the most conformist pious believers.
>
> (Freud, 1930a, p. 145)

I started teaching in 1969. I began analysis in 1981. Much of the material in this chapter is based on my own experiences with both, and reflects the difficulty I had in summarizing so much that seems so close. In Chapters 3 and 4, I relied on primary and secondary sources to present the history of the relationship between education and psychoanalysis as it evolved between 1910 and the mid-1960s. But as I began to sort through materials from the last four decades, I found myself overwhelmed. My own memories and fantasies rushed in to mix with the materials, such that there seemed too much to synopsize, and a synopsis seemed both too abstract—these were living memories to me—and too unwieldy—how could I summarize a relationship between two professions that underwent such dramatic changes in three decades. The task appeared particularly hard, given that the emancipatory project of psychoanalysis has been kept alive in the field of education, since the 1970s, only through the efforts of a group of curriculum theorists, most of whom I know personally and whose efforts I wanted to recognize. It was also hard for me to separate the upheavals in the relationship between education and psychoanalysis from those in my own life.

When in 1969 I took a teaching job at the prep school I had attended as a boy, I had just had my first brief—it lasted a few months—and anxious—I was a nervous wreck and shut down for most of it—encounter with therapy. I was living at home, and took the teaching job because I needed to work. Over the next ten years I earned a master's degree and doctorate, taught English in three different high schools, and worked as a guidance counselor in one. When I look back on that period from 1969 to 1980, my life seems typical in two very different senses. On one hand I pursued an established career path. On the other hand I engaged in all the experimentation with politics, sexuality, living arrangements, and philosophies that so many young people at the time did. In the late 1960s and 70s the seemingly more unconventional behavior was part of a revolution that offered solidarity to all those who participated in it. In the hands of scholars, such as Norman O. Brown, radical analysts such as R.D. Laing, and critical theorists such as Herbert Marcuse, psychoanalysis encouraged living the revolution now. Meeting professional expectations or staying on professional track, on the other hand, appeared in some ways to be colluding with the system. By the 1980s, of course, such revolutionary gestures were treated as acting out or had been criminalized, while diligently showing up for work and pursuing professional goals were once again signs of psychological maturity. My point here is that whether or not I was acting out or taking small steps for social equality and justice, whether I was growing up or selling-out, such evaluations have nothing to do with psychoanalytic theory in terms of its emancipatory project. Such a project is interested in articulating, rather than categorizing, the psychic co-ordinates and the unconscious pulls and pushes that have led us to where we are. These co-ordinates and psychic rip tides cannot be separated from the social. Indeed they are deeply implicated in the social, but they cannot be reduced to it.

When I finally began analysis in 1981, it was not as a result of the revolutionary excesses of the 1960s and 70s, nor was it as a result of running on a professional track. I entered because I felt depressed, scared, stuck, and adrift, all at the same time. Psychoanalysis didn't help me grow up or mature. It did not enable me to throw off the harness of work or bear it more lightly. Nor did it help me find, stay in, or leave relationships. As Freud warns in the quote at the top of this chapter, it did not bring me consolation. It did, however, give me a perspective. That perspective, which is an interminable, sometimes intolerable, analysis, has more than anything taught me that while I cannot escape a destiny that has brought me to this moment, I am also responsible for the moment by moment unfolding of that destiny. As I age, I hear and see more and more my mother and father in my own words and gestures, the ways I seek intimacy with my daughters, the patterns I fall into when I teach. I know there is no escaping what Freud called the family romance and the social that mingles with and enters through it, but the point here, again, is not to pass judgment, although I do plenty of that myself. The point is to attend to the myriad known and unknown ways the past lives, forever, in the present. And yet that past is always historicized by the present's new thinking as well as its new defenses. Surely that is what is happening as I try to reconstruct the history of the relationship between psychoanalysis and education.

If I can stay attuned to the minor shocks of feeling, the transit of memories, the shriveling up of words as I try to reconstruct the recent past of the relationship between psychoanalysis and education, I may be able to provide myself and the reader with a history of the present that is open to its own unconscious and a different future.

Let us then return to that history. I begin with an overview.

1968 to the Present: An Overview

Between the mid-1960s and the first decade of the twenty-first century, education seemed to career from one extreme to another desperately trying to respond to profound social shifts and relentless demands to transform itself or transform society. It moved from a focus in the 1950s and 60s on academicism in the curriculum and behaviorism and mental hygiene in teacher education to a tumultuous love affair with the open school movement of the 1960s and 70s. Then, beginning with the election of Ronald Reagan, it swung completely in the opposite direction, with attempts to impose a professionalization agenda of accountability and to restore standards. Initially these attempts hit resistance from multiculturalists and radical educators who were protesting not only the conservative backlash in education but the absence of attention to oppressed groups and the crippling structures of schooling that sustained white supremacy, ruling class and heterosexist ideologies, and patriarchy.

In the academy and schools, the conflict took the form of what were called the canon wars or culture wars. Eventually both sides reached a kind of accord. For the last decade K-12 education has more and more resembled a job preparation conveyer belt with various check points along the way, almost always high stakes tests (Taubman, 2009). Higher education has moved to a corporate model (see in particular Bok, 2003; Kirp, 2003; Readings, 1996), intent on ensuring high enrollment and consumer satisfaction, which means guaranteeing the relevancy of students' educations to their future employment. Teacher education has become synonymous with a professionalization agenda that is on one hand tempered by the social justice agenda and on the other appears to be accommodating what was initially a conservative but is now simply a neoliberal move to de-regulate public education and reduce it to job training.

I chose 1968 as the break with the previous twenty-five years because that year marked the high point of the social unrest that had been brewing in the United States for some time and, more importantly, because "1968 saw the beginning of the surge of free school growth" (Graubard,1972, p. 40). While the civil rights movement and anti-war movement were already well underway, the events of that year—the murders of King and Kennedy, the Tet offensive, My Lai, the urban riots, the siege at Columbia, the televised demonstrations and police riot at the Democratic convention, student revolts throughout Europe, Prague Spring, NOW's demonstration at the Miss America Pageant, the successes of the Black Panthers and Young Lords in gaining community support, Ocean Hill-Brownsville and the New York teachers' strike, the list seems endless—suggested that 1968 could serve as a violent break with the previous quarter of a century. Such social eruption was bound to affect education and psychoanalysis and the relationship between them.

The open school or free school movement that blossomed at the end of the 1960s and then limped along through much of the 1970s revived, with little acknowledgment, the earlier progressive movement and its experiments in revolutionary pedagogy, student freedom, and curricular experimentation. Although the movement didn't transform American education, it did influence the conversation on education and how teachers were themselves taught in schools of education. While the open school movement responded to the civil rights and anti-war movement of the time, and while it clearly responded to what educators agreed was a "crisis in the classroom," it also served as a portal for the often unacknowledged introduction of psychoanalytic theory into education. The new movement owed much to the work of A.S. Neill and Sylvia Ashton-Warner, both influenced by psychoanalysis, to humanistic psychology, particularly the work of Carl Rogers and Abraham Maslow, and, to a lesser degree, to the radical utopian energies of cultural and social critics, such as Herbert Marcuse, R.D. Laing, and Norman O. Brown, whose work was psychoanalytically informed.

Prior to 1968 the psychoanalysis that had influenced education had encouraged adjustment to the status quo, pathologized unconventional behavior, and disavowed Freud's more radical insights. It had adhered to the therapeutic project of psychoanalysis, but a particularly medicalized one. Starting in the mid-1960s humanistic psychologists had begun to import into education views that questioned the educational status quo, although these views were directed toward curing what ailed education. The theories promulgated by these psychologists, who were aligned with the therapeutic project of psychoanalysis, rendered psychoanalysis even more optimistic and devoid of the otherness of sexuality than the mental hygiene movement's rendering. Nevertheless during the open school movement of the 1960s and 70s, humanistic psychologists, while downplaying Freud, did often appear more open to the emancipatory project of psychoanalysis than had psychoanalysts and psychologists involved in education in the post World War II period.

In the late 1960s and 1970s psychoanalysis in the United States cemented its alliance with medicine, but also splintered into a myriad of training institutes and eclectic psychotherapeutic modalities. Concurrently, psychoanalysis, particularly its therapeutic project, came under attack from feminists, Marxists and neo-Marxists, people of color, the gay liberation movement, and poststructuralists. These groups forced psychoanalysts to question their diagnostic categories and their procedures. Some responded. Generally, however, psychoanalysis retreated into the training institutions and the medical establishment (Hale, 1995b, pp. 360–79). In the popular media psychoanalysis emerged as the butt of jokes or object of scorn. Psychoanalysts had lost their glory, paradoxically, in large part, as Zaretsky (2004) argues, because they chased after the status they believed medicine and science could bring. As their theories hardened into doxa and lost their disturbing critique of social and cultural conventions as well as their tragic view of life, and as psychoanalytic theory was increasingly subjected to its use value in curing patients, psychoanalysis seemed to lose its way.

In part thanks to theorists like Marcuse, Brown, and Laing, who offered political activists a more palatable psychoanalysis, but also in large part due to the efforts of feminists who began in the 1970s to reinterpret Freud and re-conceptualize object relations theory, psychoanalytic theory's emancipatory project remained alive, but not in psychiatric psychoanalysis. Even there, though, the political challenges forced a reconsideration of classificatory systems and what behaviors were deemed patho-logical. As the 1970s unfolded and feminist criticism of psychoanalysis intensified, some feminists such as Nancy Friday (1977) tried to understand mother-daughter relationships through psychoanalytic theory and directed their work to the general public. Feminist scholars such as Nancy Chodorow (1978), and Dorothy Dinner-stein (1977), used the work of object relations theory to re-conceptualize gender and sexuality. That work influenced educators in the field of curriculum theory (see in particular; Grumet, 1981; Pinar, 1981, 1983), as well as some psychologists, like Carol Gilligan (1982), who while not referring to object relations theory, did seem to think through it in her theorization of gender differences in moral development. Her popular books revealed a reconceived psychoanalytic approach to gender and did impact views of girls' education.

With the election of Ronald Reagan in 1980, the already fading euphoria over the open school movement evaporated. As had so often been the case "most policy talk and policy action … proceeded as a conscious reaction to the period that pre-ceded it" (Tyack and Cuban, 1995, p. 53). Education rushed headlong in the opposite direction. The standards and accountability movement, with its ties to the learning sciences, came to dominate discussions of education and teacher education. Although competency based and mastery learning approaches had intruded into many teacher education programs in the 1970s, an alternative discourse in teacher education had also clearly existed. That changed in the 1980s. Other than the field of curriculum theory, psychoanalytic theory vanished from schools of education, as teacher educators solidified their alliance with psychology departments, which pro-vided the behavioral and cognitive theoretical foundations for their work. Man-dated courses for prospective teachers focused on learning theory, as understood by Kohlberg, Piaget, and Vygotsky, and for secondary school teachers, Erik Erikson, whose psychosocial stages students studied. Psychoanalytic theory, already under siege from social activists, retreated from education and schools of education. Even in curriculum theory, where its emancipatory project had been taken up by various scholars, psychoanalytic theory moved to the sidelines during the 1980s canon wars and focus on identity politics.

Had it not been for the arrival of Jacques Lacan, the relationship between psychoanalysis and education would in all probability have ended. Lacan's return to Freud, which challenged the therapeutic project of psychoanalysis and, in particular, took ego psychology to task, revived interest in Freud's more unsettling insights.

Along with Lacan's writing, feminist theorists influenced by him, particularly Shoshanna Felman, Jane Gallop, Luce Irigaray, Julia Kristeva, and Jacqueline Rose captured the attention of humanities departments in the 1980s. There psychoanalytic theory emerged as a self-questioning hermeneutic that could be used to understand the various disciplinary objects under study or to disrupt disciplinary boundaries. English departments in particular used psychoanalytic theory as an interpretive strategy, and several prominent composition theorists employed psychoanalytic theory as a way to understand and teach the writing process. Lacanian theory also briefly exerted its influence in departments of sociology and anthropology. And in post-colonial studies, Franz Fanon's work took on new significance.

In the last decade, while psychoanalytic theory continues to get a hearing in humanities departments, due mainly to the popularity of Slavoj Žižek's work and Judith Butler's theorization of power, its cozy corner there grows smaller. Even film criticism, which since the 1980s had relied on psychoanalytic theory, seems to have turned to cognitive science to help explain films and how audiences see them (see Bordwell and Carroll, 1996). Psychoanalysis certainly has made no comeback in departments of psychology. And other than its presence in curriculum theory, where it can barely make its voice heard over the cries for social justice and democratic education, psychoanalysis is today absent from the field of education.

It is a stunning absence to anyone who remembers the heady days of the 1960s and 70s and the open school movement, let alone the early history of the relationship between psychoanalysis and education. It is as if a great repression had occurred, or, more accurately a final disavowal of psychoanalytic knowledge. To understand how things changed so quickly, let us look more closely at the last forty years of the relationship between psychoanalysis and education.

A.S. Neill, Summerhill, and Eric Fromm

> [T]he alternative-free school movement of the 1960s fused
> A.S. Neill's Freudian-based pedagogy with the 'return to
> nature' philosophy of Rousseau.
>
> (Bowers, 1987, p. 20)

A.S. Neill's school, Summerhill, had been founded in 1921, but the book *Summerhill* was not published until 1960. It became such a best seller that by 1970 it "was selling an amazing 200,000 copies a year and was required reading in at least six hundred university courses" (Ravitch, 2000, p. 387). The book presents Neill's philosophy and description of the daily life in his school. Basically, Neill believed in allowing students to discover their own interests, make their own rules, ask for lessons when they chose, and explore their own sexual and emotional relationships. Like many of the psychoanalytically influenced pedagogues in the early part of the century, particularly those in Austria and Germany, Neill believed in lifting all repressive disciplinary and academic rules and requirements. There were no grades, no enforced classes, no rules other than those the students made, and no boundaries between kids or between adults and kids. The one stipulation Neill did make was that there was to be no violence or threat of violence between or among students and teachers.

According to Neill's autobiography, *Neill, Neill, Orange Peel!*, although he had been born in 1883, he had not heard of Freud until World War I, but his interest in psychoanalysis intensified once he began reading Freud's writing. Eventually Neill was analyzed by Wilhelm Reich and Wilhelm Stekel, both Freudians, and Maurice Nicoll, a Jungian. Stekel had been an early member of Freud's Vienna circle and had been analyzed by Freud. He broke with Freud a few years after the Clark Conference and the two men never reconciled. Stekel would eventually take his own life in 1940, while he lived in London.

Reich had a more powerful influence on Neill. Reich, Neill wrote, was "the man for whom I have been searching for years, the man to link the soma to the psyche" (1972, p. 190). From 1937 to 1939, the analysis with Reich unfolded, and even when it ended, the two men remained friends. While Neill admitted Reich's effect on him personally, he claimed he had no effect on his running of Summerhill (p. 193), which is a bit hard to believe, given that Neill attributed to Reich the freeing of his emotions around sex. According to Roazen (1992), unlike Freud, Reich "thought that health depended on orgiastic potency, and … was in favor of full and free sexual satisfaction" (p. 503). He was particularly interested in adolescence and believed that if teenagers could freely express their sexuality, many problems would be avoided later. Certainly such views were in evidence at Summerhill. A committed Marxist, Reich also believed, not unlike R.D. Laing, that the nuclear family should be destroyed, since it bred mental illness. In Vienna Reich had pushed Freud to take up socio/political programs, and when Reich was turned down by Freud for analysis, he broke with the Vienna Circle. Eventually, of course, he was arrested in the United States for his experiments with orgone therapy, and he died in prison.

One of my two roommates at New York University, a boy named Joseph, was the son of Reich's partner. When I met him in 1965, I was struck by his refusal to bathe, his derby, his bottle-neck guitar playing, and his talk of orgone energy accumulators. I was intrigued and repulsed, and grateful that he rarely slept in the room. It would be several years before I would pick up Reich's *Character Analysis*, but when I did in 1973, I was teaching in Philadelphia, and, accepting its views of character armor, asked my ninth grade students to tense various parts of their body where they imagined they held tension, to become those parts, and to write poems from the point of view of the constricted muscles. I also read *Summerhill* in the early 1970s and, when I taught in those years, attempted to follow Neill's philosophy, at least as much as was possible given the school rules. I allowed students to cut classes, I hung out with them outside school, I shared cigarettes with them (smoking was allowed then), I let them choose the books they wished to read, and I encouraged them to follow their own interests. In my classes I also tried to integrate, with little preparation or structure, the psychoanalysis that had come to me in my T-group work at Teachers College. There, in the early 1970s, I had pursued a masters degree in counseling in an experimental program, started by Ed Gordon, that used modules, did away with grades, and focused on sensitivity training, organizational development, community organizing and counseling techniques. While I brought a mishmash of all these influences into my teaching, I was most drawn to Neill.

Rather than Reich, Neill cites as influences on his educational theory Carl Rogers, Paul Goodman, Bruno Bettelheim, and Goodwin Watson among others. One of his greatest admirers as well as heroes was Henry Miller, with whom he sustained a friendship for several years. But, if we go by what he says in *Summerhill: A Radical Approach to Child Rearing* (1960), it would seem, *contra* his comments in his autobiography, that Freud was the greatest influence.

> Freud showed that every neurosis is founded on sex repression. I said, "I'll have a school in which there will be no sex repression." Freud said that the unconscious was infinitely more important and powerful than the conscious. I said, "In my school we won't censure, punish or moralize. We will allow every child to live according to his deep impulse ... I gradually learned that my territory was prophylaxis – not curing. (p. 294)

Neill's comments echo the views held by the early psycho-pedagogues, but his ideas appeared to educators involved in the open school movement as shockingly new. Bill Ayers writes in his *On the Side of the Child: Summerhill Revisited* (2003) that when he began teaching in 1965, Neill's educational philosophy was for him and so many others at the time a brilliant, new idea (p. 4).

Noteworthy is that among those Neill lists as influences and admired friends there are no women. In fact most of the well known radical educators of the 1960s and early 1970s, whom we associate with psychoanalysis were men. There was one prominent exception whose work appeared in the early 1960s, and I shall discuss Sylvia Ashton Warner in a moment, but let us look at Neill's school Summerhill a bit more by way of the introduction to his book.

The introduction to the 1960 edition of *Summerhill* was written by Erich Fromm, a psychoanalyst who would achieve celebrity for his books *The Art of Love* and *Escape from Freedom*, both of which proposed that humans were capable of surpassing their limitations and achieving a more harmonious society. Fromm had been analyzed in Berlin and was a practicing psychoanalyst, but he had also, upon his arrival in the United States, moved away from Freudian psychoanalysis. He found it dualistic, too focused on sexuality, and too pessimistic. A committed socialist, Fromm believed that humans needed to embrace their freedom, which meant not conforming, and forge bonds with their fellow humans to change society. He understood love as a creative capacity rather than as an emotion and believed very much that the analyst should reveal his own personality in the analytic situation.

In his introduction to *Summerhill* Fromm repudiated the assumptions of the life adjustment movement and ego psychology of the 1940s and 50s. He praised Neill's criticism of conformist education, which produced "mass-man" and which trained children to accept the barbarism of war. As Fromm (1960) put it, "Neill does not try to educate children to fit well into the existing order, but endeavors to rear children who will become happy human beings, men and women whose values are not to *have much*, not to *use* much, but to *be* much" (p. xiv). Neill valued, above all else, Fromm exclaimed, authenticity, individuality, and "full human development" (p. xiv). The focus on authenticity would take on enormous importance as humanistic psychology entered education.

Finally Fromm suggested that Neill's educational philosophy, if put into practice, which he said was unlikely and not yet happening in the United States, would create individuals who could transform society for the good of all. "Children reared by such methods will develop within themselves the qualities of reason, love, integrity, and courage" (p. xv).

Interestingly one of the few reservations Fromm voiced about Neill concerned sexuality. He wrote, "I feel that Neill … is steeped in the assumptions of Freud; and as I see it, he somewhat overestimates the significance of sex, as Freudians tend to do" (p. xiv). This downplaying of sexuality, which we have seen all the way back to Putnam, accompanied Fromm's optimism about the future. "If it can happen once in Summerhill," he wrote, "it can happen everywhere – *once the people are ready for it*. Indeed there are no *problem children* as the author says, but only 'problem parents' and a 'problem humanity'" (p. xv, italics in orginal). But of course there are problem children, if we mean by problem children those who aren't compliant or who are aggressive, mean, or obnoxious. Certainly Freud taught us that children were not innocent, vulnerable creatures, but were filled with envy, rage, anxiety, and aggression. Certainly August Aichhorn didn't consider his charges all sweetness and light. Fromm's romanticizing of children doesn't really capture Neill's views either. They could be monsters, Neill believed, but that didn't mean one didn't work with them, respect them, or bring to them a compassionate curiosity, as Aichhorn had done.

But Fromm's reticence about sexuality points to what I would call a symptom of the open school movement, in this case, as understood by Neill and Fromm. The sexuality that Fromm associates with Summerhill and with Freud is really a romanticized "natural" sexuality, a kind of coherent, continuous sexuality, which is either repressed or liberated. It is not the radical otherness of sexuality that I would argue Freud's work pursues.

Fromm concluded his introduction on an optimistic and prescient note. "Neill's work," he predicted, "is a seed which will germinate. In time, his ideas will become generally recognized in a new society in which man himself and his unfolding are the supreme aim of all social effort" (p. xv). He would not have long to wait.

Although Summerhill was in England, Neill's book had an enormous effect on the open school movement in the United States. So too did another book that appeared in 1963, Sylvia Ashton-Warner's *Teacher*. Ashton-Warner never explicitly acknowledged the influence of psychoanalysis, but its presence as an emancipatory project is clear in her book. So is A.S. Neill's presence, whom Ashton-Warner recounts thinking of one day as she contemplates opening a school like his (p. 197). Eric Fromm also appears in the book as a memory reminding her that "destructiveness is the outcome of an unlived life" (p. 93). It is an interesting phrase "an unlived life," as if one could have a life but not live it. For Ashton-Warner living a life meant living it with passion, following one's instincts, and living in the moment. It meant infusing the erotic into one's teaching. "When I teach people," she would say, "I marry them. ... They become part of me, like a lover. ... All the rules of love-making apply to these spiritual and intellectual fusions" (1986, pp. 209–13). For both Neill and Ashton-Warner, as it was for so many of the early educators influenced by psychoanalysis, teaching could not be separated from the libidinal and aggressive forces that streamed through pedagogical relationships, although we know that today in education every effort is made to defend against such eroticism. The defenses take the form of repression both on the far right and often on the left. While conservatives oppose sex education, liberals often champion GLBT groups but confine discussions to identity and bias rather than open up for study and conversation a more dangerous eroticism.

Sylvia Ashton-Warner

> Education, fundamentally, is the increase of the percentage
> of the conscious in relation to the unconscious.
>
> (Ashton-Warner, 1986, p. 207)

> Your only allowable comment is one of natural interest. ... [I]t all boils down
> to whether [the teacher] is a good conversationalist;
> whether or not she has the gift of wisdom to listen to another; the
> ability to draw out and preserve that other's line of thought.
>
> (Ashton-Warner, 1986, p. 58)

Teacher covers nine years of Ashton-Warner's teaching life, from 1931 to 1940. In 1939 Ashton-Warner had a breakdown and was in treatment with Dr. Allen, a Freudian psychoanalyst, but, according to one of her biographers, Lynley Hood (1988), despite analysis and her reading of Freud, "she retained a curious tunnel vision concerning the connections between childhood trauma and adult behavior" (p. 90). When "she considered her own behavior and that of her Maori pupils, she never looked to the past" (p. 91). According to Sue Middleton (2006), however, Ashton-Warner "placed the 'sex drive' firmly in the center of her educational theory" (p. 52). She quotes Ashton-Warner: "Inspiration is the richest nation I know, the most powerful on earth. Sexual energy Freud calls it; the capital of desire I call it; it pays for both mental and physical expenditure" (quoted in Middleton, p. 52).

It's clear from *Teacher* that Ashton-Warner was not afraid of integrating the erotic into her teaching. She also was not afraid of her own aggressive impulses. As both Hood (1988) and Robertson (2006) point out, Ashton-Warner would occasionally beat her students. What seemed to fill her classroom was passion.

There are two important aspects of her teaching that exemplify the emancipatory project. First, through her reading of psychoanalytic texts, including those by Jung, Ashton-Warner seems to have understood the importance of the child's sexual researches. In "Analysis Terminable and Interminable," Freud pointed out that simply telling a patient what was wrong with him wouldn't work, since "[w]e have increased his knowledge but altered nothing else in him" (1937b, p. 233). Freud suggested that while there is nothing wrong with enlightening children about sexuality—in fact, sex education is fine—it will not necessarily interrupt or change the more fantastic theories children have about where they come from and who they are to their parents. "[T]hey are by no means ready," he wrote, "to sacrifice those sexual theories which may be said to be a natural growth and which they have constructed in harmony with and in dependence on their undeveloped libidinal organization" (p. 233). It is not easy for us to give up our beliefs.

Ashton-Warner seemed intuitively to have known this, because while she didn't shy away from answering the children's questions about sex, she approached their researches circuitously. Judith Robertson (2006) writes:

> A crucial feature of the teacher's pedagogical innovation comes from the incorporation of children's unconscious thoughts, which have a linguistic structure, into learning material ... In a pedagogical restaging of the psycho-analytic method, not only does [Ashton-Warner] elicit primary process thinking from children, but ... she uses it as creative material to decode ... reading and writing. ... The children's sex and aggression words ... pose striking challenges to the respectable lingua franca of ... basal readers, [but] Ashton-Warner ... reconstruct[s] their latent and unconscious intentionality, which she then demonstrates as crucial to the learning process. (p. 182)

In allowing the sexual researches to emerge on the border between the unconscious and conscious, and helping students re-symbolize and explore their questions, she neither engaged in the therapeutic project of requiring students to express feelings in the service of some higher moral goal, nor did she reduce the sexual researches to sex education. She didn't try to replace students' theories with the correct ones but rather encouraged the students to play with their theories, to bring the same erotic energy to their sexual researches or theories about life and themselves and their world that they might bring to their own bodies, which of course was a more complicated attitude than she might have expected.

The second aspect of the emancipatory project embodied in Ashton-Warner's teaching was a particular *style* of listening. She listened without passing judgment. Sounding like George Green's "psychanalysis," "You've no right," she wrote, "to criticize the content of another's mind" (1986, p. 57). If you are attending to your own evaluations you can't listen because hearing "requires [one's] whole attention" (p. 17). What she was listening to was the unconscious, in dreams (p. 69), in the artwork, in the words the students chose. "[Y]ou find," she wrote, "that of the two kinds of orders, the conscious and the unconscious order, only one is real. It's the order in the deep hidden places. ... [I]t is accessible to anyone" (p. 87). "[C]ultivate the order in the unconscious" (p. 86). Teachers cultivate it through art, music, writing, but also through developing positive transferences with students. Like Aichhorn, Ashton-Warner was able to place convention aside to engage in deeper conversations with students. She described sharing a cigarette with a kid (p. 121) and swearing with another. Sounding like Jacques Lacan, Ashton-Warner wrote, "I teach style and only style" (p. 103). It was a style of listening.

Ashton-Warner's book was an enormous success when it appeared in the early 1960s, but she turned down several speaking engagements in the United States, claiming, much like Freud, that America was obsessed with the dollar (Hood, 1988, p. 204). Her approach did strike a chord with educators engaged in the open school movement, and in the early 1970s she was invited to Aspen Colorado to teach at the Aspen Community School, a non-hierarchical, parent run, public, alternative school. Her experience was a disaster for her and for the school. Hood describes a year of collapsing relationships with colleagues and children, increasing alcohol and drug consumption, and little success in the classroom. Ashton-Warner's radical methods with the Maori suddenly seemed, to the teachers and some of the parents in Aspen, conservative. She wanted to use the belt, she argued there was not enough structure in the school, and she called for more discipline. The failed year is interesting to me because it spotlights something symptomatic about the relationship between education and psychoanalysis as it was understood in these projects of Neill and Ashton-Warner. Looking at such a symptom might allow us to re-construct a different past for the future.

Between 1973 and 1975, I taught at a large, suburban prep school. There I tried a variety of approaches to teaching, ranging from having students grade themselves, to running the class as a T-group, to allowing the curriculum to be whatever students wanted to discuss. I provoked, disclosed, and broke down divisions between student and teacher. Influenced by Beatrice and Ronald Gross' book, *The Children's Rights Movement: Overcoming the Oppression of Young People*, and by the Gray Panthers' lectures on ageism, I socialized with students and fought with the administration. Students seemed to like me and some did interesting work, often much more than I asked. When I left I received lots of letters. I moved from there to an alternative, public high school in Philadelphia. I was not successful there, and I felt bored and lost. But why? And why did Ashton-Warner's year of teaching in Aspen dissolve into frequent absences? And why did Neill's experiment remain islolated?

I suspect, in part, we needed a firm structure to define ourselves against—perhaps a paternal phallus to hate—and we needed the love of those in whose eyes we were the unusual ones, the ones who were special, the ones who were different. At the

Aspen Community School and at the alternative, public school in Philadelphia, *all* the teachers were different. A conservative group in Aspen referred to the Community School as run by hippies, and quite a few of the teachers at the alternative school in Philadelphia would have fitted that label. It was, however, not only a question of being counter-dependent—defining oneself in opposition to—that is noticeable here. Nor was it simply the assumption, and here I can only speak for myself, that the person in charge should know better, should be doing something differently, and deserves our rage because he or she should have the answer. Such needs and assumptions may echo family dramas, in which anxieties about separation, engulfment, or retribution from parents eventuate in ambivalence and confusion about one's difference from and dependence on others.

I think what is more important here is that in the efforts of Neill and of Ashton-Warner and in my own modest and not well thought out attempts to liberate students, the mirror image of ego psychology and the mental hygiene movement appear. Rather than an ego adapted to social reality, rather than a well adjusted and well adapted, normal child, we all sought to develop an autonomous, unconventional, authentic individual, even a rebel. And, at least in my own efforts, I yearned also to be different, to be seen as unique and special—not like any of those other teachers, but more authentic, more unconventional, more independent. I couldn't play that role in the alternative school in Philadelphia.

I am suggesting that in their pursuit of individuality and liberation from repression, the psychoanalytically informed educational theories of Neill and Ashton-Warner, and perhaps those of many open school educators, not only repeated the focus on lifting repression found in the early psycho-pedagogy, but sought to create another *kind* of well adjusted kid. So, for all the emphasis on freedom and on students finding themselves, there were, within these theories, a desire to control and a disavowal of the radical otherness of both the unconscious and sexuality. I am not claiming that Neill, Ashton-Warner, or I and those educators who allowed students just to be themselves, should have done anything differently. Nor am I making any sweeping claims about those educators who were committed to open schools and interested in psychoanalytic theory. I simply mean to say that in the small details, for example Ashton-Warner's and my dreary flops at these two schools, lies the trace of a symptom whose recovery may open another future for the relationship between psychoanalysis and education, a future whose contours were present but not fulfilled. What would it mean to teach but to relinquish control? Not control as it was understood by the open school movement or the early psycho-pedagogues, but control in terms of a focus on outcomes or making something happen or curing someone of their ignorance or illness. Such a pedagogy would be premised on and strive to take into account the radical otherness of the unconscious and sexuality.

While Ashton-Warner's and Neill's work would be read in teacher education courses throughout the 1970s, and while *Teacher* continues on syllabi in childhood education courses, although rarely in secondary education courses, neither of these writers would have the influence on education that another movement did, one which was much more wedded to the therapeutic project, but which would keep psychoanalytic theory alive in academia and teacher education for a little while longer.

The Third Force: Humanistic Psychology

Early challenges to the Tylerian paradigm emerged from humanistic psychology identified with Abraham Maslow, Gordon Allport, Erich Fromm, Carl Rogers and Erik Erikson.

(Pinar et al., 1995, p. 178)

The humanists called themselves a 'third force' by which they meant that they were forging a path distinct from both psychoanalysis and behaviorism.

(Herman, 1995, p. 265)

According to Ellen Herman (1995) both Abraham Maslow and Carl Rogers traced their intellectual roots back to Fromm, Karen Horney, and Harry Stack Sullivan. They also claimed John Dewey as an intellectual mentor. It is difficult to measure the influence that these two men had on the open school movement and teacher education at the end of the 1960s and throughout the 1970s. The optimistic version of human potential and growth that these third force psychologists presented certainly appealed to educators rebelling at what they saw as the oppressive conventions of public education. Criticisms of schools had begun to proliferate in the late 1960s, not in terms of their low standards—those criticisms had ended the life adjustment movement and ushered in the academic curriculum of the 1950s and early 1960s—but in terms of their soul deadening procedures. Charles Silberman captured the criticism when he wrote in *Crisis in the Classroom*, "It is not possible to spend any prolonged period visiting public school classrooms without being appalled by the mutilation visible everywhere – mutilation of spontaneity, of the joy of learning, of pleasure in creating, of sense of self" (p. 10). Books promoting the ecstasy of learning (Leonard, 1968) and describing how children fail (Holt, 1964), how they die at an early age (Kozol, 1967), and how teaching can be a subversive activity (Postman and Weingartner, 1969) were "part of the bumper crop of radical critiques of the public schools that were published during the 1960s and early 1970s" (Ravitch, 2000, p. 389). While many of the books demanded that education be more democratic, less racist, and more egalitarian, all of the books argued that education should focus on the emotional development of the student, on making the curriculum relevant to students' interests, on student choice, on treating students as equals, on lifting repressive codes of conduct and rigid academic requirements, and on freeing students to find and be themselves. Above all else education should create authentic individuals who do not simply go along with conventions or the status quo. That emphasis on authenticity was presented to educators largely through humanistic psychology, with its roots, however disavowed, in Freudian psychoanalysis.

Carl Rogers

> It seems to me that anything that can be taught to another
> is relatively inconsequential, and has little or no significant
> influence on behavior.
>
> (Rogers, quoted in Kirschenbaum, 1979, p. 308)

Carl Rogers was a clinical psychologist who played an important role in establishing the *bona fides* of clinical psychology within the American Psychological Association. He is most often associated with what he termed client-centered therapy, listening with the third ear, and non-directive therapy. His approach to therapy was to listen intently to what the client—no longer called a patient—said, and to reflect back the emotional subtext or the sentiments expressed. He believed firmly in the capacity of clients to realize their full potential and grow into healthy individuals, if they were provided with an empathic, non-judgmental, and engaged therapist. Obviously such a view contradicted many of the tenets of Freudian psychoanalytic theory.

Although he rarely mentioned Freud in his writings, Rogers had been exposed to psychoanalytic theory when he was a young man. Arriving in New York in 1924 to study at the Union Theological Seminary for the ministry, he met Goodwin Watson, whom we encountered earlier. Watson would be key to the development of the T-group and laboratory methods of human relations training and would introduce Rogers to psychoanalytic theory. Rogers also took courses at Teachers College with Kilpatrick and Edward Thorndike. In 1926, when he was twenty-four, Rogers started working at the newly formed Institute for Child Guidance in New York, where he concentrated on interpreting various psychological tests, and where he became more familiar with Freud's theory. According to his biographer, Howard Kirschenbaum (1979), Rogers' "reading of Freud was relatively shallow" (p. 84), "his training in psychological testing and measurement ... inclined him to be somewhat scornful of ... concepts like id, ego, superego, Oedipus complex and the like" (p. 245), and his "whole nature and training were opposed to the elaborate theoretical superstructure and method of psychoanalysis which Freud had introduced" (p. 83). Absent from Rogers' theory was any sense that the unconscious was a thinking that occurred elsewhere, that it was inherently disruptive and radically unknowable, that we are, all of us, limited by symptoms that for the most part we can only partially come to understand, and that at best analysis can turn human suffering into more interesting meanings and psychic stasis into modest movement.

Rogerian theory seemed to out-Putnam Putnam and to reject most of Freud's ideas, except for one: a non-judgmental approach. While in his own practice Freud was known to lecture, ramble, and admonish, his theory advocated a neutral, free-floating attention and interpretations emptied of moral evaluations. He also became less and less apt to offer interpretations, since, prematurely offered, they could arouse resistance in the patient. Perhaps there was one other similarity. Both Freud and Rogers had no appetite for getting people to adjust to the norm. Unlike Freud, however, when it came to education, Rogers saw only possibility.

Freedom to Learn appeared in 1969. Comprised of essays Rogers had written over two decades, the book presented his thinking about education and teaching. Well into the 1970s the book frequently appeared in education courses around the country. In *Freedom to Learn* Rogers argued that the goal of education was the facilitation of learning (p. 105). That goal might easily be approved of by today's gurus of standards and accountability as well as the current scientists of learning, but there is a fundamental difference. According to Rogers the "facilitation of significant learning rests upon certain attitudinal qualities which exist in the personal *relationship* between the facilitator and the learner" (p. 106, italics in original). It doesn't rest on curricular materials, or on the teacher's knowledge, or on teaching techniques, or on proper planning. It rests on personal qualities. These qualities are first, "realness" that is a kind of authenticity and being in touch with one's feelings; second, an attitude of caring for or cherishing the student such that the teacher/facilitator can focus on the student's good qualities, praise the student's efforts, and not take personally the student's moods or reactions; and, third, empathy for the student. Just as Ashton-Warner had done, Rogers urged teachers/facilitators to refrain from judgments but also not to hide their own reactions or attribute them to the student. They should understand their reactions as being about their own psychic states rather than those of the student.

This last point may recall both Ferenczi's sharing of personal material in the analytic session as well as Freud's insistence that the analyst understand his or her counter-transferential relations. Roger's emphasis on assuming a non-judgmental attitude, striving for an awareness of how one is feeling at all times, and understanding that the cause of one's feelings is not simply or only or even mainly located in the student but rather is in oneself are all aspects of Freudian psychoanalytic theory. Rogers, however, never acknowledged the influence.

Possessing these qualities was enough, according to Rogers, for the teacher to facilitate learning. But learning of what? Rogers thought the student should determine what he or she learned. He advised teachers to provide lots of resources and allow students to discover their own interests. He also wished to make emotional growth or self-knowledge, both the student's and the teacher's, the center of the curriculum and to that end he proposed that schools integrate encounter groups or sensitivity training as a pedagogy *and* curriculum. Rogers was of course familiar with the group work that had been implemented in the 1950s and early 1960s, but he proposed that such groups not be in the extra-curriculum but rather in the curriculum.

While Rogers' views entered education, bringing with them versions of psychoanalytic theory, it is important to remember that Rogers was an academic psychologist. That affiliation led him or pushed him to verify his theories. In the late 1960s and early 1970s he conducted a series of controlled experiments on the effects of his approaches. Using personality tests and achievement tests, Rogers obtained results showing that his method increased scores on both. The focus on tests was not the only example of Rogers' allegiance to the academy. Humanistic psychology presented itself as a third way, one between psychoanalysis and behaviorism. Rogers employed language much more familiar to behaviorists than analysts. He talked about the intrinsic nature of the human organism, the role of environment in eliciting self-actualizing behaviors, and the emergence of species wide directional tendencies toward positive social relationships. Such discursive links to behaviorism made it easier for Rogers' theories to find a place in teacher education programs, which in the 1970s had one foot in competency based learning and mastery learning and the other foot in the revolution that was occurring outside the school house window.

Abraham Maslow

While Carl Rogers encouraged teachers to become self-actualizing facilitators, Abraham Maslow encouraged them to lead students up a hierarchy of needs, which ranged from basic needs to the need for self-actualization. At the top of the hierarchy were individuals who were "perceptive, self-accepting, spontaneous, autonomous, empathic, and creative" and reported what Maslow labeled "peak experiences" (Herman, 1995, p. 271). The willingness to address almost mystical states in his popular book *Toward a Psychology of Being* (1968) opened his work up in the 1970s to those educators who liked the idea of higher consciousness or cosmic consciousness, an idea that had gained in popularity along with various Eastern religions and practices.

The drive toward self-actualization and the rejection of adjusting to social norms placed Maslow in the same camp as Fromm and Rogers. "Adjusted to what?" Maslow asked. "To a bad culture? To dominating parents? What shall we think of the well-adjusted slave?" (Maslow, 1968, p. 8). This repudiation of conformity in the name of self-actualization coupled with his belief that for individuals to reach the upper limits of the needs hierarchy, the environment had to provide for the basic needs, made him a favorite of liberal and radical educators. Even though he supported the Vietnam War, Maslow was credited by Abbie Hoffman as having "laid down a solid foundation for launching the optimism of the sixties" (Hoffman, quoted in Herman, 1995, p. 274). And indeed Maslow like Rogers and Fromm believed that if people were provided with safe, nurturing environments, if they had the freedom to be themselves and the support to follow their own journeys of self-discovery, then those individuals would not only achieve mental well being but could rise to the top of the needs hierarchy and achieve self-realization.

Such a view had implications for education. In an interview conducted in 1971, Maslow said about education:

If you leave things to individual choice, they will generally, statistically, in the long run choose well rather than badly; if you give freedom, it will be well used if the people are reasonably decent to start with. ... Now acting on that assumption works pretty well in education but not with the establishment education, which acts on different assumptions and therefore, I think, is partially a failure.

(Frick, 1971, p. 33)

According to Maslow the involvement among young people in such an education would, he believed, lead them to focus their efforts on self-actualization, and experiments in open education would test these hypotheses. Maslow's emphasis on student choice and its realization in the elective curriculum in many U.S. schools in the early 1970s would elicit charges in the 1980s of schools becoming shopping malls (Powell, Farrar, and Cohen, 1986). As did Rogers, Maslow suggested the efficacy of using sensitivity groups in schools to help students achieve greater self-awareness, and he reported in an interview (Frick, 1971, p. 38) that in one of his college classes he let the students fall into a spontaneous T-group and take charge. He left the room and when he came back found the students had had a powerful experience where they dropped their defenses and found a "sense of communion, of belongingness" (p. 37). The fact that they "had thrown the content away and communed" (p. 37) left Maslow sad, but only because they hadn't had such an experience earlier.

While Maslow entered psychology as a behaviorist, he did study with Ruth Benedict, who recall had studied cultures as personalities, and who was part of a circle of friends that included Erikson, Frank, Lewin, Spock, and Zachry. More than Rogers did, Maslow cites Freud in his work. In referring to the life-long project that is self-actualization, Maslow actually sounds Freudian when he states that beginners are "in psychoanalytic terms, apt to put too great a stress on insight and not enough on working through" (Frick, 1971, p. 36), but then he says something that is odd. He states that from Freud he learned "that if you cleared away the rubbish, and the neuroses and the garbage and so on, then the person would blossom out, that he'd find his own way" (p. 37). Now Freud never said anything like that, although such a tenet was essential to humanistic psychology. But after Maslow makes this claim about Freud, he continues that he, Maslow, is troubled by his findings that there are people who do have all their needs met on the hierarchy, but for some reason regress. In other words there is *not* an inherent movement to self-actualization or fulfilling one's potential. Some of the young people who are pretty well gratified fall into depressions. Certainly this would not surprise Freud, but Maslow, sounding like Putnam, states that these findings make him feel "like more of a missionary than ever" (p. 38). He needs to get the word out about what values are of most worth.

Echoing Erich Fromm, who believed that if "people would truly accept the Buddhist Eightfold Path as the effective principle to guide their lives, a dramatic change in the whole culture would take place" (quoted in Jacoby, 1997, p. 14), Maslow seemed to believe that if you just told people what was important they would do it. Nevertheless, it is an odd moment in the interview, and it is followed by Maslow's claim that perhaps there are constitutional factors that account for such self-destructive behaviors. It is at this point that one can see how the human potential movement would come to shift ever so gradually into neuropsychology and pharmacology. If the goal were self-actualization and happiness, then surely if psychopharmacology or neuroscience could provide a faster way to get there, what would be the problem? But that was yet to come.

The human potential movement and humanistic psychology introduced into education, at the level of public schools and teacher education programs, certain insights and emphases that were much more closely associated with psychoanalysis than were those of the mental hygiene movement, ego psychology, the life adjustment movement, or even, in some respects, the medicalized psychoanalysis of psychiatry. How is that the case?

First, humanistic psychology challenged the status quo and the view that mental health consisted of adapting oneself to reality. It suggested that each of us has an idiosyncratic relationship with the social world and that that relationship is largely psychically determined, although we can choose to change it. Second, humanistic psychology emphasized openness to one's feelings. Because authenticity was so clearly valued, individuals were encouraged to "tell it like it is." But that meant that one had to know what one was feeling, and so self-reflection, a kind of Calvinist introspection but in the language of psychology and feelings, found its way into classrooms and teacher education programs. While such self-disclosure was never an end point for Freudian psychoanalytic theory, it did become one for humanistic psychology. It also became a particular way to validate one's views of others or the world. Attaching "I feel that" to "you are a jerk," somehow authenticated the accusation, now phrased as a feeling. Nevertheless, support for a kind of emotional free association was certainly more in line with Freud's theory than the kind of disclosure in the service of adaptation so much a part of ego psychology and the mental hygiene movement. Third, because humanistic psychology tied learning to the attitudes of teachers, it pushed teachers to focus on their own self-development, take responsibility for their own reactions rather than blaming them on students, and work to refrain from judgments. Here we see the similarity to, for example, the pedagogical approaches of the early psycho-pedagogues, to George Green's educational theory, and to Arthur Jersild's work in the 1950s and early 1960s. Fourth, the goal of self-actualization undermined the push to define oneself in terms of or adapt one's ego to social norms or society, both of which ego psychology and the mental hygiene movement had equated with the reality principle. Finally, humanistic psychology placed the psychic development of the individual at the heart of education— not the cognitive, or moral, or physical development but the psychic development of each individual. One result was that schools and teacher education programs integrated sensitivity training, but more important they shifted from the discourse of personality and adjustment to the discourse of self-analysis. Autobiographical work, critical self-reflection and reflective practice emerged as important in teacher education.

Of course, what is so surprising about the impact of humanistic psychology on education is that it never really acknowledged its roots in psychoanalysis, nor did it refer back to the early progressive movement, which as we have seen championed so many of the same reforms. As the schools adjusted to address individuals' different potentials, as open education gave attention to the emotional life of the students, even mainstream educators got on the bandwagon. The U.S. commissioner of education was the speaker at the Philadelphia's Parkway Program's graduation in 1970 (Ravitch, 2000, p. 394). That program not only allowed students to pursue their own interests, hold weekly town halls, study in mixed age groups, come to class as they pleased, and avoid classrooms and grades, but also encouraged teachers to give primary importance to the students' emotional life (Bremer and von Moschzisker, 1971).

By the end of the 1960s and throughout the 1970s emotions and the body would take center stage not as pathological or in need of adjustment but as holding the promise of a future utopia. Some psychoanalytically informed critics, however, were advocating utopia was possible now!

Radical psychoanalysis: R.D. Laing, Herbert Marcuse, and Norman O. Brown

> In seeking to obliterate distinctions, to keep everything
> and everyone together, and to transform the world as a
> whole, the 1960s generation turned to such utopian Freudians
> as Herbert Marcuse and Norman O. Brown, as well as to R.D. Laing
> … who described society, not the individual as mad.
>
> (Zaretsky, 2004, p. 317)

According to Eli Zaretsky (2004) the utopian or radical current in psychoanalysis, as exemplified by R.D. Laing, Herbert Marcuse, and Norman O. Brown, was channeled in three directions by the New Left (p. 317). First, it pursued freeing the erotic, overthrowing the bourgeois conformity of the nuclear family, and liberating homosexuality and polymorphous perversity. Second, it, like humanistic psychology, "rejected repression and sublimation in favor of authenticity, expressive freedom and play" (p. 317). And third, it rejected technocentrism and instrumentalism.

While Zaretsky captures how leftist activists may have deployed Laing's, Marcuse's, and Brown's psychoanalytic insights, there are other currents in the thought of these men that we need to acknowledge. First, Laing, Marcuse, and Brown attacked the concept of the ego that had been advanced by ego psychology. In many ways their work resembled the assault on the ego Lacan was already launching in France. They viewed the ego as fundamentally alienated, a product of a sick society. Only by shattering that ego or understanding its aetiology could we free ourselves from the madness of our society. Second, these three suggested that madness itself was not to be avoided but rather faced and gone through on the way to a de-alienated state. Laing and Brown in particular envisioned the journey into madness as bordering on the mystical. The dark side of the human soul had to be faced, and the sunny, up-beat views of Rogers and Maslow deceived people into a false optimism. For example, to R.D. Laing, Maslow was a "vacuous" "American bourgeoisified Nietzsche" (quoted in Mullan, 1955, p. 211) and Rogers, who "wouldn't admit a trace of evil in himself or knowledge of it" was "one of the least personable people" (quoted in Mullan, 1955, p. 210) he'd ever met. Finally, Laing, Marcuse, and Brown explicitly championed strains within the emancipatory project of psycho-analysis. Here is Marcuse, writing at the end of *One-Dimensional Man: Studies in the Ideology of Advanced Industrial Society* (1968). He describes positivist philosophy in terms of its desire to cure. His words could as easily describe the therapeutic project, which both education and psychoanalysis have taken up at different periods.

> The therapeutic character of the philosophic analysis is strongly emphasized – to cure from illusions, deceptions, obscurities, unsolvable riddles, unanswerable questions. ... There is indeed a goodly portion of psychoanalysis in this phi-losophy – analysis without Freud's fundamental insight that the patient's trouble is rooted in a general sickness which cannot be cured by analytic therapy. (p. 183)

The true philosopher, on the other hand, like Freud, "is not a physician; his job is not to cure individuals but to comprehend the world in which they live" (p. 183). Laing, Marcuse, and Brown did not view psychoanalysis as a method of cure, but as a way to understand how the insanity of the world infects us, how we collude in that infection, and how we might, through understanding, move to a less determined realm. On the other hand each of these writers shared one central dif-ference from Freud: they believed, as did Rogers and Maslow, that humans have within themselves the potential of becoming authentic or at least not alienated. For these writers, particularly Laing and unlike Maslow and Rogers, madness or mental illness is an understandable response to, or strategy to cope with, an alienated world into which we are born.

If their approach is reminiscent of Lawrence Frank's views expressed in his 1948 *Society as the Patient: Essays on Culture and Personality* the differences are more pronounced than the similarities. While all these writers saw society as the problem, Frank wanted to help students overcome the bad social influences while developing a healthy and socially adjusted personality. Laing, Marcuse, and Brown advocated social and psychic revolution.

Much more so than the theories elaborated by Rogers and Maslow, those of Laing, Marcuse, and Brown are too complex to summarize here, so I shall touch on only a few of the many dimensions of their analyses that influenced the open school movement and radical educators.

R.D. Laing

> The relevance of Freud to our time is largely his insight
> and, to a very considerable extent, his demonstration that
> the ordinary person is a shriveled, desiccated fragment of
> what a person can be.
>
> (Laing, 1967, p. 10)

> [W]e are ... so estranged from the inner world that many
> are arguing that it does not exist.
>
> (Laing, 1967, p. 33)

Laing is most often associated with the Tavistock Institute in London, where he was supervised by D.W. Winnicott and where he studied object relations theory. His commitment to the emancipatory project of psychoanalysis radiates from his writing, and to read him today seems a powerful tonic or elixir. We have become so used to the positivistic, neutral language of science, which according to Laing drains out the "sense of possibility, of passion, of joy, delight, passion, sex, violence" (Laing, 1967, p. 40), that we can barely remember that teachers have a powerful internal life. In fact, one of the most striking differences between Laing and those educators, today, who focus on techniques of teaching or observable performance, is that Laing talks about experience rather than behavior. For Laing, the focus on behavior impoverishes our understanding of relationships, because it fails to take into account the complexity and richness of one's experience, which he understands not only in terms of what we make of what we perceive but also in terms of our fantasy life, our dreams, and our unconscious life. It is not just language, however, that disfigures and mystifies our experience.

According to Laing, society in general, the family, and school all work to ignore or deny our experiences, such that we assume our experiences that don't accord with the norm aren't real, that they must be figments of our imagination. Just as social critics argued at the time that society made women, minorities, and non-conformists doubt their own experience, Laing argued that these institutions made all of us doubt or deny our experiences of reality, distort our emotional lives, and hallucinate relationships, which, under such conditions, were really nothing but shared, normalized fantasies. "Only by the most outrageous violation of ourselves," Laing wrote, "have we achieved the capacity to [adjust] to a civilization apparently driven to its own destruction" (1967, p. 49). Such a view, of course, had serious implications for schooling.

In *The Politics of Experience* Laing approvingly quotes the anthropologist Jules Henry, whose work was at the time often included in education courses. Henry had visited several American schools and described scenes that Laing interpreted as filled with behaviors that drove children mad. Teachers were indirect, students were continually put into Batesonian double-binds, e.g., be compliant/be creative; follow my directions/think for yourself, and the entire apparatus of the school worked to de-value or deny each student's existential experience of what was going on. While neither Laing nor Henry focused on the double-binds in which teachers were placed, e.g., the demand to treat each child as an individual coupled with the requirement to assess each child by group tests, the implication was clear: schools made us schizophrenic, and schizophrenia was an understandable response to the insanity in schools. In that sense schizophrenia and madness were political statements.

Laing also introduced the idea that if there was a way out of the insanity, and he was not sure there was, it would be through a de-alienation process that involved deep soul searching and going through one's own alienation or madness. It is important to remember that Laing adamantly opposed any move to pathologize experience. Institutional categories of illness or of developmental stages created only further alienation and disconnection between humans. People act, according to Laing, the way they are labeled and treated. Treat a student as a sneaky kid or as a child in need of discipline, and the student will act that way. Many educators translated this into treating students as people, but that missed Laing's point. People were already alienated. Laing hoped that if individuals could first enter their own world, experience their actual feelings, however violent, erotic, or terrifying, they would be less apt to judge others' experiences as weird or different or pathological. They would begin to accept that psychosis lived in them, that although they were normal adults, they harbored within themselves terrified, ecstatic, and playful children, anxious and exuberant adolescents, schzophrenics, murderers, rapists, saviors—the entire panoply of human possibilities.

Such work required individuals to dissolve their ego, which for Laing was not only alienated but armored, a composite of defenses that kept us alienated. "True sanity," Laing wrote, "entails in one way or another the dissolution of the normal ego, that false self competently adjusted to our alienated social reality" (p. 101). Radical educators would find in those words and Laing's belief that "what we call 'normal' is a product of repression, denial, splitting, projection, introjection and other forms of destructive action" (p. 11), support for their own view that the educational system was oppressive and its acceptance of business-as-usual mind numbing and soul deadening.

Perhaps no essay on education would capture Laing's views as eloquently as "Sanity, Madness, and the School" by William Pinar, which appeared in 1975. In that essay Pinar concluded that the "cumulative effect of the schooling experience is devastating" (p. 381). The solution, according to Pinar, was for teachers and student to begin to attend to "one's 'within'" (p. 382) and to reclaim and revive an atrophied subjectivity. That project found expression in the 1970s in personal writing, auto-biography, and the focus on getting in touch with one's feelings. Unfortunately, unlike Pinar, most teachers who pursued such work had little sense of its psychoanalytic foundations.

It is, as I said exhilarating to read Laing today. I doubt, though, that his work is widely read in the academy. Certainly it does not appear on syllabi in teacher education courses. That may be because while it shocks, it also seems somehow dated or, conversely, too much like science fiction, which seems the only genre to hold utopian aspirations (Jameson, 2005). I suspect that the absence of Laing's work also has to do with the diminishing of utopian energies and how much we take reality for the only way things can be. It is as if a perfect feed-back loop existed between what we do and the reality we see outside ourselves. In such a closed circuit, we disavow our own subjectivity and with it the psychoanalytic knowledge that makes it possible. The fact that today's leading educators, such as Linda Darling-Hammond and John Bransford can write that effective teachers are the ones who "have good grounding in normal development, [and] an appreciation of the variations of normal development" so they can employ these "for instructional purposes" (Horowitz, Darling-Hammond, and Bransford, 2005, p. 117) reveals how far the discourse on education has come since Laing was writing and how much reality is taken for granted as simply being what it is. The popular saying, "It is what it is" suggests the impossibility of subjectivizing reality, the intractability of external circumstances, and the disavowal of psychoanalytic knowledge that looks at our own complicity in the fantasmatic construction of our realities. It is as if we believe we know reality, and the choices seem to be between accepting society as sick and cynically enjoying it, so much so that the very word "sick" now means good, or clinging to a frenzied optimism and "can-do" attitude, meant to signify health. In teacher education, the cynical resignation of teachers who joke about how bad things are accompanies the compulsive touting of each new reform or best practice that comes on the market.

The point I want to make here, is not another gloss on contemporary culture's cynicism or manic boosterism. It is that Laing's work did sustain much of the emancipatory project of both psychoanalysis and education, in the face of an increasingly militarized, bureaucratized, and corporatized life world, and it continues to challenge our assumptions about what we present to students as the true reality. We can so easily succumb to the practical and expedient—what some educators take for pragmatism. Conversations about twenty-first century skills, the gold standards of best practices, or how to get students to do … well, whatever it takes to do well, long ago replaced discussions about our own psychic investments in teaching or what it means to be authentic or what the educational value of the journey inward might be. There do continue to be discussions of social justice, however, although in most instances they do not hearken back to the cultural critique of critical theorists such as Herbert Marcuse.

Herbert Marcuse

"Polymorphous sexuality" was the term which I used
to indicate that the new direction of progress would depend
completely on the opportunity … to make the human body
an instrument of pleasure rather than labor.

(Marcuse, 1968, p. ii)

Marcuse was a prominent figure in the Frankfurt School and achieved celebrity in the late 1960s and early 1970s among the New Left. His books *One Dimensional Man: Studies in the Ideology of Advanced Industrial Society* and *Eros and Civilization: A Philosophical Inquiry into Freud* reflect critical theory's indebtedness to Freud, although today critical pedagogy, which claims its link to the Frankfurt School and Marcuse, disavows or at most downplays any roots in psychoanalytic theory (see Daniel Cho, 2006 and 2009 for an exception to this). Marcuse, more even than Laing or Brown, and certainly more than the psychological humanists, committed himself to the emancipatory project of psychoanalysis. In *Eros and Civilization* he wrote:

> This essay moves exclusively in the field of theory, and it keeps outside the technical discipline which psychoanalysis has become. Freud developed a theory of man, a "psycho-logy" in the strict sense. With this theory, Freud placed himself in the great tradition of philosophy and under philosophical criteria. Our concern is not with a corrected or improved interpretation of Freudian concepts but with their philosophical and sociological implications. ... [N]o therapeutic argument should hamper the development of a theoretical construction which aims, not at curing individual sickness, but at diagnosing the general disorder. (p. 7)

It is interesting to note that Marcuse's commitment to theory irritated Erich Fromm who accused him of neglecting the practical. Fromm's (1968) *The Revolution of Hope: Toward a Humanized Technology* had called on individuals to take that first step to creating a better society by joining clubs that would advance such a cause. Marcuse found such practical solutions complicit with the rein of instrumental rationality and blind to the unconscious conflicts that render such gestures at best suspect. The urgency to act often sustains the compulsion to repeat.

Marcuse's project was to rethink Freud's work on Eros and Thanatos and historicize the dynamics of repression presented in *Civilization and Its Discontents*. Marcuse argued that the technological advances in the West and accompanying demise of scarcity had made some repression, what he called surplus repression, unnecessary, and therefore our erotic lives did not, as Freud had suggested, have to be repressed in the service of civilization. Furthermore, Marcuse attacked the healthy ego conceptualized by ego psychologists as autonomous and free of conflict. He also rethought Freud's primary narcissism in terms of a pre-Oedipal, oceanic oneness—a state of polymorphous perversity. Such a state, Marcuse argued, could on one hand interrupt the isolation of consumer driven individuals, blurring boundaries between them, and, on the other hand, replace the instrumental rationality of life adjustment, ego psychology, and a medicalized psychoanalysis with an eroticized rationality, a fluid sexuality, and openness to communal life.

Similar to Laing, and even Rogers and Maslow, Marcuse sought a more authentic human being, one whose subjectivity was not frozen over by the historical sedimentation that constituted our ego, our normalized or prosthetic sexuality, and our purported individuality, which Marcuse considered as idiosyncratic as the toothpaste under its variegated packaging. His work advocated a revolution that took into account society, the economy, and the psyche. Marcuse believed that instrumental reasoning and technical rationality emerged with what he termed genital supremacy—patriarchy. He suggested that the gay liberation and women's liberation movements were in the vanguard of the revolution, not only because they challenged the nuclear family, but also because they challenged normalized and commodified sexualities, particularly normative masculine heterosexuality. These reified or what I would label prosthetic sexualities isolated individuals, were confused with erotic potential, and helped sustain instrumental reasoning.

While Marcuse's work was not widely adopted by educators in the open school movement, radical educators and some curriculum theorists such as James Macdonald (see B. Macdonald, 1995) found in Marcuse's work an antidote to the regnant behaviorism and technocentrism of mainstream education. The relaxation of codes governing sexual behavior in schools was at the time in part attributable to Marcuse's work and through it to Freud. More important, however, are two other facts about Marcuse's work. First, very few critical pedagogues who appealed to Marcuse's work acknowledged the psychoanalytic influence in that work or his call to reclaim a subjectivity that was not synonymous with individuality, social identity, or personality. There are, however, some scholars in education who currently do work to reclaim the psychoanalytic influences on critical pedagogy. Here I am thinking particularly of the work of Daniel Cho (2009), whose work looks at Freire's indebtedness to Lacan and Freud, and Stephen Appel's work (1999) which has contributed to our understanding of the relationship between psychoanalysis and critical pedagogy. Second, Marcuse's work served as a bridge between feminism, critical theory, and psychoanalysis. In the last public speech he gave before his death, Marcuse stated that the women's movement is "perhaps the most important and potentially the most radical political movement we have" (Marcuse, quoted in Buhle, 1998, p. 299). That feminism and psychoanalysis exist today as absences within teacher education is a sad commentary on Marcuse's hope for the future.

Norman O. Brown

> Today even the survival of humanity is a utopian hope.
>
> (Brown, 1970, p. 305)

Norman O. Brown was a classicist who turned to Freud for two reasons. First, he had become disillusioned with what he considered the failures of Marxism and second, he sought to understand the role of repression and sublimation in disfiguring our psychic life. Brown followed Freud's theory of repression, i.e., repression was a result of the conflict between the reality principle and the pleasure principle, and agreed with Freud that "the symptom is … a substitute for sexual satisfaction denied by reality" (Brown, 1970, p. 23). But contra Freud he argued that childhood sexuality is a kind of anarchic, polymorphously perverse state, which "is the ultimate essence of our desires and our being" and offers "nothing more or less than delight in the active life of all the human body" (p. 30). Further Brown collapsed the distinctions Freud had made between identification, aim, and object choice and argued that love has "one essential aim over and above pleasure, which is to become one with the objects in the world" (p. 44). The search for oneness became a theme in Brown's work.

That search led Brown to conclude that psychoanalysis' own dualisms prevented it from its true aim, which consisted of reuniting psyche and body. According to Brown, what orthodox psychoanalysis, particularly ego psychology, considered the goals of development—personal autonomy, genital sexuality, sublimation—were inherently repressive. Brown, not unlike the early progressive educators who had turned to Freud, saw repression as the bane of our existence. We are capable of working through this repression, if we return to a state of polymorphous perversity, a state that corresponds to transcendence of the self.

Brown agreed with Freud that all sublimation was sublimation of sexual impulses. But since sublimation, in whatever form it took, e.g., art, work, scientific creation, was a form of repression, there seemed to be no way out of living with repression. If analysis allowed sexual impulses to come under the control of the ego and thus free the individual from a neurosis caused by repression of those impulses, where would the impulses go then? Freud had offered three choices: refrain from acting on them, act on them, or sublimate them, and he himself was pessimistic about the success of any of them. Brown argued that sublimating them or not acting on them amounted to repression, and claimed that "clearly the outcome of therapy could only be a more erotic mode of behavior in the real world" (p. 140). Sublimation is "no way out of the human neurosis but leads to its aggravation" (p. 307). How then do we get out of this trap? Brown's answer is complicated, so my summary does it injustice, but basically he argued that the sexuality that is repressed is a normalized, genitally focused sexuality, which itself emerges as the ego's defensive reaction to fear of separation. That fear of separation links with a fear of death. If we can release the polymorphous sexuality trapped beneath the normalized one, it will not only infuse rationality with a new life, but also allow us to continue to build a culture.

> Sublimation negates the body of childhood and seeks to construct the lost body of childhood in the external world. Infantile sexuality is an autoplastic compensation for the loss of Other; sublimation is alloplastic compensation for the loss of self. ...
>
> Hence the hidden aim of sublimation and cultural process is the progressive discovery of the lost body of childhood. (p. 170)

Brown argued the path to breaking free from the crippling effects of repression consisted in re-finding the lost body of childhood within. In other words, if we allowed ourselves to take pleasure in our own and others' bodies, not in a genitally fixated way but in a polymorphously perverse way, a way beyond oppressive norms and conventions governing sexuality, we would sustain culture and thought but they would now be infused with the erotic.

Brown's importance for education must seem at first glance minimal. But when we consider the movements over the last four decades that have transformed attitudes toward sexuality, and how these changes have impacted education, perhaps his influence was greater than it first appears. Furthermore, Brown's focus on release, on looking within, and on lifting repression, coincided with the general trend in the late 1960s and 1970s to talk about feelings, to let it all out, to tell it like it is, to be authentic, and to express oneself. As evidence, we need only consider Jerry Farber's controversial but widely read 1969 essay, "The Student as Nigger," which advocated an open recognition of sex in the schools, student rights, getting rid of grades, and the lifting of sexual repression. Such an essay today would be considered outrageous, but at the time it seemed compellingly revolutionary. That particular ethos of revolution certainly spread into the schools and teacher education programs.

Perhaps George Dennison (1969) summed the movement up best. In *The Lives of Children* he wrote:

> We made much of freedom of choice and freedom of movement; and of the reality of encounters between teachers and students. ... We abolished tests and grades and Lesson Plans. We abolished Superiors too. ... We abolished homework (unless asked for), we abolished the category of truant. ... [W]e laid bare the deeper motivations and powers which contribute to what might be called 'internal order,' i.e., a structuring of activities based upon the child's innate desire to learn, and upon ... the needs of the children. (p. 6)

All the teacher could do, "[was] cease to attempt to control the young. Beyond this he (could) ally himself with the student's quest for wholeness" (p. 103). Dennison's views, clearly informed by humanistic psychology, and the views of Laing, Marcuse, and Brown, and shared widely by radical educators at the time, also recall the earlier reforms of the Progressive Era and the psycho-pedagogy from the beginning of the century. The attempt to put into practice those views would not last.

Demise of the Open School Movement

Whatever impact the open school movement and radical educators had on public education and teacher education is hard to determine. Cuban (1993) concludes that "in the academic organization of the classroom, whole group instruction, reliance on textbook for authoritative knowledge, and homework assignments still captured the majority of high school teaching practices in the 1970s" (p. 204). Writing in 1974, David Tyack had this to say about that period, although it could apply to the entire history of psychoanalysis and education:

[A] small libertarian wing of educational progressives ... sought to make the school conform to the trajectory of the individual child's growth. They drew on Freud and avant-garde artists and intellectuals to criticize the repressiveness of the traditional school structure and curriculum and to urge the individual self-expression of the child instead. ... [T]he libertarians ... had little practical impact on urban schools. (p. 196)

On the other hand, Diane Ravitch (2000) argued that schools cut "back on graduation requirements, expand[ed] electives, eliminate[ed] dress codes, and eas[ed] disciplinary rules" (p. 402). It is clear something happened.

My own experiences teaching at the end of the 1960s and in the early 1970s suggest that relationships between teachers and students became more fluid, teachers tried to make the curriculum relevant and integrated their own and student's interests into class content, and group dynamics seemed a part of teacher education programs, as did studying critiques of oppressive educational practices. Self-actualization or self-exploration often emerged as a focal point of the curriculum and courses on methods of teaching. What was considered educational reform, if not educational revolution, consisted of many of the approaches implemented in pre-World War I Vienna and Berlin, as well as in progressive schools in the U.S. Educators who appealed to the work of Laing, Marcuse, and Brown saw themselves as true educational revolutionaries. One gets a sense of how what passes for educational reform today differs from that of the late 1960s and 1970s, if one considers that today's reformers focus on raising test scores.

The psychoanalytic *origins* of the changes propounded in the 1960s and 70s by the open school movement were rarely acknowledged, studied, or discussed. Humanistic psychology might have been an explicit part of the teacher preparation curriculum, and students might have read Laing, Marcuse, or Brown, but Freud was generally not on the reading lists in education courses. No attention was paid to the history of the relationship between education and psychoanalysis.

What is so striking about this period is that although it clearly had effects that persist today: using small groups for assignments and to confront issues of bias; asking students to relate their feelings, often as opposed to ideas, about a topic; incorporating self-reflection, and journal writing; trying to make the curriculum relevant to student interest and socially relevant, and offering students electives, by and large one could sit in education courses today, visit schools and classrooms, and never know that an open school movement existed, let alone one influenced by psychoanalytic theory. Even the mental hygiene movement's influence on classroom practices seems to have left few traces. Emotional life has been shuttled off to the guidance counselor or social worker. We are so fearful of emotional disturbances that any sign, whether in creative writing assignments, dress, or words, that a student might feel violent toward him or herself or others sends us running to the experts. Irrational outbursts, violent and otherwise, are shuttled off to the psychologists who repeat the same explanations. Teachers are advised to leave students' emotional lives to the experts. Sex education has been largely eliminated from schools (Levine, 2002), and while what some would consider alienated forms of sexuality are rampant, eroticism seems sadly lacking. Zero tolerance, metal detectors, and relentless testing have replaced self-exploration, following one's interests, and journeys through madness.

On the other hand, the hope that the therapeutic project of either psychoanalysis or education could transform society or individuals may in fact have contributed to education's historical amnesia and its seemingly endless cycles of reform, followed by crises, followed by reforms, followed by disillusionment. If, as Freud argued, repetition is the sign of forgetting, certainly the forgetting of the historical relationship between psychoanalysis and education, and the disavowal of psychoanalytic knowledge can be seen to have contributed to the repetition compulsion of educational reform movements. In aligning itself with and aspiring to the perceived status of science and medicine, psychoanalysis and education fell prey to the historical amnesia that haunts both science and medicine. Physicists, biologists, and physicians rarely study the history of their fields, other than as a minor topic of interest. Psychoanalysis and education simply followed suit.

That failure to remember or to think back through history constituted a disavowal of the radical knowledge of psychoanalysis. If the unconscious returns to us as symptoms, dreams, failures—as memories not consciously remembered—then its disavowal condemns us to repeat what has not been remembered, to repeat those failures and reproduce those symptoms. Now Freud argues in several places that what we fail to remember we repeat, but he also suggested that what was remembered or reconstructed was not really what was significant. What psychoanalysis offers is not a remembered past but a way of reconstructing the past. It is not that we learn the secret of our own family romances or lift the amnesia about the losses, wounds, and angers that fill our early life, although these certainly appear at times. Rather what is developed is a way of attending to the past in the present such that we can try, often unsuccessfully, to trace what we are feeling at any given moment back to the possible psychic coordinates that produce the ideation or fantasies or perceptions provoking such feelings. In the transferences that adhere in analysis and in associations to dreams, slips—whatever comes to our mind—we can re-construct the psychic layers through which we experience life, and in doing so, we can ever so slightly loosen ourselves from our own over-determined entanglements in the present. The memories or histories we produce are much less important than the way we come to attend to our reactions and to figuring out to whom we are or were speaking, who is or was speaking within us, and what our own desires are or were.

The explosions in the late 1960s and 70s provided an orgasmic sense of freedom in the face of what appeared to be the release of repressed material. Suddenly we were all finding out how it really was. Nothing was hidden. And we wanted students to let it all hang out also. But the assumption was that the truth lay in what had been repressed and that, in knowing this, causal chains could be divined and constructed, that what hung out was free of unconscious determinants. Educators calling for the end to repression paradoxically wound up repeating the same experiments that had been tried in the early part of the century. The exposures of histories of oppression, of war crimes, and of injustices, and the revelation of patterns of abuse were all important, but simply learning about them didn't mean those patterns would not be repeated. The release of feelings, interests, desires, and dreams didn't mean that these were, in and of themselves, innocent of social and historical determinants as these had been passed on through families. The belief that students' expressions of their now unfettered interests and emotions would lead to a healthier, better educated, and, most of all, more egalitarian society appealed to a version of Freudian psychoanalysis stripped of its tragic dimension and impossibility. This ameliorative version adopted by educators would contribute to the very demise of the open school movement and the psychoanalytically informed radical reforms advocated in the late 1960s and 1970s, since the results never measured up to the promises. How could they, when the very radical nature of the unconscious these reforms seemed to take into account, subverted the utopian assumptions implicit in the educational reforms? Rather than consider the dream of education itself and what it might reveal about education's unconscious, radical educators took the dream as an aspiration that could be realized if particular educational approaches were put in place. Rather than sift what was released through the analytic perspectives of psychoanalysis and disciplinary knowledge, radical educators assumed the release itself would generate a new world and a better educated student.

Studying the history of the relationship between education and psychoanalysis will not guarantee that that history is not repeated, anymore than studying the history of our educational system will guarantee that we interrupt the repetition compulsion in which education has been stuck for a century. It is in the ways we re-construct that history through its symptoms, slips, and dreams that we might find another future in the past one that wasn't achieved. In doing so we might interrupt these deadening compulsions to repeat.

Feminist Critiques of Psychoanalysis and Feminist Responses

> The idealizations of Freud and of psychoanalysis and the
> identification of psychoanalysis with the psychiatric establishment
> inevitably inspired disillusionment and disagreement.
>
> (Hale, 1995b, p. 349)

One of the reasons educators may have been loath at the time to discuss the psychoanalytic roots of the open school movement and radical educational experiments in the 1960s and 70s concerned the public perception of psychoanalysis and what was seen as its conservatism.

The alliance between psychoanalysis and medicine had brought prestige to psychoanalysis in the 1950s and 1960s, but as psychoanalysis hardened into dogma and as the civil rights, women's, and gay liberation movements grew in strength, psychoanalysis came in for some devastating critiques. Furthermore, academic psychologists began challenging psychoanalysis' claims to scientific status. And finally, some social critics like Christopher Lasch (1979) accused psychoanalysis of having lost its radical edge and fragmented into a million therapies circulating in a culture of narcissism. Nathan Hale (1995b) recalls the films and novels from the 1970s, which, unlike those of a decade or two earlier, satirized shrinks and depicted psychoanalysis as a form of mind control. Ken Kesey's *One Flew over the Cuckoo's Nest* is perhaps the best example of this genre.

I don't think there is any need to review the charges against psychoanalysis of being racist, classist, homophobic, heterosexist, and sexist. What is important to keep in mind is that those American feminists who grappled with psychoanalysis and found in it a way to understand gender arrangements did influence curriculum theory in the late 1970s and early 1980s. Thus the work of Nancy Chodorow (1978), Dorothy Dinnerstein (1977), and Gayle Rubin (1975), all of whom had turned to psychoanalytic theory, influenced the curriculum theorizing of Madeleine Grumet, Janet Miller, and William Pinar, and, while their influence was never directly acknowledged by her, of Carol Gilligan. In turn Gilligan's work supported diverse educational efforts ranging from defenses of Title IX to greater attention being given to middle school girls' participation in classroom discussions.

Women analysts had occupied a central place in psychoanalysis' early history, but as psychoanalysis had allied itself with medicine, their participation dwindled. Alice Balint, Anna Freud, Karen Horney, Melanie Klein, and Margaret Mahler, all had taken Freud's views further and struggled to work through the patriarchal bias in his theorizing. Klein, Mahler, and Balint, more than Horney, influenced the psychoanalytic theorizing of feminists in the 1970s, in particular the work of Nancy Chodorow.

Nancy Chodorow

In essence Chodorow argued that the fact that women are primary caretakers in society fixes the configuration of the Oedipal crisis and produces an asymmetry in male and female experience and in relational potentials. Emphasizing the pre-Oedipal origins of gender identity, Chodorow argued that initially both infants identify with and love the mother. Thus the boy's primary identity is female and his primary relational valence is heterosexual and the girl's is female and lesbian. Their *normative* developmental tasks are therefore different: the boy must achieve masculinity and the girl must achieve heterosexuality. Given those projects the fact that girls and then women stereotypically express more interest in relationships, particularly with the opposite sex, and feel more comfortable being physically affectionate with other females, and boys stereotypically show more interest in proving their masculinity, competing with other males, and repudiating their feminine qualities is not surprising. Gilligan extended this analysis to argue that girls' and women's ethics tend to be relationally oriented, while boys' and men's ethical or moral approaches tend to be rule governed. She pointed out that there was not one developmental trajectory for moral development but two and that girls' ethical sensibilities were in some ways superior to the rule-governed ethical decision making of boys.

For Chodorow the asymmetrical childrearing arrangements rather than any biologically based proclivity accounted for the fact that women mothered. It also accounted for women's ability to sustain intimacy and relationships. Dinnerstein, who had been more influenced by Melanie Klein than Chodorow had been, viewed the asymmetry in terms of the infant's reactions to maternal omnipotence. She contended that boys and then men, still unconsciously ambivalent about their mother's power, seek to control women. They also experience intense jealousy but find it difficult to commit given that dependence on a woman evokes unconscious primal anxieties of engulfment. Women, on the other hand, according to Dinnerstein, never overcome their initial guilt for separating from their mother and therefore work to establish all encompassing love relationships with their primary other (Buhle, 1998, p. 252). Both Dinnerstein and Chodorow concluded that only dual parenting would transform a situation that was unhealthy for both men and women.

Central to the insights of those feminists working psychoanalytically was that gender was not based in biology, that the pre-Oedipal period more so than the Oedipal drama influenced later gender identity, and that how men and women created relationships resulted from a woman being the first love object of both and being the basis of their earliest identification. Those insights, however, were taken in two directions. On one hand writers such as Jean Baker Miller (1976) argued that women were essentially more relation oriented and thus superior. On the other hand, Chodorow argued that the assignment of mothering solely to women led to male dominance and denied women autonomy. Chodorow's theorization of gender soon made its way into the field of curriculum theory.

William Pinar (1981) relied on the theory to argue, for example, that males in the undifferentiated pre-Oedipal union with the mother take in the mother's desire for the father and thus have stitched into their psyches a homoerotic potential. Such a subversion of normative notions of sexuality challenged the heteronormativity in schools and the curriculum. Grumet (1979) used the psychoanalytic theories of Chodorow and Dinnerstein to explore the epistemological categories of subject/object and to locate these categories within the asymmetry of childrearing practices. She argued that constructivist epistemology "mirror[ed] the configurations of the symbiosis of the mother/child bond and the extension of that continuity beyond the oedipal crisis in the mother/daughter relationship" while "the dyadic structure of materialist and idealist epistemologies" mirrored the "repression of the mother/son preoedipal bond" (pp. 15–16). Curriculum, according to Grumet, could contradict these epistemologies that reproduced intrapsychic structures developed in culturally constructed asymmetries in childrearing.

While in the late 1970s and early 1980s psychoanalytic theory did come into education and teacher education through these theorists, its influence on teachers seems minimal. Reviewing articles in the *Journal of Teacher Education* during the late 1970s and the 1980s, I could find no articles that explicitly talked about psychoanalysis. Feminism, of course, did influence curricular decisions and pedagogical approaches, but in general the feminism that entered education carried with it a socio/cultural analysis that positioned psychoanalysis as conservative and regressive, or did not mention it at all (see Belenky, Clinchy, Goldberger, and Tarule, 1986 and Culley and Portugues, 1985 for typical examples of women's ways of knowing and classroom applications of feminism).

Looking back on this period, I recall how the theorization of object relations appealed to me because it provided a lucid and logical explanation for a whole range of behaviors, including my own relational issues. But there was also something that bothered me about it, and initially I approached that discomfort from a Foucauldian perspective. I think, now, that my discomfort had more to do with the failure within object relations theory to recognize as Jacqueline Rose (1983) put it, how the "unconscious constantly reveals the 'failure' of identity" (p. 9).

> '[F]ailure' is something endlessly repeated and relived moment by moment throughout our individual histories. It appears not only in the symptoms, but also in dreams, in slips of the tongue and in forms of sexual pleasure which are pushed to the sidelines of the norms. Feminism's affinity with psychoanalysis rests above all ... with this recognition that there is a resistance to identity which lies at the very heart of psychic life. ... [P]sychoanalysis becomes one of the few places in our culture where it is recognized as more than a fact of individual psychology that most women do not painlessly slip into their roles as women, if, indeed, they do at all. (p. 9).

Rose's reminder of the radical otherness of the unconscious challenged Chodorow's developmental schema. It also put in question any move to contain psychic phenomena within conceptual frames that didn't attend to the strange workings of the unconscious and to language. Language would come to take on greater and greater importance in the relationship between education and psychoanalysis as the 1970s ended, but so would identity.

When Ronald Reagan took the presidency in 1980 and the conservative movement took power, many teachers and teacher educators turned their attention to identity politics and then to poststructuralism. It seemed as if psychoanalysis, in the form of either the therapeutic or emancipatory project, was about to be left behind.

The Great Repression and the Return to Freud

In 1983 *A Nation at Risk* appeared. That work, comparing the educational efforts of teachers and schools in the United States to an attack by an enemy country inaugurated a movement to institute standards and hold teachers, students, and schools accountable. The movement gained public attention not only through media hysteria over "our failing schools" but also through the publication of a slew of books blaming the excesses of the 1960s and 70s for declining test scores, cultural malaise, and the dumbing down of America. Allan Bloom's *The Closing of the American Mind* (1987), E.D. Hirsh's *Cultural Literacy* (1987) and Diane Ravitch and Chester Finn's *What Our 17-year Olds Don't Know* (1987) exemplified the jeremiads excoriating the educational experiments of the previous decade. "All things considered," Ravitch wrote, "the hedonistic, individualistic, anarchic spirit of the sixties were good for neither the educational mission of the schools nor the intellect, health, and well being of young people" (Ravitch, 2000, p. 407). Freud, along with Dewey and Rousseau, according to these educational conservatives, offered false panaceas and nihilistic visions. "Freud saw only one focus in the soul," wrote Bloom (1987), "the same one as the brutes have" (p. 137). He continued "Freudian psychology has ... no more intellectual appeal" than "engineering or banking" (p. 137). The closing of the American mind apparently could at least partially be blamed on Freud. Within education the great repression that was occurring in society increasingly was applied to psychoanalysis.

It is likely that psychoanalysis would have vanished from academia and from the field of education had it not been for the arrival in the United States of an analyst who claimed that the then current psychoanalytic theories, particularly ego psychology, had betrayed Freud. Not only was he critical of the psychoanalytic theories of the day, but he envisioned his own theory as a return to Freud. Jacques Lacan wanted to fulfill the emancipatory project of psychoanalysis and put into question the therapeutic project. His work would have a profound influence on humanities departments in the academy and, in education, on curriculum theory.

Jacques Lacan

> What you as revolutionaries aspire to is a Master.
> You will have one.
>
> (Lacan, 1990, p. 126)

I have no illusions that I can possible summarize in any comprehensible way Lacan's psychoanalytic theory. Not only is his theory difficult, not only did he himself revise and contradict himself as his theory evolved, but an industry of Lacanian exegesis has grown over the last two decades, producing often contradictory interpretations. Furthermore, current interpretations rely extensively on Slavoj Žižek's reading of Lacan, so much so that it is no longer clear in such work where Lacan begins and Žižek ends. What follows is my attempt to provide snapshots of some of Lacan's central concepts and use them to construct a story of psychic unfolding. I have concentrated on those concepts that curriculum theorists have most often relied on when they have turned to Lacan: the unconscious and language, the ego and mirror stage, the Symbolic and Imaginary registers, the subject, *jouissance*, and transference.

Fifty-five years after Freud visited America, Jacques Lacan visited Johns Hopkins University, where Hall, Dewey, and Myers had taught and studied. The Baltimore lectures as they came to be called, in part because Lacan (1966) had half-jokingly described the unconscious as Baltimore in the early morning, introduced the audience to Lacan's conception of the unconscious. The view Lacan saw from his hotel in Baltimore was of a completely thought environment—cars, buildings, planes—the result as he put it, "of thoughts actively thinking thoughts, where the function played by the subject … was there in the rather intermittent or fading spectator" (p. 5) of a flashing light in the distant cityscape. As cryptic as that sounds, the unconscious, for Lacan, its fading presence in traces in our world, does not fundamentally differ from the one Freud theorized, except on one major point, which Lacan said was implicit anyway in Freud's theory. That point has to do with language.

Language and the Unconscious

According to Lacan, the unconscious only emerges in, through, and as a result of language. By language Lacan was referring to words, the words we speak and write, the words that bind us into a community of speakers for whom language is a storehouse of endless meanings which exist as other words. Words. Not images or feelings—these require language to make sense. Language for Lacan knows the world for us, or at least brings it to us and into us. He wrote, "It is the world of words which creates the world of things – the things originally confused in the *hic et nunc* of the all-in-the-process-of-becoming – by giving its concrete being to their essence and its ubiquity to what has always been" (2006, p. 229). We cannot escape language other than in psychosis, a mute world of piercing, incoherent, and fragmented sensations. "Before speech, nothing either is or isn't. … There is neither true nor false prior to speech. Truth is introduced along with it and so is the lie" (Lacan, 1988a, p. 228). The ideas that Freud said were repressed are for Lacan always-already constituted within language, as are the free associations that may bring the unconscious to us, an unconscious only inferred from those traces. When Lacan talks of repression, then, he refers to words that are repressed, fragments of words, a name, a phrase, and these words form signifying chains that literally think elsewhere, but think without any self-consciousness. But let us move slowly.

The language or discourse that brings the world to us, that enters us is always-already social; it provides the social link. Lacan designated the field of social relations as discourse, "because there's no other way to designate it once we realize that the social link is instated only by anchoring itself in the way language is situated over and etched into what the place is crawling with, namely, speaking beings" (1998, p. 54). He would also designate that field as the Symbolic. Discourse, the Symbolic, language, the total field of words—they are by and large interchangeable for Lacan. This is why there is no metalanguage for Lacan. Metalanguages are only more words.

We cannot do without the Symbolic. Our entry into it *marks* our loss of a forever unknowable but often fantasized primal, pre-Oedipal oneness and it consolidates our sense of who we are. Our arrival within language not only alienates us and castrates us, dividing us from an imagined pre-Oedipal unity, but it also provides access to our humanity. This rethinking of the unconscious in terms of language allowed Lacan to further dissolve the boundaries between inside and outside, to render them in terms of a Mobius strip, and to suggest that what he called the Big Other equates with the following: the field of social relations, conventions, laws, rules and opinion; the parents who act as a conduit for these but also convey through language their own desires; and the unconscious. All of these insist in and exist in language. In that sense the unconscious is both within and without. The unconscious is structured as a language. It is the language of the Other. And that language, particularly that of the parents always carries desires that the child is forever trying to decode. What do they want of me? Who am I to them? Who are they to one another? These questions are Lacan's elaboration of Freud's concept of the child's sexual researches. And these are questions that haunt us as adults.

Lacan was not suggesting that language was all there was, only that without it, without words, we are reduced to our animality. But he understood that sensations pass through us and arrest us. We sense things. And we are riven by drives. If we had no language we couldn't articulate these sensations or mark them or even separate them out from the flow of sensations—we would react to them only by pure instinct, the way a dog follows a familiar scent until another breaks in—but they are there. And the drives too, they come to us not as animal instincts but as already shaped by language. These body based sensations and drives affect us as humans, then, only as they enter through language, through the Symbolic. And it is as linguistic formations, as words, that these drives will be repressed when confronted with the implicit and explicit social rules that come also through the Symbolic as carried by one's parents. These linguistic formations will speak in us. These are the words that constitute the thinking elsewhere that Lacan talks about. They constitute our unconscious. For Lacan this thinking elsewhere, this *ça*, as he called it, that appears in failed actions, jokes, and dreams—"it all fails, laughs, and dreams" as he would write (2008, p. 81)—thinks "at a level where it does not grasp itself as thought at all" because "it does not want to be grasped at all" (2008, p. 103). We are thus always split between our conscious talk—the talk we address to others as well as our interior monologue, stuttered phrases, half spoken thoughts—and our unconscious—this *ça* that thinks elsewhere.

But our entry into the Symbolic, while it marks for Lacan our castration, does not constitute our first or primal splitting and alienation. Before we are produced through language, before the Symbolic interrupts the dyadic relationship between mother and child, before the Symbolic opens up this lexical unconscious, Lacan theorized that we had a precarious, fluid sense of our self as separate, as an ego.

The Ego, the Mirror Stage and the Imaginary

Lacan postulated what he called the Imaginary register. The Imaginary has nothing to do with imagination, although it consists of unconscious fantasies and specular images. The Imaginary, for Lacan, is a realm, like the Symbolic, of alienation. We can get lost in it, and if we do, the result will be madness. But for Lacan it is exactly that madness that we take as normalcy.

The basis of the Imaginary is the ego, which arises in what Lacan called the mirror stage. The mirror provided Lacan with a metaphor for the exchange of images between the mother and the child. The infant is jubilant to experience him or herself as a unity in the eyes and words and gestures of the mother or intimate other and at the same time identifies with that other. I am me in your gaze, and I am you, as you gaze at me. This unity that the child takes as self, and also self-as-other is superimposed on an inchoate, quivering bundle of sensation, impulses, and labile sense of oneness with the mother. It is a labile sense because the oneness is already shot through with the infant's rage, libidinal joy, and anguish. So while the infant identifies with the (M)Other who provides an image of the infant's unity, the infant also experiences a separateness that is still dependent on that (M)Other, because it is in the eyes of the mother that the infant finds that unified image of itself. Perhaps I can phrase the interplay as follows, understanding that it unfolds before the entry into the Symbolic: I am me only insofar as you tell me who I am. I am also you. Such an exchange between infant and mother, in effect, reproduces the initial trauma and jubilance of birth. Before the umbilical cord is cut, later reproduced by the intrusion of the Symbolic, the infant is itself, but still part of the mother.

The image that the mirror, mother, or parent throws back at the child can never, of course, capture who that child is, anymore than when we look in the mirror what we see captures who we are. For Lacan the mirror and our image in it suggest the initial dynamics of how our ego is formed in the eyes of the other, and anticipates later dynamics of identification and ego formation. "The mirror stage is a drama whose internal thrust is precipitated from insufficiency"—the infant's dispersed fragmented body—"to anticipation"—the infant's looking and being fascinated with a unified image of itself provided by the mirroring gaze of the mother. "The succession of fantasies that extends from a fragmented body-image to a form of its totality" Lacan calls "orthopaedic" (2006, p. 4). For Lacan the infant's identification with that unity constitutes "the assumption of the armor of an alienating identity which will mark with its rigid structure the subject's entire mental development" (2006, p. 4). We are fascinated by the image of unity and the "uncoordinated incoherent diversity of the primitive fragmentation gains in unity in so far as it is fascinated" (1988b, p. 50). That armor, that unity is the ego.

As infants grow that ego is developed and adopted in the relationship with the mother, or father, or intimate others. As the Symbolic intrudes that ego hardens and layers are added, but the fundamental structures are laid down in infancy and early childhood. When we are infants and children, others in our life convey to us through gestures, vibrations, looks, words, sounds, touch, who we are or should be or should want to be. They provide us with images of who we are, insist on who we are or should be, and we come to take these images and words for who we are, who we want to be, and the place from which we look at ourselves. This ego for Lacan consists of "that set of defenses, of denials, of dams, of inhibitions, of funda-mental fantasies which orient and direct the subject" (1988a, p. 17). Furthermore, such an ego is rent with aggressivity, anguish, and longing. The infant is torn between all that is me/ego and that which is left out or in excess of ego, and between a sense of unity and a sense that such unity depends on the (M)Other. The infant's ego is itself riven with conflict.

This obviously is not the ego of ego psychology. Lacan understood the ego as being fundamentally alienated, consisting of nothing but "the superimposition of various coats borrowed from what I call the bric-a-brac shop of its props depart-ment" (1988b, p. 155). This ego, however, is not synonymous with the kernel of our being.

> There's no doubt that the real I is not the ego. But that isn't enough, for one can always fall into thinking that the ego is a mistake of the I a partial point of view ... The ego isn't the I, isn't a mistake ... It is something else – a particular object within the experience of the subject. Literally the ego is an object – an object which fills certain function which we here call the imaginary function. (1988b, p. 44)

Such an ego appears as soon as we talk about ourselves as being a particular way: "Oh, I am such and such," or, "you know me, I am ... " fill in the blank. In the same way, Lacan would say that the commoner who takes himself for a king is quite mad, but the king who takes himself for a king is equally as mad. Such a move, naturally, has serious implications for anyone wishing to hold onto a fixed identity. It certainly undermined the ego of Hartmann, Loewenstein, and Kris since for Lacan there is no healthy, autonomous ego. In fact, sounding like R.D. Laing, Lacan saw the ego as a deadly symptom, "the mental illness of man" (1988a, p. 16), but, nevertheless, a symptom or illness we can't ultimately do without, although he advised analysts to work toward that end.

The ego is a fiction, a necessary one, but a fiction, and it certainly isn't synonymous with the subject. In fact the more we misrecognize ourselves as that ego the more aggressive we can feel, and that aggression, paradoxically can emerge as guilt. There is in us something more than that ego and that something irrupts, reminds us, if we listen, that we are more than that ego, less than, or other than that ego. This irruption can be quite unsettling. The more identified with the ego we are, the more unsettling these irruptions can be and the more we react by fabricating or rationalizing the shock. If, for example, we imagine ourselves as not competitive and then we find we hate someone who has won a prize, we may rationalize the irruption by saying the person won it unfairly or the system is corrupt and that explains our anger. If we imagine ourselves good teachers and our students fail, however we define failure, we imagine all sorts of reasons for the failure. In fact, often when we tell *ourselves* or another how we are really a good person or a bad teacher or an inconsistent partner, such summations, by themselves, often eventuate in an aggression directed toward that ego or outward toward another. Because the ego is so tied up with self-image the entire mental apparatus that accompanies it is often invested in attributing to others or to what one takes for one's nature the very problems about which one complains. My class went badly because those students are horrible; my class went badly because I am a horrible teacher. That person is beautiful, smart, etc.; I am envious, less than, etc. For Lacan, then, suffering in part results from the constant back and forth between "it's me who is to blame, no it's you who is to blame" and the belief that there is some fixed reality out there that mirrors the fixed reality of our ego.

The ego, for Lacan, also accounts for that running commentary in our heads as we become self-conscious—uh oh, I wonder how I appear to them, or what they think of me, or what effect I am having on them. Ego in the Imaginary register, then, is tied up with self-image.

The ego is even more complicated than this, however, because it is what we take for the agent of our conscious intentionality. When for example, in analysis, we tell the analyst something and say, "This is what I mean," that intention and meaning refer to what we consciously think we mean, when in fact, according to Lacan, that meaning is imaginary. Thus the analyst listens not to the meaning but to what the patient actually says—the words. And the analyst allows those words to enter his or her own unconscious, provoking other thoughts/words that one hopes are not as bound to the analyst's ego as are the meanings the patient makes to his or hers. This, too, is why Lacan could argue that patients really had no idea what they were saying, why they were saying it, to whom they were speaking, or even who was speaking. As Bruce Fink writes, "It is when patients begin to throw ... the when, what, why, and who of their utterances [into question] ... that they are genuinely engaged in analysis" (1997, p. 25). Part of the goal of analysis then is to provoke in the patient the analytic attitude that asks such questions in and out of analysis—thus making analysis interminable.

But if the ego is a fiction, a symptom, our prison, and our compass, if we cannot live without it but it distorts our relationships, how do we find another way? How do we escape the mirages of the ego? And who, what, and where is the subject? To answer these questions we need to return for a moment to the Symbolic.

The Symbolic instantiates in language the losses, joys, alienation, omnipotence, and pain experienced in the Imaginary. It is our tragedy and possibility. It separates the child from the imagined pre-Oedipal bliss of oneness with the mother and allows the child to enter the social. It castrates us, provides us with a sense of self—however illusory—and our power. First, though, in severing us from the fantasized paradisiacal maternal oneness—fantasized because it was always torn by loss and rage as well as ecstasy—the Symbolic marks the beginning of desire, desire to be whatever it is we imagine the M(O)ther desires, so we can regain that oneness. But because we can never fathom the enigma of the mother's desire, and never achieve this fantasized bliss of pre-Oedipal union, we wind up looking for the answer to the question and the lost oneness in all sorts of substitutions, which we demand. But even if our demands are satisfied, even if we have all the love, money, fame we think will satisfy us, we remain unsatisfied. Why? Because our demands are only pale shadows of the real need we have for that fantasized pre-Oedipal paradise or the answer to the M(O)ther's desire or to the question What do they want from me? Never bringing the satisfaction we hope for, our demands leave us craving something else and that craving or desire transforms into other demands. This is why Lacan could state that desire is demand subtracted from need. Language carries our demand, which, when satisfied, only yields more desire because the demand can never completely articulate our primal need and even if it could, such a need can never be satisfied. It never was.

The Subject is an Other

> "Where the reign of sleep was, I must come."
>
> (Lacan, 2008, p. 83)

Lacan located the subject in the unconscious. "The unconscious" is the unknown subject of the ego, [and] it is misrecognized by the ego" (1988b, p. 43). The subject "does not coincide with the ego" (1988b, p. 44). The subject is what remains after the inchoate infant is "jammed, sucked in by the image, the deceiving and realized image, of the other, or equally by its own specular image" (1988b, p. 54). The subject then is only knowable to the ego as a fading trace that can be caught in slips of the tongue, bungled actions, dreams, and what the individual (the ego) thinks of as his or her symptom. "In the unconscious, excluded from the system of the ego, the subject speaks" (1988b, p. 58). Thus the subject is an other—the Other as language, recall that language constitutes the unconscious; the Other as mother or parent, recall that the desires for and of the parent are carried by words that are repressed; and the Other as the unconscious itself, recall that the unconscious is both inside and outside us.

It sounds then as if we are composed of two agencies—the ego and the unconscious, which Lacan seems, most of the time, to equate with the subject. The question then is: What does analysis offer? Certainly for Lacan it does not mean strengthening the ego; that would be equivalent to making us even more mentally ill. If we were to fall completely into the unconscious, however, we would break human ties—we would appear as irrational as a steady stream of free associations might. What then does psychoanalysis offer?

Transference and Analysis

> The basic thing about analysis is that people finally
> realize they've been talking nonsense for years.
>
> (Lacan, 2008, p. 71)

> Analytic listening and analytic understanding are more
> salient than promises of analytic cure.
>
> (Turkle, 1992, p. 7)

When the patient enters analysis the patient doesn't know what is really wrong, only what has brought him or her into analysis—depression, a string of broken relationships, obsessing over someone or something—suffering. The patient does, however, believe the analyst knows or will know what the real problem is, what is behind the presenting problem. It is that assumption, according to Lacan, that jump starts the transference—the patient's assumption that he or she is in the presence of the one presumed to know. What we presume the analyst knows could be any of the following: the real reason we are suffering, the hidden truth about ourselves, wisdom we don't feel we possess, knowledge about how to really enjoy life, or how to be a good person or how to possess or be what we desire or the Other desires. This person presumed to know ignites the transference.

The transference, as Freud and Lacan understood it, is the reproduction in the present of older patterns of relating with important figures from one's childhood—parents or siblings. The patient, for example, may become or give what he or she thinks will please the analyst. The patient may wish to become the analyst or may treat the analyst as judge and jury. Such transferences go on all the time in our regular lives. We meet someone who occupies the position of the one supposed to know, and we find ourselves acting as that person's rebellious servant or resentful victim or imperious boss or needy child, or we contort ourselves trying to become the object of that person's desire or to avoid such desire. All of this goes on unconsciously, but we then suffer the consequences of such adapting to the other person, only we don't understand what is happening. Why are they acting so aloof or hurt or angry or distant? Why do I get treated like an ingénue or minor character in a play? The ways we unconsciously act with others have been set a long time ago in our childhoods and relate to how our own egos were formed.

In analysis however the patient does act through words, and whatever the patient does say registers on the free floating attention of the analyst who listens to his or her own counter-transference to provide clues to what the patient wants, to whose desire is really speaking through the patient, and to who the analyst is to the patient. The analyst listens to the patient talk about him or herself, listens to the linguistic layers of the ego and its communicative patterns unfold, listens to the words, and watches as he or she becomes the Other for the patient. The analyst tries to understand the patient's desires, who is actually desiring, whom the desire is for, and what forms it takes. And the analyst makes interventions, such that the patient begins to think about the various voices, knots, words that make-up his or her being. The confirmation of such interventions is provided by the patient's associations that follow. The more they flow out, the more the patient has for the moment anyway, broken the transference. When speech dries up, Lacan (1988a) claimed, transference is in effect (p. 40). Free association cuts "off the moorings of the conversation with the other" (1988a, pp. 174–75) so that the patient better understands the illusory nature of the ego.

> For the subject, the uncoupling of his relations to the other causes the image of his ego to fluctuate, to shimmer, to oscillate, renders it complete and incomplete. So that he can recognize all the stages of his desire, all the objects which have given consistency, nourishment and body to this image, he has to perceive it in its completeness, to which he has never had access. (1988a, p. 181)

For Lacan the aim of analysis is not to strengthen the ego. It is not to bring up a traumatic memory such that the patient will be released from it. It is not to point the patient in the right direction or re-educate him. Who, after all, is the analyst to assume he or she can re-educate? Refusing all certainties, the analyst must never assume, as his or her real position, the position of the one presumed to know. Such a thought would be the ego of the analyst speaking—worth listening to but not identifying with. The aim of analysis certainly is not to have the analyst as master or expert cure the patient back to health. Nor, finally is it to get the patient back on track or get in touch with various emotions. The aim, if there were an aim in analysis, and Lacan maintained it was not cure, is to move the patient to assume responsibility for his or her own over-determined existence. What does that mean?

The aim of analysis is to move the unconscious into the ego, such that the unconscious moves into consciousness *as* the ego accepts its own destiny and past. "Where it was, the Ich – the subject, not psychology – the subject, must come into existence" (1981, p. 45) was Lacan's translation of Freud's "*Wo es war, sol ich warden.*" Or, in a more elaborated form Lacan wrote, "Where it was just now, where it was for a short while, between an extinction that is still glowing and an opening up that stumbles, *I* can come into being by disappearing from my statement" (2006, p. 802). We can see this is almost the obverse of how Freud's words have generally been translated, which is as "where id was there ego shall be."

Lacan's translation suggested that the most we can hope for is that we will take full responsibility for and provide an existential meaning to our symptoms. But to reach this freedom of embracing one's destiny we must "suspend [our] certainties until their last mirages have been consumed" (2006, p. 43). We must see the symptom of our own ego and accept the limits of our own desire.

> Man can adumbrate his situation in a field made up of rediscovered knowledge only if he has previously experienced the limits within which, like desire, he is bound. Love, which it seems to some, I have downgraded, can be posited only in that beyond, where, at first, it renounces its object. (1981, p. 276)

We must assume our history, make it our own. This entails coming to understand that the Other—the one presumed to know—is as castrated as we ourselves are. Furthermore, in analysis we may come to understand that not only are we castrated—castrated by language, by our separation from a fantasized paradisiacal unity—but also that no one demanded our castration. Rather it came as the price of being human. In other words, there are no ultimate solutions, answers, or certainties. We can never know what our parents wanted of us or who we were to them. We can never be or possess what we believe them to have been or to have had, because they didn't possess "it" either, nor were they "it." We are all fallible. What we take for reality, our loves and hates, our sexual relations, our moans and groans about others, all these we have fashioned unconsciously. They have emerged as we took in from our parents the words that carried them or formed them.

> Here we discover ... that the unconscious is the discourse of the other ... It is the discourse of my father for instance, in so far as my father made mistakes which I am absolutely condemned to reproduce. ... because I am obliged to pick up again the discourse which he bequeathed to me. ... and it is precisely my duty to transmit it in its aberrant form to someone else. I have put into someone else the problem of a situation of life and death in which the chances are that it is just as likely that he will falter. (1988b, p. 89).

The only way out of such a circuit, if there in fact is one, is to acknowledge it, understanding that the aberration each of us makes of it offers a small space for our difference, our humanity—we are not simply stations transmitting the same discourse. It is the suffering that such discourses bring that takes us into analysis and humanizes us. There, in analysis, we come to understand that while we were not the cause of the madness we find around us, we are fully responsible for it.

Implications

Lacan's theory of language, the ego, desire, and the unconscious suggested that there is no fixed boundary between self and society: the ego consists of various sedimentations of the social. It also suggested there is no natural human essence: the subject comes into being as already alienated in the Imaginary, and then further alienated in the Symbolic. Even drives, as Freud had suggested, are not for Lacan biological instincts, but rather already shaped by and inseparable from language. He suggested, too, that the subject is not the ego, not the individual, not the "I" of language but in fact the unconscious, speaking through these other veils. The small crack of freedom we might have comes from opening up or weakening the ego to admit the subject of the unconscious. Thus Lacan could say that we always speak from where we are not, and that whether we are lying or not we always speak the truth of the unconscious. "I always speak the truth. Not the whole truth, because there's no way to say it all. Saying it all is literally impossible: words fail. Yet it's through this very impossibility that the truth holds onto the real" (1990, p. 3). His theorization of the ego also led him to critique knowledge which hung "on the notion of totality, of unitary functioning, [and] which presuppose[d] a given unity accessible to … an instantaneous, theoretical apprehension" (1988b, p. 78). Finally, the concepts I have adumbrated here suggest, much as Freud had suggested, that the best we can do is turn suffering or misery or the illusions of the ego into an interminable analysis. That analysis reveals our own complicity in and responsibility for what we find "out there," the dangers of ideals and hope, and the reality that *we* cannot and perhaps should not try to control or cure others.

Lacan elaborated on and changed his ideas over time. He maintained the three registers, of the Imaginary, the Symbolic and the Real. The latter refers to that which exceeds the Symbolic and Imaginary, to that which introduces, with the unconscious, contingency and instability into all our unities and certitudes, and to that which keeps Lacan from being a postmodernist à la Rorty or Braudrillard, i.e., not everything is dissolved in discourse. Lacan paid increasing attention to the Real and less to the Imaginary at the end of his career. His concept of *jouissance*—a kind of ecstasy in pain or intense pleasure from a repetitive effort or pleasure mixed with disgust took on a more prominent role in his theorizing as did the concept of the *sinthome*, basically a symptom which knots together who we are and is suffused with a *jouissance* thus making it difficult to give up. There were of course other concepts, but I chose the ones that seemed central to much of the scholarship undertaken by educators who tried to think about teaching and education through Lacanian theory.

But what were or are the implications of Lacanian theory for teaching and curriculum? I want to suggest three, although there are, of course, many more. The first is that treating the identity of the teacher or the curriculum as fixed and invulnerable to the subjectivities of the teacher and student renders life in the classroom as a strange masquerade or Kafkaesque exercise carried out in the name of whatever reality is deemed important for students to accommodate to or whatever goal is deemed important for students to achieve. For the teacher to take him or herself absolutely as the one who knows, as the one who is the teacher, rather than as the one who at different times occupies the position of teacher, is for the teacher to seal him or herself in an armor or costume that silences the teacher's subjectivity. For the curriculum to be treated as a fixed body, a carapace, totalized and transparent to itself, rather than as a living, contingent, and re-symbolizable response to our desires, fears, and dreams is to excise the teacher's and student's subjectivity. The end result, apparent today in the countless books touting sure-fire techniques for teaching, in the packaged curricular outcomes based on standards, and in programs of cultural literacy, is a vision of two machines transmitting, receiving, and returning information. If psychosis is a form of automaticity, that is experience fully stripped of the existential subjectivity that loosens our imprisonment in stimulus response circuits or in maddening compulsions, then the automatic behaviors current educational reforms depict as desirable are a form of psychosis.

The second implication is that we must accept our own complicity in the realities we discover in the classroom. This is not the same as the old saying that a student's failure means the teacher has not done his or her job. Rather, it is to suggest that we are responsible for the meanings we ascribe to our experiences and that those meanings, themselves, are shaped by our unconscious investments. Thus, the more we can articulate and analyze why we respond as we do without immediately placing the cause outside us in someone or something else or thinking in terms of cause and effect, the more we will be able to fully assume our own destiny as it unfolds in the classroom.

The third and perhaps most important implication is that there is no absolutely knowable essence of a human being. Our sexuality, our so-called inner being, our deepest emotions, our most heartfelt interests are themselves shaped by social determinants and over-determined by unconscious investments. Most of all they are shaped by and in language. There is no natural self to be expressed. No natural voice to be found. No transparent interests to be valorized. Such a view contradicts the urge among the psycho-pedagogues in the early twentieth century and their counter-parts in the 1960s and 70s to make the child's sexuality or interests or the child's inner life the content of the curriculum.

I think there is no question that Lacan's work revived the emancipatory project in psychoanalysis. In rendering the subject as the subject of the unconscious, in articulating the impossibility of a transparent language and of self-identical knowledge, and in revealing the illness of the ego, Lacan advanced an interminable analysis. But the writing was difficult and off-putting and seemed to provoke a good deal of aggression in the form of either competition or contempt. In part the dismissal of Lacan within teacher education can be attributed to his rejection of a therapeutic project that, for good or bad, teachers hold close.

The disavowal of the emancipatory project and of the radical questions and theorizing that Freud and then Lacan raised and performed has condemned teacher education to compulsively repeat the same cycle of recriminations, reform, and return. Although we teachers cannot renounce the therapeutic project, we can allow it to rub up against the emancipatory project. It was the therapeutic project that Lacan was gesturing toward in the quote that opens the above section on him. When he told the students at Vincennes in 1968 that they wanted a master and that they would have one, he was not suggesting that they should stop complaining and provide an alternative to what is—a kind of live in the solution not the problem—but rather that they should understand that the big Other to whom they were addressing their demands didn't know what it was doing either, was as castrated as they were. If they didn't know that, they would simply put another Master in its place. Of course, this is exactly what we continue to do in education. We condemn the old pedagogy or approaches to education as wrong and then look to new ones for the final solution.

While the influence of Lacan and Lacanian studies in the field of education has been slight, other than in curriculum studies, it did have a dramatic impact in the humanities and continues to influence humanities scholars.

Lacan Goes to School

The impact of Lacan's theories was immense—in the academy. It had less of an impact on psychoanalysis itself. Nathan Hale's two volume history of psychoanalysis in the United States goes up to 1985, and there is one sentence devoted to Lacan. There exist today two training institutes in the United States devoted to Lacanian analysis, the Lacanian School of Psychoanalysis in San Francisco, and *Après-Coup* in New York, although the latter's website has not been updated since 2007–8. There are Lacanian analysts, particularly in urban centers, but in general Lacanian psychoanalysis is not taught in training institutes, other than as an elective or part of a course. It is clearly alive in the university, however.

By the end of the 1970s and early 1980s psychoanalysis in America had been by and large repudiated by feminism and the gay liberation movement. The utopian psychoanalysis of Laing, Marcuse, and Brown had dissipated with the end of the war and the beginning of Reagan's great repression. When Lacan's theory arrived in the United States, generally in departments of literature, it not only captured the imagination of academics but it also opened a rift in feminism between those who followed Lacan and the French and American feminists influenced by him, such as Gallop, Grosz, Kristeva, and Rose, and those who championed a pre-theory feminism, such as Nancy Miller (on this division see Buhle, 1998, pp. 330–45). Eventually these divisions were passed over, and today undergraduate and graduate students in departments of literature, film, art history, cultural studies, women's studies, and language departments may have read excerpts from Lacan's oeuvre, or if not then articles by Kristeva or Žižek.

In the 1980s and 90s psychoanalysis also made inroads in anthropology and sociology (see in particular Heald and Deluz, 1994 for anthropology and Endleman, 1981 for sociology) but by 2000, psychoanalysis had lost some of the little foothold it had in those departments. In part this had to do with the on-going debates over identity and its formation, debates which came to be more focused on post-colonial theory, Deleuzian theory, and Foucauldian studies of governmentality, and in part it had to do with the growing concern and critique of the effects of neoliberalism and Bush era policies. Nevertheless in anthropology Henrietta Moore's work and James Weiner's essays have sustained the interest in psychoanalysis in that discipline (see for example, Moore, 2007 and Weiner, 1995). Sherry Ortner's work has also contributed to a psychoanalytic presence in socio/cultural work (see for example, Ortner, 2006). Unfortunately, however, their work has not made inroads into education.

Psychoanalysis, more generally understood, established itself in humanities departments, particularly in English departments, as a possible method of teaching reading and writing. In the 1980s courses in psychoanalytic interpretation proliferated. Terry Eagleton's (1983) *Literary Theory: An introduction* devoted one of its four chapters on literary criticism to psychoanalysis, and the focus was on Lacan, and secondarily Norman Holland, Harold Bloom, and Julia Kristeva. David Bleich's *Subjective Criticism* (1978), while published in the 1970s, was followed by other books offering a reader response theory that incorporated psychoanalysis.

In composition studies, Mark Bracher's (1999a) *The Writing Cure: Psychoanalysis, Composition and the Aims of Education* worked on the border of Lacanian psychoanalysis, English, and education. Bracher, a professor of English argued that "[o]nly a psychoanalytic pedagogy can successfully address [the psychic] dimension of social problems" (p. 192) because it "would allow students to confront the contingency of their identity and the ineluctability of their unconscious desires and gratifications at their own pace" (p. 6). Bracher's book was one of a few that appeared in the 1990s and 2000s trying to build bridges between Lacanian psychoanalysis and critical pedagogy. The title of his book, however, suggests its commitment to the therapeutic project of psychoanalysis.

Lad Tobin (1993, 2004), on the other hand, seemed less interested in curing students than in using writing and psychoanalysis as ways to explore what it means to write or teach writing. Tobin argued for an approach to working with writers and writing teachers that urged teachers to become aware of their unconscious reactions. He argued that teacher writing groups could serve to explore these reactions. Tobin also wrote about his own transferential issues in the classroom and how he handled the emotional messiness of teaching the personal narrative. In one essay he suggested that the writing teacher "play patient" (2004, p. 51). In other words Tobin encouraged the writing teacher to freely associate to the student's text. But he also wondered if teachers might not read the text as if they were listening to it with the free floating attention of an analyst and "rely on metaphorical rather than directive language" (2004, p. 54) when commenting on the text. Such responses would, he urged, provoke more and fuller writing. Tobin (1993) also cautioned us against holding onto ideals and standards that can mask aggression returned to us in the form of resistance in the classroom. More than most composition theorists and teachers of writing, he has seemed willing to allow the unconscious to interrupt, complicate, or simply burst the teacher's ego, the Imaginary dialectics of the writing classroom, and the endless demands for better writing.

Wendy Bishop (1993) another English professor also struggled with the question of whether or not teaching is therapy, and Robert Brooke (1987) has explored how transference works in the classroom. Dawn Skorczewski (2005) has narrated how the teacher's and student's unconscious can irrupt in the classroom, disturbing teacher and student. In particular Skorczewksi has examined the teacher's counter-transference in the classroom and "the teacher's embodied experiences and unconscious expressions of what it feels like to be the instructor in the writing class" (p. 4). In the 1980s *College English* and *College Composition and Communication* published several articles on psychoanalysis and writing and reading, and on transference in the English classroom. These articles appeared amidst a slew of books on the role of psychoanalysis in teaching writing, although the number of articles declined after 2000 (for articles see in particular Baumlin and Baumlin, 1989; Baumlin and Weaver, 2000; Davis, 1987; Jay, 1987; McGee, 1987; Murphy, 1989; Penley, 1986; Perelman, 1986; Samuels, 2003. For books see Alcorn, 1994, 2002; Berman, 1994, 2001; Fetterly, 1977; Kurzweil and Phillips, 1983).

Interesting about these articles and books written by professors of English and composition is that while they discuss education, there are few references to teacher educators or curriculum theorists. If there are, they tend to cite Paulo Freire, Henry

Giroux, and Peter McLaren—critical pedagogues. On the other hand, teacher educators and curriculum theorists who have written about psychoanalysis and teaching have often ignored these literary and composition scholars.

Also of note is the similarity between the issues these writers raise and those raised by psychoanalytically informed educators at the beginning of the twentieth century: the importance of transference, how imperative it is that teachers take note of their own counter-transference, the anxiety produced in classes when emotions are released into the air, how free association has a pedagogical role, and how much psychic relationships affect learning. The difference is, however, that Lacan's influence, particularly his linguistic focus, interrupted any take-for-granted unities and continuities of self, knowledge, identity, sexuality, or the unconscious.

Shoshana Felman

One essay that appeared in *Yale French Studies* in 1982 and then was collected that same year in an edited volume by Barbara Johnson entitled *The Pedagogical Imperative: Teaching as a Literary Genre* would profoundly influence curriculum theorists. The essay was entitled "Psychoanalysis and Education: Teaching Terminable and Interminable." Its author was Shoshana Felman. Felman was a professor in comparative literature and French at Yale University and had previously written about Lacan, but in this essay she would think about pedagogy by way of Lacan's return to Freud.

Felman (1997) begins her essay by quoting Socrates and Freud. Both, she reminds us, said that teaching was impossible. But if teaching is impossible, she asks, "What are we teachers doing?" (p. 18) By way of answering that question she states that teachers have misunderstood Socrates', Freud's, and, she adds, Lacan's claim that education is an impossible profession. Mistaking it to mean that we teachers have nothing to teach, educators have been satisfied with either a critique of education, or a call to give up authority and take the position of student, or the call that we should lift repressive structures to allow for the student to express him or herself. The problem Felman points out is that these calls fail to see the didactic function of the *utterances* as opposed to the content of the statements (p. 20). "They fail to see, in other words, the pedagogical situation—the pedagogical dynamic in which statements function not as simple truths but as performative speech acts" or "the way of teaching" (p. 20) as opposed to the what of teaching.

What does that mean? For Felman it means that teaching needs to take into account the unconscious not only as a force that continually interrupts the conscious communication between student and teacher, but also as the place from which words come and to which they speak. Recalling Lacan, Felman suggests that the communication we take for real in the classroom is really only part of the picture, and a minor part. Felman argues that students and teachers also speak from where they are not—from their unconscious. In other words they always mean more than they say and say more than they mean. Just as the analyst never knows who is speaking, from where or to whom, neither does the teacher know this when the student speaks or, for that matter, when the teacher him or herself speaks. Not only does the unconscious complicate any simple definition of learning but it also shapes the student's and the teachers' complicity in what they know and don't know, what they desire to know and what they desire not to know. And this unconscious dynamic is complicated by the transferential relationships that obtain in the classroom. The teacher, or the context, i.e. school and books, is positioned as the one who is presumed to know, and this kicks off the transference.

For Felman (1997) the pedagogical exists then in the relationship between the student and teacher. "Knowledge," she writes, "is not a substance but a structural dynamic; it is not contained by any individual but comes about out of mutual apprenticeship between two partially unconscious speeches that both say more than they know" (p. 29). The teacher then can do only three things: listen to the words as they emerge from the student, paying attention to the words as words before compressing them into a settled meaning and seeing where the student's resistance is located; listen to his or her own associations as they bubble up; and offer questions and interpretations that are not directives, not coming from a place of mastery, but are questions and interpretations that, perhaps metaphoric, create the condition such that the student continues to talk, to produce more meaning.

Such a pedagogy proceeds through "breakthroughs, leaps, discontinuities, regressions, and deferred action" (p. 23) and it puts into question the "traditional pedagogical belief in perfectability, the progressivist view of learning as a simple one-way road from ignorance to knowledge" (p. 23). We can see how unsettling such an approach is to the cognitive, outcomes based education of today.

In Felman's approach knowledge emerges as never identical to itself, never totalizable, never authoritative because it is always subject to the vicissitudes of the unconscious intermingled with one's own unconscious knowledge. It is thus impossible to teach as most teachers understand that activity—getting a student to know something. In fact, much knowledge and knowing are bound up with the desire not to know, and so the "pedagogical question becomes: "Where does it resist? Where does the text … resist interpretation? Where does what I see—and what I read [in others words, actions or demeanor as well as texts] resist my understanding?" (p. 27) As teachers, our questions and interpretations that emerge from our own listening to our unconscious and the places where our students' answers resist are all we have; all else is impossible.

Once we understand the impossibility of teaching, once we understand how the unconscious disrupts the illusions of mastery, ego, and conscious intention, we, as teachers and as students are freed to explore the meanings that do surface and that we can read as texts. We are free to create the conditions of knowledge. In some ways this is similar to what Lad Tobin was gesturing toward. The difference perhaps is that Tobin has a content—writing—and it is not clear, in Felman's essay, what the content is that she has in mind. In her later work (1992), however, on trauma, history itself and our present relationship to it constitute the content and teaching is rendered as testifying, making "something happen, and not just transmit[ing] a passive knowledge, pass[ing] on information that is preconceived" (p. 53). For Freud and Lacan the content was the suffering of the patient brought into contact with the unconscious of an analyst who had learned or metabolized an analytic. The patient speaks about his life. Tobin's students speak about their writing, which, given the personal nature of that writing, is another way of speaking about themselves. While we know they say much more than that and what they say comes from somewhere other than they may think, they like Freud's and Lacan's patients are explicitly talking about themselves. But what if one is teaching chemistry? Or teaching how to teach? These are questions Felman didn't address in her startling essay, although she suggests in her later essay that teaching, no matter what the content, must provoke a crisis in the classroom (1992, p. 53). She did, however, show us that "psychoanalysis has opened up unprecedented teaching possibilities, renewing both the questions and the practice of education" (1997, p. 18). In the 1980s and 90s, and early 2000s curriculum theorists were ready to think through that opening.

Curriculum Theory

> Curriculum theory is the interdisciplinary study of educational experience.
>
> (Pinar, 2004, p. 2)

In large measure the opening of the field of curriculum to a variety of approaches can be attributed to what has been referred to as the re-conceptualization of the curriculum field (Pinar, et al., 1995, pp. 211–39). The re-conceptualization of curriculum was in large part premised on the idea that curriculum consists of what individuals *make* of their education. In other words it is not what we are presented with in life or school, but what we make of this. We might say then that the re-conceptualization understood education and curriculum in terms of what Freud called an "after-education." For Freud after-education referred to the overcoming of resistance (1905b, p. 267), the way analysis helps us reconstruct the inhibitions, knots, lacunae, disturbances, and defenses that result from our early education. Such reconstruction unfolded in the transference (1916, p. 312), but its aim was to free the patient from crippling blocks and thus allow him or her to love and work and find more compelling meaning. Curriculum theory often argued for teaching as a kind of *via negativa*, that is as an exposure and stripping away of the psychic and social obstacles—unquestioned assumptions, conditioned responses, social biases, unconscious fears and desires, and blind emotional investments—that inhere in disciplinary knowledge but also that prevent students from engaging with disciplinary knowledge in order to more fully explore their lives.

Those curriculum theorists involved in the re-conceptualization of the field attempted to reclaim subjectivity at a moment when psychology and the sociology of education had turned curriculum and teaching into developmentally or politically appropriate strategies, had instrumentalized teaching, and had rendered subjectivity in terms of observed behaviors, cognitive schemas, or as epiphenomenal to structures of class. They often looked to the humanities and psychoanalysis to articulate that subjectivity and to illuminate educational experience. For over thirty years, now, a good many curriculum scholars have worked through psychoanalytic concepts to gain a better understanding of what happens in the classroom, schools, and in education, conceived in the broader sense.

I cannot possibly review all the psychoanalytically informed curricular work carried out by scholars in the United States, and I would add Canada, since Canadian work has been central to bringing psychoanalysis into the field of curriculum theory. I know personally most of the individual curricularists who work psychoanalytically, and most of them know one another. There are far too many articles and edited collections written by curriculum theorists that work with psychoanalytic theory for me to include them all. Among those scholars who have solo-authored psycho-analytically informed books and whose work has advanced the relationship between education and psychoanalysis are the following: Stephen Appel (1996, 1999), Wendy Atwell-Vesey (1998), Deborah Britzman (1998, 2003, 2006, 2009, 2010), Brian Casemore (2007), Daniel Cho (2009), Mary Doll (1995, 2000), Susan Edgerton (1996), Liz Ellsworth (1997, 2005), Madeleine Grumet (1988), jan jagodzinski (1996, 2004), Ursula Kelly (1997), Janet Miller (1990), Marla Morris (2001, 2008, 2009), Joanne Pagano (1990), William Pinar (1994, 2001, 2004, 2006b), Alice Pitt (2003), Paula Salvio (2007), Jonathan Silin (1995), Peter Taubman (2009), and Sharon Todd (1997, 2003). These scholars have relied on the work of British and American object relations theorists, Lacan and various Lacanian theorists, Jung and Jungian scholars, and, of course, Freud.

These curriculum scholars, as well as the many others who have written psycho-analytically informed essays and edited books, have kept alive a relationship between education and psychoanalysis. They continue to work with and through the radical otherness of the unconscious and sexuality. Their writing has created curricular con-ditions for teachers and students to acknowledge and re-symbolize the singularity of the unconscious without losing sight of its social determinants.

Unfortunately, while many curriculum theorists were willing to work through psychoanalytic theory, and, in the Winnicottian sense, "use" its concepts, teacher educators have seemed reluctant to discuss psychoanalysis at all. The goal of understanding educational experience, so central to curriculum theory and curriculum studies, was not necessarily shared by teacher educators who desired, hoped for, and pursued practical and dependable solutions to problems in the classroom. In the 1980s through today, teacher educators have not looked to psychoanalysis to understand their work.

Reviewing issues of *Harvard Educational Review*, *Educational Researcher*, *Teachers College Record*, and the *Journal of Teacher Education* between 1980 and 2009, I found only a handful of articles addressing psychoanalysis. Between 1980 and today, *The Review of Research in Education* had no articles on psychoanalysis and education. On the other hand the main journals in the field of curriculum: *Curriculum Inquiry*,

Journal of Curriculum Theorizing, Curriculum Studies and journals in educational foundations: *Educational Theory, The Journal of Philosophy of Education* had several articles.

What is it about teaching and teacher education that has made it so difficult for psychoanalytic theory, particularly its emancipatory project to find a home there? One answer is that as teaching became applied psychology, the hegemony of the learning sciences and the exile of psychoanalysis from psychology departments resulted in the silencing of psychoanalysis in our discussions of teaching.

Another possibility is that teacher education never experienced the re-conceptualization that the field of curriculum underwent in the 1970s. Its approaches, policies, and theories seemed to come from psychology, sociology, and the business world. Rarely did teacher educators turn to the humanities for ways to understand teaching. Perhaps as a result there have been few initiatives by teacher educators to introduce psychoanalytic theory as a way to think about teaching.

A third possibility is that at a moment when the national conversation on education seems breathless over scientific certainty and collapses teaching into strategies that are as dependable as medical protocols, teachers and teacher educators find the radical knowledge of and from the unconscious annoyingly troubling. It disturbs their belief in and desire for a method or set curriculum that will guarantee a particular outcome. That belief, that if we just do x, then y will result, captures the aspiration of so many educators today who wish to make teaching into a science. It is a belief, as we have seen, that is central to the therapeutic project. It is also a belief threatened by the radical knowledge of and from the unconscious, a knowledge that subverts attempts to predict and claim certainty of method. In teacher education, in educational policy, and in the conversation about teaching, the unconscious itself has been all but silenced. But as has always been the case it returns, often in painful ways.

6

CONCLUSION

Another History

> Psychoanalysis is an account of the meaning of life. ...
> Psychoanalytic knowledge is knowledge of poets, novelists,
> and playwrights, rendered more systematic and for this reason
> somewhat less subtle.
>
> (Alford, 2003, p. 50)

In my attempt to reconstruct the history of the relationship between education and psychoanalysis, I have sought to find within that history, the outlines of another one, one that is only in the process of emerging and that may point to a future different from the one promised by today's educational reformers. In reconstructing the history of that relationship, in exploring the disavowed knowledge within both psychoanalysis and education and its effects on their relationship, I combined a psychoanalytic approach with an historical one.

In analysis the patient or analysand begins by narrating what appears to be an obviously true narrative of a life, one in which are located the presumed causes for the felt confusion or stasis or suffering. Gradually the patient forms a different narrative of the past, one based on a shift in his or her understanding of the present, an understanding that arrives through an analysis of symptoms, dreams, slips, associations, and bungled actions as these unfold within the transference. And finally the patient comes, however modestly, to adopt an interminable analysis, to acknowledge his or her own complicity in the reality found, and to transform misery and compulsions into existential meaning and some freedom.

In much the same way, I have sought to analyze the symptoms, dreams, and failures that haunt education. That analysis of the history of the relationship between psychoanalysis and education has emerged in the presence of and within my own transferential relationships to the figures who represent and constitute that history. The resulting shift in perspective offers the outlines of a shadow history, one not yet formed and barely glimpsed, as well as a possible future for the relationship, one that might provide alternatives to how we think about education and teaching. "Every historical rupture," Slavoj Žižek (1989) writes, "every advent of a new master signifier, changes retroactively the meaning of all tradition, restructures the narration of the past, makes it readable in another new way" (p. 56). As the history of the relationship between psychoanalysis and education came to emerge, I increasingly found within that history, within the repetition compulsions, within the dreams that lay scattered, and within the failures that littered the history, the suggestion of not only what could have been but more important the potential for what might yet be.

What became most clear, as I began to reconstruct the history was that the radical knowledge of and from the unconscious constituted the structural impossibility of education and when that knowledge was ignored it troubled the dreams of education and returned as a repetition compulsion. In "Remembering, repeating and working-through" Freud (1914) argued that the compulsion to repeat acts as a defense against remembering, and that the form of repetition is wrested from the past. "[A] thing which has not been understood," he wrote elsewhere, "inevitably reappears; like an unlaid ghost, it cannot rest until the mystery has been solved and the spell broken" (Freud, 1909, p. 122). What keeps reappearing in our educational reform efforts is the radical otherness of the unconscious.

In the face of countless daily disappointments, losses, and failures, as well as pleasures and successes, teachers and educators, confronted by the disruptions, resistances, and mysterious movements of an unconscious as it appears in classrooms, have fled from the knowledge from and of the unconscious or tried to domesticate it or romanticize it, and in doing so, have spun round and round dreaming of some solution that will ensure success, reversing course when the solutions didn't produce the promised results, and always insisting that they not only can predict and ensure educational outcomes but also are solely responsible for them. As Richard Rothstein documents in *The Way We Were? The Myths and Realities of America's Student Achievement* (1998), complaints about education and assumptions that there was some golden period in the past have circulated for a hundred years. Christopher Lucas, in *Teacher Education in America: Reform Agendas for the Twenty-first Century* (1999), makes the same point about teacher education, as he traces the laments over how poorly trained our teachers have been, laments that, no matter when they have been uttered, always portray some better but non-existent time in the past. All the reform efforts whose success has been measured by students' achievement of something: test scores, reduction in bias, revolution, higher states of consciousness, or a better way of being, all the actions that constitute the reform efforts seem to wind up in further disappointments.

"All of these actions," Laplanche and Pontalis (1973) write in *The Language of Psychoanalysis* place us "in distressing situations thereby repeating an old experience," but we do "not recall the prototype; on the contrary [we have] the strong impression that the situation is fully determined by circumstances of the moment" (p. 78). This would certainly seem to capture the plight of a good many teachers, and teacher educators, who seem forever to be stuck in cycles of crisis, reform, and more blame and who keep pursuing ways to cure, control, and predict. But because the unconscious cannot be so easily silenced, prediction and control crumble. Whether it is the eruption of the teacher's unconscious— recall Ashton-Warner's experience in Colorado and my own in an alternative school, or the unruliness of the student's unconscious—consider all those students who fell passive in the face of Bernfeld's reforms or who don't respond to the guaranteed teaching methods of a Doug Lemov (2010), the disavowal of knowledge of and from the unconscious keeps us spinning in cycles of reform, lurching between versions of the therapeutic and emancipatory projects, but almost always judging the value of our actions according to their success in attaining some pre-ordained end.

Even when the knowledge of and from the unconscious has seemed to be central to approaches to teaching, as in the work of the early psychoanalytically influenced progressive educators or the radical educators of the late 1960s and early 1970s, it has been treated as a given, as self-transparent, and as natural. Inherent to the radical education projects at the beginning of the century and in the 1960s and 70s was the belief in the fundamental potential goodness of the unconscious and sexuality. What we let out, while it might be disturbing, was healthy. Repressed desires, feelings, polymorphous sexuality—their very airing was meant to transform us and transform society. We confused Freud's radical unconscious with Rousseau's noble savage and put it in the service of Putnam's higher power. The results we know.

Also central to the project of psychoanalytically influenced early progressives and radical educators in the 1960s and 70s was the belief in the importance of the child's desires. Radical educators and early progressive educators who were influenced by Freudian psychoanalysis and who shared several aspects of the emancipatory project defined learning in terms of releasing the students' desires and interests. These educators believed we learn only what we want to learn, and that student interests are self-transparent. They believed that the child, as Adam Phillips (2006) has written "can be taught only what he wants to know" (p. 146). "[P]eople can learn but they can't be taught, or, at least they can't be taught anything of real significance. And that is partly because no one can ever know beforehand ... exactly what is of personal significance" (Phillips, 1998, p. 68). Phillips' claims capture those we have heard from educators such as A.S. Neill, Sylvia Ashton-Warner and Floyd Dell. The psycho-pedagogues in the early twentieth century and the radical educators in the 1960s and 70s seemed wedded to the idea that you teach children what they want to learn and follow where their desires lead, acting as a resource on the journey. In such a view all education is an "after-education;" we can never control what a student really learns. The implication is that one should teach to and about the students' interests and accept the fact that what students find important will change over time. These claims, however, constitute part of the very dynamic that traps us and keeps us spinning in circles of educational reform.

Phillips' claim that "[t]he child can be taught only what he wants to know" is not unlike Freud's theorization of the child's sexual theories. Until the child is ready to give them up, no amount of enlightening will take hold. But what if the child doesn't know what he or she wants to know? What if the child's needs or desires are not available in any transparent way? What, in fact, if they can't be? Please understand I am not suggesting anyone else knows them either. I am suggesting that they are radically unknown, although not without potential answers. In other words, what if we assume that the child's questions are finally unconscious, that any interest or desire expressed is always metonymic or synecdochic? Responding to such desires as if they were transparent would in fact mislead, mis-educate, just as taking the patient's stated desires or meanings as truth would prove problematic.

Phillips' other claim that "people can learn but they can't be taught, or, at least they can't be taught anything of real significance ... because no one can ever know beforehand ... exactly what is of personal significance" (1998, p. 68) also echoes the view of a good many radical educators. Recall Carl Rogers' open classroom and his comment that he had lost interest in teaching (Kirschenbaum, 1979, p. 208), Maslow's letting the students drift into conversation as he left the room, the interest in T-groups' implications for pedagogy, the laissez-faire approach at Summerhill. But for all its openness, and here I'll let Phillips' statement stand in for the various educational experiments, his claim slides over just how profoundly unsettling the unconscious is. That we can only say we learned something in retrospect seems obvious. But do we only learn what is of significance to us or does what we have learned become significant or insignificant after the fact?

If Phillips is right and we only learn what is significant to us or what will have been significant, then we would be wise to follow A.S. Neill and Carl Rogers. We will wait and see what draws the students' attention and follow up on it, sup-plementing or not as the case may be, but pulled along behind or alongside the student's desire. But if the unconscious is a thinking that occurs elsewhere, if it works in horrifyingly alien ways, then what is of most significance to us may be what we most resist and what appears least significant may be what we have the greatest trouble admitting we want. I never thought math was significant and I kept it at arm's distance, but I would suggest that it held the greatest significance to me, a significance reflective of an anesthetized psychic relationship to numbers, to that which was terrifyingly fixed in their definitions. Had I understood that in fact numbers could be ambiguous, fluid, flexible, playful, and slippery I suspect my relationship with them might have been quite different. And such associations take me, of course, to my own familial positioning as well as to the alterity of sexuality. But these have no room, in the seemingly radical but in fact normalizing claims of Phillips or the practices of Rogers and Neill.

If the potential monstrousness of the unconscious has at times been romanticized in the service of applying psychoanalysis in the classroom, as it perhaps was by early progressives and later radical educators, it has simply been ignored or domesticated by those educators overly wedded to the therapeutic project. We have seen, for example, how the mental hygiene movement appropriated knowledge of and from the unconscious, applying it to its endeavor to achieve curative ends for students and the nation. Even when the goals of teaching and teaching itself are defined in the most limited ways, for example as higher test scores and scripts for teachers, as they are today, the unruliness of the unconscious subverts even these operationalized and narrow ends and practices.

Furthermore, in versions of both the emancipatory and the therapeutic projects, the student is the focus of intervention or of refraining from intervention. In either case the inner life of the teacher drains out. In the therapeutic project it collapses into best practices or the most expeditious means to an end or an ideal goal to which the student is meant to be led. In the particular versions of the emancipatory project we have looked at, the teacher's inner life is supplanted by the desires of the child. Teachers may be asked to attend to the students, or urged to face themselves, but only in the interest of helping the student. The self-evacuation that teachers subject themselves to as they sacrifice for the kids reproduces the 1950s middle class, stay-at-home mom who was urged to give up everything for her kid in her child-centered world. We know what happened to those moms (Salvio, 2007), and we know what happens to teachers. Such self-sacrifice, paradoxically, may be driving them out of teaching if not mad.

Perhaps more than anything, what has kept teacher educators and the conversation on teaching from facing the disruptive knowledge of and from the unconscious is the hope that they will find a solution to the enigmas of learning and teaching, a cure for ignorance or alienation or oppression. As Paula Salvio (1999) wrote in "Reading beyond Narratives of Cure in Curriculum Studies,"

> It is the trope of our times to locate the question of education in the realm of the *cure*. Educational discourses are becoming more and more wrought with the metaphors of disease, symptoms, and recovery. ... Narratives of cure also invoke a cultural desire for an imaginary 'ending' to the problems we face as educators. (p. 185).

The approach Salvio gestures toward rejects notions of cure and hope. Salvio argues that "by clinging to the fantasy that we can indeed cure our students of ignorance, we keep from our conscious awareness as teachers our own frailties, fears and anxieties about our competencies, intelligence, and emotional stability" (p. 187). I would add that the desire to cure and the need for hope, both so much a part of the therapeutic project, keep us from facing the terror of our own mortality which comes to us each second, if we give ourselves over to the shocking contingency of the moment. It is fear that freezes us and makes us want to freeze reality such that it can be measured, and sectioned into right and wrong answers, curriculum designs, or final solutions. But it is not only the fear of contingency that arouses the desire to cure and control. It is not just the fear of our mortality or that we won't have what we desire or have what we don't want that makes us cling today to science as offering hope for a good or better outcome. It is a much greater terror. It is the terror that the very kernel of our being, the inner real "me," is in fact not mine at all, that evokes our desire to control and cure. It is the fear that the painful reality that greets us may in fact be an answer to our own desires and questions. It is the terror that the "I" we hear in our innermost thoughts and the "me" of our conversations may consist of fossilized answers to what we imagined were others' desires. It is the fear that the very way we make love or engage in sex is gnarled and suffused with fantasies, old aches, anesthetized patches, burning questions, and irredeemable losses. This terror at the knowledge of and from the unconscious can provoke the defensive rush to cure or control others. Hope defends against such terror because it offers an undisturbed tomorrow.

In his only televised appearance, later published as *Television*, Jacques Lacan (1990) said, "I just want you to know that more than once I've seen hope—what they call bright new tomorrows—drive people … to kill themselves" (p. 43). What might it mean to teach or live without hope?

To teach without hope, to teach without focusing on outcomes, whether these be social revolution, the reduction in prejudice, or learning square roots, to teach without trying to cure is to shift our attention to the palpably invisible, to engage in a very delicate empiricism that attends to the minor tremors, and the fleeting sensations that hover around or strike the corners of consciousness. To teach in the face of education's impossibility means wading into the messiness of our being and life in the classroom and accepting our flawed humanity, and our ruptured existence. It means once again re-thinking, perhaps in light of figures such as Ashton-Warner or Aichorn or George Green the place of love in the classroom. It might mean thinking back through the history of the relationship between education and psychoanalysis so we might be startled by as well as educated by the experiments of those who thought psychoanalytically about education. By relinquishing the focus on the outcome, on the hope for its achievement, and by being present to the alterity of the unconscious, and the questions it provokes, the teacher can make possible the possibilities for the students' learning as a side effect of study, of conversation, of questioning.

If we do not focus on outcomes or assume our efforts are for a guaranteed end, we might instead focus on the unique singularity constituted by a radically other unconscious. Rather than think in terms of the fixed identities of students, of their personalities, we might, in opening as much as possible to the unconscious, try to fathom the way each of us responds to the enigmas of our existence. And rather than only allow for the free associations between words, students, thoughts, and affective states, we would always also be in dialogue with the empirical reality of life in the classroom as it is sifted through the disciplines we teach. Those educators, today almost solely curriculum theorists, who have faced the radical knowledge of and from the unconscious, embrace modest approaches to education and its relationship with psychoanalysis. To create the conditions such that an interminable analysis, an interminable questioning, one filtered through the sieve of the disciplines, is offered, is made possible, seems an aspiration that emerges from the reconstructed history of that relationship. Teaching is not about unleashing the unconscious—it is always unleashed—or freeing desires—they are always mobile. Rather teaching becomes the creation of conditions for re-symbolizing and re-constructing alternative futures that lie in scattered looks, ideas, feelings, sensations, words, gestures but have not yet come into being. Disciplinary knowledge, institutional knowledge, the arts, all these may offer forms and rhetorical structures for this re-symbolization. It is the teacher's duty to create the conditions for such re-symbolization: the conversations, the experiences, the materials. The teacher must know as much as possible about these, and fight to provide as many resources as possible, but once provided, the teacher then attunes to the unpredictable and uncontrollable swarm of feelings, responses, looks, and words that emerge.

I began this book with a quote from Bruno Bettelheim, who said, in 1969, that the relationship between education and psychoanalysis was neurotic. My effort has been to re-construct that relationship. In exploring the disavowals, splits, and repressions that constituted it, in trying to listen for the slips, examine the dreams, and tolerate the failures as the relationship unfolded, I have tried to discover another future within that past, one that might still be possible. In psychoanalyzing the relationship, I tried as much as possible to listen to my own unconscious as it rumbled and disturbed my attempts to control so much material and package it.

Ending this work, I couldn't help but be reminded of other terminations: terminations of analysis and of classes. What constitutes the end of an education? How does one end an analysis or a book or a class? These are not unrelated questions. It is easy to let the buzzer and the word count dictate the end to the class and book, but the end of analysis, as Freud (1937b) knew, is harder to ascertain. In all three cases talking can go on forever, and perhaps in all three cases an analysis is never ended; it is only interrupted to be taken up somewhere else.

BIBLIOGRAPHY

Abraham, N., & Torok, M. (1994). *The shell and the kernel*, vol. I. Edited and translated by Nicholas T. Rand. Chicago, IL: University of Chicago Press.

Aichhorn, A. (1939 [1925]). *Wayward youth*. NY: Viking Press.

Alcorn, M. (1994). *Narcissism and the literary libido: Rhetoric, text and subjectivity*. NY: New York University Press.

Alcorn, M.(2002). *Changing the subject in the English class: Discourse constructions of desire*. Carbondale, IL: Southern Illinios University Press.

Alford, C. Fred (2003). Psychoanalysis as philosophy, psychoanalysis as world view. *Psychoanalytic Knowledge*, eds. Man Cheung Chung and Colin Feltman. NY: Palgrave Press.

Alper, T. G. (1980). Psychology in New England: A retrospective look—A woman's point of view. *Journal of the History of the Behavioral Sciences, 16* (3), 220–24.

Anderson, S. (1983 [1919]). *Winesburg, Ohio*. NY: Penguin.

Appel, S. (1996). *Positioning subjects: Psychoanalysis and critical educational studies*. Wesport, CT: Bergin and Garvey.

Appel, S. (ed.). (1999). *Psychoanalysis and pedagogy*. Westport, CT: Bergin and Garvey.

Ashton-Warner, S. (1986 [1963]). *Teacher*. NY: Touchstone Books.

Atwell-Vesey, W. (1998). *Nourishing words*. Albany, NY: SUNY Press.

Auden, W. H. (1940). "In Memory of Sigmund Freud." www.poets.org/viewmedia.php/prmMID/15543.

Autio, T. (2006). *Subjectivity, curriculum and society: Between and beyond German didaktik and Anglo-American curriculum studies*. Mahway, NJ: Lawrence Erlbaum.

Avrich, P. (1980). *The modern school movement*. Princeton, NJ: Princeton University Press.

Ayers, B. (2003). *On the side of the child: Summerhill revisited*. NY: Teachers College Press.

Barford, D. (2002). *The ship of thought: Essays on psychoanalysis and learning*. London: Karnac Books.

Baumlin, J. S., & Baumlin, T. F. (1989). Psyche/logos: Mapping the terrains of mind and rhetoric. *College English, 51*, 245–61.

Baumlin, J. S., & Weaver, M. (2000). "Teaching, classroom authority, and the psychology of transference." *The Journal of General Education, 49*(2), 75–87.

Belenky, M., Clinchy, B., Goldberger, N., & Tarule, J. (1986). *Women's ways of knowing: The development of self, voice, and mind*. NY: Basic Books.

Bender, T. (1987). *New York intellect: A history of intellectual life in New York City, from 1750 to the beginning of our own time*. Baltimore, MD: The Johns Hopkins University Press.

Bender, T., & Schorske, C. (1997). *American academic culture: Fifty years, four disciplines.* Princeton, NJ: Princeton University Press.

Benjamin, L. T. (2005). A history of clinical psychology as a profession in America (and a glimpse at its future). *Annual Review of Clinical Psychology,* 1, 1–30.

Benjamin, W. (1969). *Illuminations.* Edited by Hannah Arendt. Translated by Harry Zohn. NY: Shocken Books.

Berliner, D., & Calfee, R. (eds.). (1996). *Handbook of educational psychology.* NY: Macmillan.

Berman, J. (1994). *Diaries of an English professor: Pain and growth in the classroom.* Amherst, MA: University of Massachusetts Press.

Berman, J. (2001). *Risky writing: Self-disclosure and self-transformation in the classroom.* Amherst, MA: University of Massachusetts Press.

Bernfeld, S. (1973 [1925]). *Sisyphus or the limits of education.* Translated by Fredric Lilge. Berkeley, CA: University of California Press.

Bersani, L. (1986). *The Freudian body: Psychoanalysis and art.* NY: Columbia University Press.

Bestor, A. (1953). *Educational wastelands: The retreat from learning in our schools.* Urbana, IL: University of Illinois Press.

Bettelheim, B. (1969). Psychoanalysis and education. *The School Review,* 77(2), 73–86.

Bettelheim, B., & Janowitz, M. (1950). *Dynamics of prejudice: A psychological and sociological study of veterans.* NY: Harper and Brothers.

Bion, W. (1993 [1970]). *Attention and interpretation.* London: Maresfield Library.

Bishop, W. (1993). Writing is/and therapy? Raising questions about writing classrooms and writing program administration. *Journal of Advanced Composition,* 13(2), 503–16.

Bleich, D. (1978). *Subjective criticism.* Baltimore, MD: Johns Hopkins University Press.

Bleich, D. (1998). *Know and tell: A writing pedagogy of disclosure, genre and membership.* Portsmouth, NH: Boynton/Cook.

Bloom, A. (1987). *The closing of the American mind: How higher education has failed democracy and impoverished the souls of today's students.* NY: Simon & Schuster.

Bobbitt, C. (1934). Questionable recommendations of the commission on the social studies. *School and Society,* 40, 201–8.

Bode, B. (1934). Editorial comment. *The Phi Delta Kappan,* 17, 1, 7.

Bode, B. (1931). Education at the crossroads. *Progressive Education.* 8(7), 543–49.

Bode, B. (1938). *Progressive education at the crossroads.* New York, NY: Newsom & Company.

Bok, D. (2003). *Universities in the marketplace: The commercialization of higher education.* Princeton, NJ: Princeton University Press.

Boldt, G., & Salvio, P. (eds.) (2006). *Love's return: Psychoanalytic essays on childhood, teaching and learning.* NY: Routledge.

Bordwell, D., & Carroll, N. (eds.) (1996). *Post-theory: Reconstructing film studies.* Madison, WI: University of Wisconsin Press.

Bornstein, R. F. (1988). Psychoanalysis in the undergraduate curriculum: The treatment of psychoanalytic theory in abnormal psychology texts. *Journal of Psychoanalytic Psychology,* 15(1), 83–93.

Bornstein, R. F. (2001).The impending death of psychoanalysis. *Psychoanalytic Psychology,* 18(1), 3–20.

Bowers, C. A. (1967). The ideologies of progressive education. *History of Education Quarterly,* 7(4), 452–73.

Bowers, C. A. (1987). *The promise of theory: Education and the politics of cultural change.* NY: Teachers College Press.

Boyd, W. (1931). Begin with the teacher. *Progressive Education,* 3(3), 235–37.

Bracher, M. (1999a). *The writing cure: Psychoanalysis, composition, and the aims of education.* Carbondale, IL: Southern Illinois University Press.

Bracher, M. (1999b). Psychoanalysis and education. *Journal for the Psychoanalysis of Culture and Society,* 4(2), 176–211.

Braddock, L., & Lacewing, M. (eds.) (2007). *The academic face of psychoanalysis: Papers in philosophy, the humanities and the British clinical tradition.* NY: Routledge.

Bransford, J., Darling-Hammond, L., & LePage, P. (2005). Introduction. *Preparing teachers to teach for a changing world: What teachers should learn and be able to do,* eds. Linda Darling-Hammond and John Bransford, 1–40. San Francisco: Jossey Bass.

Bremer, J., & von Moschzisker, M. (1971). *The school without walls: Philadelphia's Parkway Program.* NY: Hold, Rinehart and Winston.

Britzman, D. (1998). *Lost objects, contested objects: Toward a psychoanalytic inquiry of learning.* Albany, NY: State University of New York Press.

Britzman, D. (2003). *After-education: Anna Freud, Melanie Klein, and psychoanalytic histories of learning.* Albany, NY: State University of New York Press.

Britzman, D. (2006). *Novel education: Psychoanalytic studies of learning and not learning.* NY: Peter Lang Press.

Britzman, D. (2009). *The very thought of education: Psychoanalysis and the impossible professions.* Albany, NY: State University of New York Press.

Britzman, D. (2010). *Freud and education.* NY: Routledge Press.

Brook, R. (1987). Lacan, transference, and written instruction. *College English, 49*(6), 679–82.

Brown. N. O. (1970 [1959]). *Life against death: The psychoanalytic meaning of history.* Middletown, CT: Wesleyan University Press.

Bruner, J. (1996). *The culture of education.* Cambridge, MA: Harvard University Press.

Buhle, M. J. (1998). *Feminism and its discontents: A century of struggle with psychoanalysis.* Cambridge, MA: Harvard University Press.

Burgess, E. W. (1939). The influence of Sigmund Freud upon sociology in the United States. *The American Journal of Sociology, 45*(3), 356–74.

Burnham, J. C. (1973). The progressive era revolution in American attitudes toward sex. *The Journal of American History, 59*(4), 885–908.

Callahan, R. (1962). *Education and the cult of efficiency: A study of social forces that have shaped the administration of public schools.* Chicago, IL: University of Chicago Press.

Carroll, H. A. (1964). *Mental hygiene: The dynamics of adjustment,* 4th edition. Englewood Cliffs, NJ: Prentice Hall.

Casemore, B. (1997). *The autobiographical demand of place: Curriculum inquiry in the American south.* NY: Peter Lang.

Cheung, M., & Feltman, C. (eds.) (2003). *Psychoanalytic knowledge.* NY: Palgrave.

Cho, D. K. (2006). Thanatos and civilization: Lacan, Marcuse, and the death drive. *Policy Futures in Education, 4*(1), 18–30.

Cho, D. K. (2009). *Psychopedagogy.* NY: Palgrave Macmillan.

Chodorow, N. (1978). *The reproduction of mothering: Psychoanalysis and the sociology of gender.* Berkeley, CA: University of California Press.

Church, R. (1971). Educational psychology and social reform in the progressive era. *History of Education Quarterly, 11*(4), 390–405.

Cochran-Smith, M., & Fries, M. K. (2005). Researching teacher education in changing times: Politics and paradigms. *Studying Teacher Education: The Report of the AERA Panel on Research and Teacher Education,* 69–110. Mahwah, NJ: Lawrence Erlbaum.

Cohen, P. (2007). Freud is widely taught at universities, except in psychology departments. *New York Times,* November 25. Week in Review. http://www.nytimes.com/2007/11/25/weekinreview/25cohen.html?pagewanted

Cohen, S. (1979). In the name of the prevention of neurosis: The search for a psychoanalytic pedagogy in Europe, 1905–38. *Regulated children/liberated children: Education in psychohistorical perspective,* ed. Barbara Finkelstein 184–219. NY: Psychohistory Press.

Cohen, S. (1983). The mental hygiene movement, the development of personality and the school: The medicalization of American education. *History of Education Quarterly, 1*(2), 123–49.

Cohler, B. (1989). Psychoanalysis and education: Motive, meaning, and self. *Learning and education: Psychoanalytic perspectives*, eds. Kay Field, Bertram Cohler, & Glorye Wool. Madison, CT: International Universities Press, Inc

Cooke, B. (2007). The Kurt Lewin–Goodwin Watson FBI/CIA files: A 60th anniversary there-and-then of the here-and-now. *Human Relations*, March, 60, 435–62,

Coriat, I. H. (1926). The psycho-analytic approach to education. *Progressive Education, 3*(1), 19–25.

Counts, G. (1932a). Dare progressive education be progressive? *Progressive Education*, 1, 257–63.

Counts, G. (1932b). *Dare the schools build a new social order?* New York, NY: John Day Company.

Cremin, Lawrence. (1988). *American education: The metropolitan experience 1876–1980*. NY: Harper and Row.

Cuban, L. (1993). *How teachers taught: Constancy and change in American classrooms 1880–1990*. NY: Teachers College Press.

Culley, M., & Portuges, C. (eds.), (1985). *Gendered subjects: The dynamics of feminist teaching*. Boston, MA: Routledge & Kegan Paul.

Cushman, P. (1995). *Constructing the Self, constructing America: A cultural history of psychotherapy*. NY: Perseus Press.

Danto, E. (2005). *Freud's free clinics: Psychoanalysis and social justice, 1918–1938*. NY: Columbia University Press.

Danziger, K. (1990). *Constructing the subject: Historical origins of psychological research*. Cambridge, UK: Cambridge University Press.

Danziger, K. (1996). The practice of psychological discourse. *Historical dimensions of psychological discourse*, eds. C. F. Graumann, & K. Gergen, 17–35. Cambridge, UK: Cambridge University Press.

Danziger, K. (1997). *Naming the mind: How psychology found its language*. London: Sage Publications.

Darling-Hammond, L., & Bransford, J. (2005). *Preparing teachers to teach for a changing world: What teachers should learn and be able to do*. San Francisco, CA: Jossey Bass

Davis, R. C. (1987). Pedagogy, Lacan, and the Freudian subject. *College English 49*(7), 749–55.

de Forest, J. (2006). New York City's failed teacher selection project: Political reality trumps educational research, 1947–53. *Teachers College Record, 108*(4), 726–47.

de Forest, J. (2007). Antecedents of dispositions: Testing: Lessons from the history of the good teacher. *Journal of Educational Controversy*. http://www.wce.wwu.edu/Resources/CEP/eJournal/v002n002/a007.shtml

Dell, F. (1932). Adolescent education. *Progressive Education, 9*(7), 473–81.

Dennison, G. (1969). *The lives of children*. NY: Random House.

Detre, K. C., Thomas-Frank, T., Refsnes-Kniazzeh, C., Robinson, M. C., Rubin, J. A., & Ulman, E. (1983). Roots of art therapy: Margaret Naumburg (1890–1983) and Florence Cane (1882–1952)—A family portrait. *American Journal of Art Therapy*, 113, 114–16.

Dewey, J. (1928). Progressive education and science. *The later works of John Dewey 1927–1928*, vol. 3, ed. Jo Ann Boydston, 257–75. Carbondale, IL: Southern Illinois University Press.

Dinnerstein, D. (1977). *The mermaid and the minotaur: Sexual arrangements and human malaise*. NY: Harper Colophon Books.

Doll, M. (1995). *To the lighthouse and back: Writings on teaching and living*. NY: Peter Lang.

Doll, M. (2000). *Like letters in running water: A mythopoetics of curriculum*. Mahwah, NJ: Lawrence Erlbaum.

Dollard, J., Doob, L., Miller, N. E., Mowrer, O. H., & Sears, R. R (1939). *Frustration and aggression*. New Haven, CT: Yale University Press.

Douglas, A. (1995). *Terrible honesty: Mongrel Manhattan in the 1920s*. New York, NY: Farrar, Strauss & Giroux.

Drayer, A. (1963). *Problems and methods in high school teaching.* Boston, MA: Heath.

Dufresne T. (2004). Freud is dead. *Los Angeles Times.* February 18. http://articles.latimes. com/2004/feb/18/opinion/oe-dufresne18, retrieved June 8, 2010.

Eagleton, T. (1983). *Literary theory: An introduction.* Minneapolis, MN: University of Minnesota Press.

Edgerton, S. (1996). *Translating the curriculum: Multiculturalism into cultural studies.* NY: Routledge Press.

Edmundson, M. (2007). *The death of Sigmund Freud: The legacy of his last days.* NY: Bloomsbury.

Eigen, M. (1993). The area of faith in Winnicott, Lacan and Bion. In M. Eigen *The Electrified Tightrope,* 109–38. London: Jason Aronson, Inc.

Elkind, D. (1985). Child development research. *A century of psychology as a science,* eds. Sigmund Koch & David E. Leary, 472–88. NY: McGraw-Hill Book Company.

Ellenberger, H. F. (1970). *The discovery of the unconscious: The history and evolution of dynamic psychiatry.* NY: Basic Books.

Ellsworth, E. (1997). *Teaching positions: Difference, pedagogy, and the power of address.* NY: Teachers College Press.

Ellsworth, E. (2005). *Places of learning: Media, architecture, pedagogy.* NY: Routledge.

Elster, J. (1987). *Sour grapes: Studies in the subversion of rationality.* Cambridge, UK: Cambridge University Press.

Emerson, G. (1985). *Some American men.* NY: Simon & Schuster.

Endleman, R. (1981). *Psyche and society: Explorations in psychoanalytic sociology.* New York, NY: Columbia University Press.

Ensor, B. (1926). The new education in Europe. *Progressive Education, 3,* Jan–March, 222–29.

Eysenck, H. (1952). The effects of psychotherapy: An evaluation. *Journal of Consulting Clinical Psychology, 6,* 319–24.

Farber, J. (1969). *The student as nigger and other stories.* NY: Contact Books.

Farber, S., & Green, M. (1993). *Hollywood on the couch: A candid look at the overheated love affair between psychiatrists and moviemakers.* NY: William Morrow & Co.

Federn, E. (1967). How Freudian are the Freudians? Some remarks to an unpublished letter. *Journal of Behavioral Sciences 3*(3), 269–81.

Felman, S. (1992). *Testimony: Crisis of witnessing, psychoanalysis, and history.* NY: Routledge.

Felman, S. (1997 [1982]). Psychoanalysis and education: Teaching terminable and interminable. *Learning desire: Perspectives on pedagogy, culture and the unsaid,* ed. Sharon Todd, 19–34. NY: Routledge.

Ferenczi, S. (1949a [1908]). Psycho-analysis and education. *The International Journal of Psycho-analysis, 30,* 220–24.

Ferenczi, S. (1949b [1932]). Confusion of tongues between the adult and the child (The language of tenderness and passion). *The International Journal of Psychoanalysis, 30,* 225–30.

Fetterly, J. (1977). *The resisting reader: A feminist approach to American fiction.* Bloomington, IN: Indiana University Press.

Feuer, L. (1960). Standpoints of Dewey and Freud: A contrast and analysis. *Journal of Individual Psychology, 16*(2), 119–36.

Field, K., Cohler, B., & Wood, G. (eds.). (1989). *Learning and education: Psychoanalytic perspectives.* Madison, CT: International Universities Press. (Emotions and Behaviour Monograph Series of the Chicago Institute for Psychoanalysis, Monograph No. 6.)

Fine, B. (1947). *Our children are cheated: The crisis in American education.* NY: Henry Hold and Co.

Fink, B. (1995). *The Lacanian subject: Between language and jouissance.* Princeton, NJ: Princeton University Press.

Fink, B. (1997). *A Clinical introduction to Lacanian theory and technique.* Cambridge, MA: Harvard University Press.

Finkelstein, B. (ed.). (1979). *Regulated children/liberated children: Education in psychohistorical perspective.* NY: Psychohistory Press.

Flax, J. (1990). *Thinking fragments: Psychoanalysis, feminism, and postmodernism in the contemporary west.* Berkeley, CA: University of California Press.

Flesch, R. (1955). *Why Johnny can't read.* NY: Harper and Row.

Foote, D. (2008). *Relentless pursuit: A year in the trenches with Teach for America.* NY: Vintage Books.

Foucault, M. (1978). *The history of sexuality: An introduction.* NY: Random House.

Fraher, A. L. (2004). *A history of group study and psychodynamic organizations.* NY: Free Association.

Frank, L. K. (1948). *Society as the patient: Essays on culture and personality.* NY: Kennikat Press.

Frank, L. K. (1951). *Nature and human nature.* Rutgers, NJ: Rutgers University Press.

Frank, L. K. (1955). Summary. In *Annals of the New York Academy of Sciences, 63*(3), 429–32.

Frank, L. K. (1956). *Your adolescent at home and in school.* NY: Viking Press.

Freud, A. (1935). *Psycho-analysis for teachers and parents.* Translated by Barbara Low. NY: W. W. Norton & Co.

Freud, S. (1995 [1925]). *The standard edition of the complete psychological works of Sigmund Freud.* Edited and translated by James Strachey, in collaboration with Anna Freud, assisted by Alix Stratchey and Alan Tyson. 24 vols. London: Hogarth Press and Institute for Psychoanalysis.

Freud, S. (1900a). The interpretation of dreams. First part. SE 4, 1–338.

Freud, S. (1900b). The interpretation of dreams. Second part. SE 4, 339–685.

Freud, S. (1905a). Three essays on the theory of sexuality. SE 7, 130–245.

Freud, S. (1905b [1904]). On psychotherapy. SE 7, 257–68.

Freud, S. (1907). The sexual enlightenment of children. SE 9, 131–39.

Freud, S. (1909). Analysis of a phobia in a five-year-old boy. SE 10, 5–149.

Freud, S. (1910a [1909]). Five lectures on psycho-analysis. SE 11, 9–55.

Freud, S. (1910b). Leonardo Da Vinci and a memory of his childhood. SE 11, 63–137.

Freud, S. (1910c). The future prospects of psycho-analytic therapy. SE 11, 141–51.

Freud, S. (1910d). Wild" psychoanalysis. SE 11, 221–27.

Freud, S. (1912a). The dynamics of transference. SE 12, 99–108.

Freud, S. (1912b). Recommendations to physicians practicing psychoanalysis. SE 12, 111–20.

Freud, S. (1913a). Introduction to Pfister's *The psychoanalytic method.* SE 12, 329–31.

Freud, S. (1913b [1912–13]). Totem and taboo. SE 13, xiii–161.

Freud, S. (1913c). The claims of psycho-analysis to the interest of the non-psychological sciences. SE 13, 165–90.

Freud, S. (1914). Remembering, repeating and working-through (Further recommendations on the technique of psycho-analysis, II). SE 12, 147–71.

Freud, S. (1915a [1914]). Observations on transference-love. SE 12, 159–71.

Freud, S. (1915b). Instincts and their vicissitudes. SE 14, 117–40.

Freud, S. (1915c). The unconscious. SE 14, 166–215.

Freud, S. (1916). Some character-types met with in psycho-analytic work. SE 14, 311–33.

Freud, S. (1918 [1914]). From the history of an infantile neurosis. SE 17, 7–123.

Freud, S. (1919a). Lines of advance in psycho-analytic therapy. SE 17, 159–68.

Freud, S. (1919b[1918]). On the teaching of psycho-analysis in universities. SE 17, 171–73.

Freud, S. (1921a).Group psychology and the analysis of the ego. SE 18, 69–143.

Freud, S. (1921b). Preface to J.J. Putnam's *Address on Psychoanalysis.* SE 18, 269–70.

Freud, S. (1923). The infantile genital organization (an interpolation into the theory of sexuality). SE 19, 139–45.

Freud, S. (1924). The loss of reality in neurosis and psychosis, SE 19, 181–87.

Freud, S. (1925a). Some psychical consequences of the anatomical distinction between the sexes. SE 19, 248–58.

Freud, S. (1925b). Preface to Aichhorn's *Wayward Youth.* SE 19, 272–75.

Freud, S.(1925c [1924]). An autobiographical study. SE 20, 7–74.

Freud, S. (1926). The question of lay analysis: Conversations with an impartial person. SE 20, 183–250.

Freud, S. (1927a). The future of an illusion. SE 21, 5–56.

Freud, S. (1927b). Fetishism. SE 21, 152–57.

Freud, S. (1930a). Civilization and its discontents. SE 21, 64–157.

Freud, S. (1930b). Introduction to the special psychopathology number of the *Medical Review of Reviews*. SE 21, 254–55.

Freud S. (1933a [1932]). New introductory lectures on psychoanalysis. SE 22, 5–182.

Freud, S. (1933b [1932]). Why war? (Einstein and Freud). SE 22, 199–215.

Freud, S. (1937a). Constructions in analysis. SE 23, 257–69.

Freud, S. (1937b). Analysis terminable and interminable. SE 23, 216–53.

Freud, S. (1940a [1938]). An outline of psycho-analysis. SE 23, 144–207.

Freud, S. (1940b [1938]). Splitting of the ego in the process of defense. SE 23, 275–78.

Freud, S. (1941 [1921]). Psychoanalysis and telepathy. SE 18, 177–93.

Frick, W. (1971). *Humanistic psychology: Interviews with Maslow, Murphy, and Rogers*. Columbus, OH: Charles E. Merrill Publishing Company.

Friday, N. (1977). *My mother/My self: The daughter's search for identity*. New York, NY: Delacorte Press.

Fromm, E. (1960). Introduction. In A. S. Neill *Summerhill: A radical approach to child rearing*. NY: Hart Publishing Co., i–xv.

Fromm, E. (1968). *The revolution of hope: Toward a humanized technology*. NY: Harper & Row.

Gabbard, G. O. (1997). The psychoanalyst at the movies. *The International Journal of Psychoanalysis, 78*, 429–34.

Gabbard, G. O. (ed.) (2002). *Psychoanalysis and film*. London: Karnac Books.

Gay, P. (2006). *Freud: A life for our time*. NY: W.W. Norton & Co.

Geldard, F. A. (1980). Clark and the psychology of "Schools." *Journal of the History of the Behavioral Sciences, 14*(3), 225–27.

Gilligan, C. (1982). *In a different voice: Psychological theory and women's development*. Cambridge, MA: Harvard University Press.

Goodman, P. (1960). *Growing up absurd: Problems of youth in the organized system*. NY: Random House.

Goodman, P. (1964). *Compulsory mis-education*. NY: Horizon Press.

Gourguechon, P., & Hansell, J. (2005). Connecting undergraduates with psychoanalysis. *The American Psychoanalyst, 39*(2), 2.

Graebner, W. (1980). The unstable world of Benjamin Spock: Social engineering in a democratic culture, 1917–50. *The Journal of American History, 67*(3), 612–29.

Graubard, A. (1972). *Free the children: Radical reform and the Free School Movement*. NY: Pantheon Press.

Graumann, C. F., & Gergen, K. (eds.) (1996). *Historical dimensions of psychological discourse*. Cambridge, UK: Cambridge University Press.

Green, G. H. (1922). *Psychanalysis in the classroom*. NY: G.P. Putnam's Sons.

Gross, R., & Gross, B. (1977 [1969]). *The children's rights movement: Overcoming the oppression of young people*. Garden City, NY: Anchor Books.

Grumet, M. (1979). Conception, contradiction, and curriculum. Paper presented at the Airlie Conference, Virginia. [Also, *Bitter milk: Women and teaching*, 1989, pp. 15–16.]

Grumet, M. (1981). Conception, contradiction and curriculum. *Journal of Curriculum Theorizing, 3*(1), 287–98.

Grumet, M. (1988). *Bitter milk: Women and teaching*. Amherst, MA: University of Massachusetts Press.

Guerguechon, P., & Hansell, J. (2008). Access to psychoanalytic ideas in undergraduate institutions. *Journal of American Psychoanalytic Association, 56*(2), 391–408

Hale, N. (1995a [1971]). *Freud and the Americans: The beginnings of psychoanalysis in the United States, 1876–1917 I*, vol. 1. NY: Oxford University Press.

Hale, N. (1995b). *The rise and crisis of psychoanalysis in the United States, 1917–1984*, vol. 2. NY: Oxford University Press.

Hall, G. S. (1923). *Life and confessions of a psychologist.* NY: Appleton.

Hansen, K. (1957). *High school teaching.* Englewood Cliffs, NJ: Prentice Hall.

Hartmann, H., Kris, E., & Loewenstein, M. (1964a). The genetic approach to psychoanalysis. In *Papers on psychoanalytic psychology.* Monograph 14 of *Psychological Issues, 4*(2), 7–26.

Hartmann, H., Kris, E., & Lowenstein, M. (1964b). The function of theory in psychoanalysis. In *Papers on psychoanalytic psychology.* Monograph 14 of *Psychological Issues, 4*(2), 117–43.

H. D. (1974). *Tribute to Freud.* NY: New Directions.

Heald, S., & Deluz, A. (eds.) (1994). *Anthropology and psychoanalysis: An encounter through culture.* NY: Routledge.

Herman, E. (1995). *The romance of American psychology: Political culture in the age of experts.* Los Angeles: University of California Press.

Hilgard, E. R. (1996). History of educational psychology. In *Handbook of Educational Psychology,* eds. D. Berliner, & R. Calfee, 990–1004. NY: Simon & Schuster.

Hines, L. M. (2007). Return of the thought police: The history of teacher attitude adjustment. *Education Next.* 7(2). http://hoover.org/publications/ednext/868954.html

Hirsch, E. D. (1987). *Cultural literacy: What every American needs to know.* Boston, MA: Houghton Mifflin.

Hofstadter, Richard. (1962). *Anti-intellectualism in American Life.* NY: Vintage Press.

Holt, J. (1964). *How children fail.* NY: Pitman.

Hood, L. (1988). *Sylvia! The biography of Sylvia Ashton-Warner.* NY: Viking Press.

Hornstein, G. (1992). The return of the repressed: Psychology's problematic relations with psychoanalysis, 1909–60. *American Psychologist, 47*(2), 254–63.

Horowitz, F. D., Darling-Hammond, L., & Bransford. J. (2005). Educating teachers for developmentally appropriate practice. *Preparing teachers for a changing world,* eds. L. Darling-Hammond, & J. Bransford, 88–125. San Francisco: Jossey-Bass.

Hunt, M. (1994). *The story of psychology.* NY: Anchor Books.

Jacoby, R. (1986). *The repression of psychoanalysis: Otto Fenichel and the political Freudians.* Chicago, IL: University of Chicago Press.

Jacoby, R. (1997 [1975]). *Social amnesia: A critique of contemporary psychology.* NY: Beacon Press.

jagodzinski, j. (1996). *The anamorphic I/i: Finding my own step through the (my)nfield of pheminism and art.* Alberta, CA: Duval House.

jagodzinski, j. (2004). *Youth fantasies: The perverse landscape of the media.* NY: Palgrave, Macmillan.

jagodzinski, j. (ed.). (2002). *Pedagogical desire: Authority, seduction, transference, and the question of ethics.* Westport, CT: Bergin and Gravey.

James, W. (1958). *Talks to teachers: On psychology; and to students on some of life's ideals.* NY: W.W. Norton & Co.

Jameson, F. (2005). *Archaeologies of the future: The desire called Utopia and other science fictions.* London: Verso Press.

Jay, G. S. (1987).The subject of pedagogy: Lessons in psychoanalysis and politics. *College English 49*(7), 785–800.

Jersild, A. (1952). *In search of self: An exploration of the role of the school in promoting self-understanding.* NY: Bureau of Publications, Teachers College, Columbia University.

Jersild, A. (1953). *Education for self-understanding.* NY: Bureau of Publications, Teachers College, Columbia University.

Jersild, A. (1955) *When teachers face themselves.* NY: Bureau of Publications, Teachers College, Columbia University.

Jersild, A. (1962). *The meaning of psychotherapy in the teacher's life and work.* NY: Bureau of Publications, Teachers College, Columbia University.

Johnson, Barbara. (1982). *The pedagogical imperative: Teaching as a literary genre.* Yale French Studies 63. New Haven, CT: Yale University Press.

Jones, E. (1910a). Editorial. *Journal of Educational Psychology. 1*(1),1–3.

Jones, E. (1910b). Psychoanalysis and education. *Journal of Educational Psychology*, 1, 497–520.

Jones, E. (1912). Psycho-analysis and education: The value of sublimating processes for education and re-education. *Journal of Educational Psychology, 3*(5), 241–55.

Jones, E. (1953). *Sigmund Freud: Life and work. Vol 1: The young Freud, 1856–1900*. London: Hogarth Press.

Jones, E. (1955). *Sigmund Freud: Life and work. Vol 2: The years of maturity 1901–1919*. London: Hogarth Press.

Jones, E. (1957). *Sigmund Freud: Life and work. Vol 3: The last phase, 1919–1939*. London: Hogarth Press.

Jones, K. (1999). *Taming the troublesome child: American families, child guidance and the limits of psychiatric authority*. Cambridge, MA: Harvard University Press.

Jones, R. (1960). *An application of psychoanalysis to education*. Springfield, IL: Charles C. Thomas.

Jones, R. (1968). *Fantasy and feeling in education*. NY: Harper Collophon Books.

Journal of Educational Psychology. (1911). Editorial. *1*(1), i–ii.

Kardiner, A., & Ovesey, L. (1964.) *The mark of oppression: A psychological study of the American Negro*. NY: W.W. Norton & Co.

Kelly, U. (1997). *Schooling desire: Literacy, cultural politics and Pedagogy*. NY: Routledge.

Kerlinger, F. N. (1956). The origins of the doctrine of permissiveness in higher education. *Progressive Education, 33*(6), 161–65.

Kirp, D. (2003). *Shakespeare, Einstein, and the bottom line: The marketing of higher Education*. Cambridge, MA: Harvard University Press.

Kirschenbaum, H. (1979). *On becoming Carl Rogers*. NY: Delacorte Press.

Kliebard, H. M. (1987). *The struggle for the American curriculum, 1893–1958*. NY: Routledge & Kegan Paul.

Kliebard, H. M. (1992). *Forging the American curriculum: Essays in curriculum history and theory*. NY: Routledge.

Knoblock, P., & Goldstein, A. P. (1971). *The lonely teacher*. Boston: Allyn and Bacon.

Koch, S. (1985). The nature and limits of psychological knowledge: Lessons of a century qua 'science.' *A century of psychology as science*, eds. S. Koch & D. E. Leary, 75–97. NY: McGraw-Hill Book Company.

Koch, S., & Leary, D. E. (eds.). (1985). *A century of psychology as science*. NY: McGraw-Hill Book Company.

Kozol, J. (1967). *Death at an early age: The destruction of the hearts and minds of Negro children in the Boston Public Schools*. Boston, MA: Houghton Mifflin.

Kris, E. (1948). On psychology and education. *American Journal of Orthopsychiatry*, October 18, 622–35.

Kubie, L. (1960). Introduction. In R. Jones *An application of psychoanalysis to education*, i–ix. Springfield, IL: Charles C. Thomas.

Kurzweil, E., & Phillips, W. (eds.). (1983). *Literature and psychoanalysis*. NY: Columbia University Press.

Labaree, D. (2004). *The trouble with ed schools*. New Haven, CT: Yale University Press.

Lacan, J. (1966). Of structure as an in-mixing of an otherness prerequisite to any subject whatsoever. Talk delivered at John Hopkins University, Baltimore, MD. http://www.braungardt.com/Psychoanalysis/Lacan-Baltimore.htm

Lacan, J. (1981 [1973]). *The four fundamental concepts of psycho-analysis*. Edited by J.J. Allain-Miller. Translated by A. Sheriden. NY: W.W. Norton & Co.

Lacan, J. (1988a [1975]). *The seminar of Jacques Lacan: Book I: Freud's papers on technique 1953–1954*. Translated by John Forrester. NY: W.W. Norton & Co.

Lacan, J. (1988b [1978]). *The seminar of Jacques Lacan: Book II: The ego in Freud's theory and in the technique of psychoanalysis 1954–1955*. Translated by Sylvana Tomaselli. NY: W.W. Norton & Co.

Lacan, J. (1990). *Television*. Edited by Joan Copjec. Translated by Dennis Hollier. NY: W. W. Norton & Co.

Lacan, J. (1992 [1986]). *The seminar of Jacques Lacan: Book VII: The ethics of psychoanalysis 1959–1960.* Translated by Dennis Porter. NY: W.W. Norton & Co.

Lacan, J. (1993 [1981]). *The seminar of Jacques Lacan: Book III: The psychoses 1955–1956.* Translated by Russell Grigg. NY: W.W. Norton & Co.

Lacan, J. (1998 [1975]). *The seminar of Jacques Lacan: Book XX: Encore on feminine sexuality and the limits of love and knowledge, 1972–73.* Translated by Bruce Fink. NY: W.W. Norton & Co.

Lacan, J. (2006 [1970]). *Ecrits.* Translated by Bruce Fink in collaboration with Héloïse Fink & Rusell Grigg. NY: W.W. Norton & Co.

Lacan, J. (2007 [1991]). *The seminar of Jacques Lacan: Book XVII: The other side of psychoanalysis.* Translated by Russell Grigg. NY: W.W. Norton & Co.

Lacan, J. (2008). *My teaching.* Translated by David Macey. NY: Verso Press.

Lagemann, E. (1989). *The politics of knowledge: The Carnegie Corporation, philanthropy, and public policy.* Chicago, IL: University of Chicago Press.

Lagemann, E. (2000). *An elusive science: The troubling history of education research.* Chicago, IL: University of Chicago Press.

Laing, R. D. (1967). *The politics of experience.* New York, NY: Pantheon Books.

Laplanche, Jean. (1989). *New foundations for psychoanalysis.* Translated by David Macey. Cambridge, UK: Basil Blackwell.

Laplanche, J. (1999). Interpretation between determinism and hermeneutics: A restatement of the problem. In *Essays on otherness.* Translated by Philip Slotkin. London: Routledge, 138–65.

Laplanche, J., & Pontalis, J. B. (1973). *The language of psychoanalysis.* Translated by Donald Nicholson-Smith. NY: W.W. Norton & Co.

Lasch, C. (1997 [1974]). Introduction. In R. Jacoby *Social amnesia: A critique of contemporary psychology.* New Brunswick, NJ: Transaction Publishers.

Lasch, C. (1979). *The culture of narcissism: American life in an age of diminishing expectations.* NY: W.W. Norton & Co.

Lay, W. (1917). *Man's unconscious conflict: A popular exposition of psychoanalysis.* NY: Dodd, Mead & Co.

Lemov, D. (2010). *Teaching like a champion: 49 techniques that put students on the path to college.* San Francisco, CA: Jossey-Bass.

Leonard, G. (1968). *Education and ecstasy.* NY: Delacorte Press.

Levine, J. (2002). *Harmful to minors: The perils of protecting children from sex.* Minneapolis, MN: University of Minnesota Press.

Leys, R., & Evans, R. (eds.). (1990). *The correspondence between Adolf Meyer and Bradford Titchener.* Baltimore, MD: Johns Hopkins University Press.

Lindner, R. (1955). *The fifty minute hour.* NY: Holt, Rinehart.

Low, B. (1920). Man's unconscious passion: by Wilfrid Lay. *International Journal of Psycho-analysis, II,* 234–37.

Low, B. (1928). *The unconscious in action.* London: University of London Press.

Low, B. (1929). A note on the influence of psycho-analysis upon English education during the last eighteen years. *International Journal of Psycho-analysis, 10,* 314–20.

Low, B. J. (2004). The hand that rocked the cradle: A critical analysis of Rockefeller Philanthropic Funding, 1920–60. *Historical Studies in Education/Revue d'histoire de l'éducation,* Spring, 33–62.

Lucas, C. (1999). *Teacher education in America: Reform agendas for the twenty-first century.* NY: St. Martin's Press.

Macdonald, B. (ed). (1995). *Theory as a prayerful act: The collected essays of James B. Macdonald.* NY: Peter Lang.

Makari, G. (2008). *Revolution in the mind: The creation of psychoanalysis.* NY: HarperCollins.

Malcolm, J. (1981). *Psychoanalysis: The impossible profession.* New York, NY: Random House.

Marcuse, H. (1966 [1955]). *Eros and civilization: A philosophical inquiry into Freud.* Boston, MA: Beacon Press.

Marcuse, H. (1968 [1964]). *One-dimensional man: Studies in the ideology of advanced industrial society.* Boston, MA: Beacon Press.

Maslow, A. (1968). *Toward a psychology of being.* Princeton, NJ: Van Nostrand.

Masson, J. M. (ed.). (1985). *The complete letters of Sigmund Freud to Wilhelm Fliess 1987–1904.* Translated by Jeffrey Moussaieff Masson. Cambridge, MA: Harvard University Press.

McCourt, F. (2005). *Teacher man: A memoir.* NY: Scribner.

McDougall, W. (1926). Introduction. In G. H. Green *Psychoanalysis in the Classroom,* v–vi. New York: G.P. Putnam and Sons.

McGee, P. (1987). Truth and resistance: Teaching as a form of analysis. *College English, 49*(6), 667–78.

McGowan, T. (2004). *The end of dissatisfaction? Jacques Lacan and the emerging society of enjoyment.* Albany, NY: State University of New York Press.

McGrath, G. (1960). *A student manual for methods of teaching.* NY: Putnam.

Menand, L. (2001). *The metaphysical club.* NY: Farrar, Straus and Giroux.

Middleton, S. (2006). I am my own professor: Ashton-Warner as New Zealand educational theorist 1940–60. *Provocations: Sylvia Ashton-Warner and excitability in education,* eds. J. P. Robertson, & C. McConaghy, 33–62. NY: Peter Lang,

Midgley, N. (2008). The 'Matchbox School' (1927–32): Anna Freud and the idea of psychoanalytically informed education. *Journal of Child Psychotherapy, 34*(1), 23–42.

Miller, H. (1962). The professional use of the self through group work in teacher education. *Journal of Educational Sociology, 36*(4), 170–80.

Miller, J. (1990). *Creating spaces and finding voices.* Albany, NY: SUNY Press.

Miller, J.-A. (1990). Microscopia: An introduction to the reading of television. In Jacques Lacan *Television: A challenge to the psychoanalytic establishment.* Translated by Denis Hollier, Rosalind Krauss, & Annette Michelson. Edited by Joan Copjec. NY: W.W. Norton & Co.

Miller, J. B. (1976). *Toward a new psychology of women.* NY: Beacon Press.

Mitchell, S., & Black, M. (1995). *Freud and beyond: A history of modern psychoanalytic thought.* NY: Basic Books.

Moore, H. (2007). *The subject of anthropology: Gender, symbolism and psychoanalysis.* Malden, MA: Polity Press.

Morris, M. (2001). *Curriculum and the holocaust: Competing sites of memory and representation.* NY: Lawrence Erlbaum.

Morris, M. (2008). *Teaching through the ill body: A spiritual and aesthetic approach to pedagogy and illness.* Rotterdam, Netherlands: Sense Publishers.

Morris, M. (2009). *On not being able to play: Scholars, musicians and the crisis of psyche.* Rotterdam, Netherlands: Sense Publishers.

Moynihan, P. (1965). *The Moynihan Report. The Negro family: The case for national action.* Washington: DC: Office of Policy Planning and Research, U.S. Department of Labor.

Mullan, Bob. (1995). *Mad to be normal: Conversations with R.D. Laing.* London: Free Association Books.

Murphy, A. (1989). Transference and resistance in the basic writing classroom: Problematics and praxis. *College Composition and Communication, 40*(2), 175–87.

Naumberg, M. 1928. *Child and the world: Dialogues in modern education.* NY: Harcourt Brace.

Naumberg, M. (1947). *Studies of the "free" expression of behavior problem children and adolescents as means of diagnosing therapy.* Nervous and Mental Disease Monographs, 1947, No. 71. NY: Coolidge Foundation.

Naumberg, M. (1950). *Schizophrenic art: Its meaning in psychotherapy.* NY: Grune and Stratton.

Naumberg, M. (1966). *Dynamically oriented art therapy: Its principles and practices.* NY: Grune and Stratton.

Neill, A.S. (1960). *Summerhill: A radical approach to child rearing.* NY: Hart Publishing Co.

Neill, A.S. (1972). *Neill, Neill, orange peel!* NY: Hart Publishing Co.

Norfleet, B. (2001). *When we liked Ike: Looking for postwar America.* NY: W.W. Norton & Co.

Nosofksy, W. (1949). Psychoanalysis and rational social change. *Journal of Educational Sociology, 22*(6), 381–93.

Nunberg, H., & Federn, E. (1910). *Minutes of the Vienna psychoanalytic society, Vol. II: 1908–1910.* Translated by M. Nunberg. NY: International Universities Press.

Oberndorf, C. (1953). *A history of psychoanalysis in America.* NY: Harper Torchbooks.

Ortner, S. (2006). *Anthropology and social theory: Culture, power and the acting subject.* Durham, NC: Duke University Press.

Pabst, G.W. (1926). *Secrets of a soul.* Produced by Hans Neumann. NY: Kino International Corp.

Pagano, J. (1990). *Exiles and communities: Teaching in the patriarchal wasteland.* Albany, NY: State University of New York Press.

Park, D. G. (1931). Freudian influence on academic psychology. *Psychological Review, 38,* 73–85.

Pearson, G. H. J. (1954). *Psychoanalysis and the education of the child.* NY: W.W. Norton & Co.

Penley, C. (1986). Teaching in your sleep: Feminism and psychoanalysis. *Theory in the classroom,* ed. C. Nelson, 129–48. Urbana, IL: University of Illinois Press.

Perelman, L. (1986). The context of classroom writing. *College English I, 48,* 471–79.

Petrina, S. (2004). Luella Cole, Sidney Pressey, and educational psychoanalysis, 1921–1931. *History of Education Quarterly, 44*(4), 1–29.

Petrina, S. (2006). The medicalization of education: A historiographic synthesis. *History of Education Quarterly, 46*(4), 504–31.

Phillips, A. (1998). *The beast in the nursery: On curiosity and other appetites.* NY: Pantheon Books.

Phillips, A. (2006). *Side effects.* London: Penguin.

Pinar, W. (1975). Sanity, madness, and the school. *Curriculum theorizing: The reconceptualists,* ed. William Pinar. Berkeley, CA: McCutchan.

Pinar, W. (1981). Understanding curriculum as gender text: notes on reproduction, resistance, and male–male relations. In W. Pinar *Autobiography, politics and sexuality: Essays in curriculum theory, 1972–1992,* 151–77. NY: Peter Lang Press.

Pinar, W. (1983). The corporate production of feminism and the case of Boy George. *Autobiography, Politics and sexuality: Essays in curriculum theory, 1972–1992.*183–89. NY: Peter Lang Press

Pinar, W. (1994). *Autobiography, politics and sexuality: Essays in curriculum theory,1972–1992.* NY: Peter Lang Press.

Pinar, W. (2001). *The gender of racial politics and violence in America: Lynching, prison rape and the crisis of masculinity.* NY: Peter Lang Press.

Pinar, W. (2004). *What is curriculum theory?* NY: Lawrence Erlbaum.

Pinar, W. (2006a). *The synoptic text today and other essays.* NY: Peter Lang.

Pinar, W. (2006b). *Race, religion, and a curriculum of reparation.* NY: Palgrave.

Pinar, W. (2006c). *Bildung* and the internationalization of curriculum studies. In *Transnational Curriculum Inquiry, 3*(2), (2006). http://ojs.library.ubc.ca/index.php/tci/article/viewFile/27/49

Pinar W. (2009). The unaddressed 'I' of ideology critique. *Power and Education,* 1(2), 189–200.

Pinar, W., Reynolds, W., Slattery, P., & Taubman, P. (eds.). (1995). *Understanding curriculum.* NY: Peter Lang.

Pitt, A. (2003). *The play of the personal: Psychoanalytic narratives of feminist education.* NY: Peter Lang Publishing.

Pollack, R. (1997). *The creation of Dr. B: A biography of Bruno Bettelheim.* NY: Simon& Schuster.

Postman, N., & Weingartner, C. (1969). *Teaching as a subversive activity.* NY: DelacortePress.

Powell, A, Farrar, E., & Cohen, D. (1986). *The shopping mall high school: Winners and losers in the educational marketplace.* Boston: Houghton Mifflin.

The President's Task Force on Manpower Conservation. (1964). *One-third of a nation: A report on young men found unqualified for military service.* January 1. Washington, DC: The White House.

Prochnik, G. (2006). *Putnam Camp: Sigmund Freud, James Jackson Putnam, and the purpose of American psychology.* NY: Other Press.

Putnam, James J. (1915). *Human motives.* Boston, MA: Little, Brown & Co.

Rajchman, J. (1991). *Truth and eros: Foucault, Lacan, and the question of ethics.* NY: Routledge Press.

Ravitch, D. (2000). *Left back: A century of battles over school reform.* NY: Touchstone Books.

Ravitch, D., & Finn, C. (1987). *What do our 17-year-olds know? A report on the first national assessment of history and literature.* NY: Harper and Row.

Readings, B. (1996). *The university in ruins.* Cambridge, MA: Harvard University Press.

Redmond, J., & Shulman, M. (2008). Access to psychoanalytic ideas in American undergraduate institutions. *Journal of American Psychoanalytic Association,* 56, 391–408.

Reich, W. (1972 [1949]). *Character analysis.* Translated by Vincent R. Carfagno. NY: Farrar, Straus and Giroux.

Rice, C. E. (2000). Uncertain genesis: The academic institutionalization of American-psychology in 1900. *American Psychologist,* 55(5), 488–91.

Richardson, T. (1989). *The century of the child: The mental hygiene movement and social policy in the United States and Canada.* NY: State University of New York Press.

Rieff, P. (1966). *The triumph of the therapeutic: Uses of faith after Freud.* Chicago, IL: University of Chicago Press.

Rieff, P. (1979 [1959]). *Freud: The mind of the moralist.* Chicago, IL: University of Chicago Press.

Riesman, D., Glazer, N., & Denney, R. (1955). *The lonely crowd: A study of the changing American character.* New Haven, CT: Simon & Schuster.

Roazen, P. (1992). *Freud and his followers.* NY: Da Capo Press.

Roazen, P. (2001). *The historiography of psychoanalysis.* New Brunswick, NJ: Transactions Publishers.

Robertson, J. P. (2006). Recovering education as provocation: Keeping countenance with Sylvia Ashton-Warner. *Provocations: Sylvia Ashton-Warner and excitability in education,* eds J. P. Robertson, & C. McConaghy, 173–194. NY: Peter Lang.

Robertson, J. P., & McConaghy, C, (eds.). (2006). *Provocations: Sylvia Ashton-Warner and excitability in education.* NY: Peter Lang.

Rogers, C. (1969). *Freedom to learn.* Columbus. OH: Charles Merrill Publishing Company.

Rose, J. (1983). Femininity and its discontents. *Feminist Review 14,* 5–21.

Rosenzweig, S. (1994). *The historic expedition to America (1909): Freud, Jung and Hall and the King-maker.* St. Louis, MO: Rana House.

Rothstein, R. (1998). *The way we were? The myths and realities of America's student achievement.* NY: The Century Foundation Press.

Roudinesco, E. (2001). *Why psychoanalysis?* Translated by Rachel Bowlby. NY: Columbia University Press.

Rudnick, L. P. (1984). *Mabel Dodge Luhan: New Mexico. New Worlds.* Albuquerque, NM: University of New Mexico Press.

Rubin, G. (1975). The traffic in women: Notes on the 'political economy' of sex. *Toward an anthropology of women,* ed. R. Reiter, 113–132. NY: Monthly Review Press.

Rugg, H. (ed.). (1941). *Readings in the foundations of education,* vol. I. NY: Teachers College, Columbia University.

Salvio, P. M. (1994). What can a body know? Refiguring pedagogic intention into teacher education. *Journal of Teacher Education 45*(1), 53–61.

Salvio, P. M. (1998). On using the literacy portfolio to prepare teachers for "Willful World Traveling." *Curriculum: Toward New Identities,* ed. W. F. Pinar, 41–74. NY: Garland Publishing, Inc.

Salvio, P. M. (1999). Reading beyond narratives of cure in curriculum studies. *JCT: Journal of Curriculum Theorizing, 15*(2), 185–88.

Salvio, P. M. (2007). *Anne Sexton: Teacher of weird abundance.* Albany, NY: SUNY Press.

Samuels, R. (2003). Teaching about the Holocaust and the subject of objectivity: Psychoanalysis, trauma, and counter-transference in an advanced writing course. *Journal of the Psychoanalysis of Culture & Society, 8*(1), 133–40.

Santner, E. (1990). *Stranded objects: Mourning, memory, and film in postwar Germany.* Ithaca, NY: Cornell University Press.

Santner, E. (2006). *On creaturely life: Rilke/Benjamin/Sebald.* Chicago, IL: University of Chicago Press.

Schmuck, R., & Schmuck, P. (1983). *Group processes in the classroom.* Dubuque, IA: Wm. C. Brown.

Schneiderman, S. (1980). *Returning to Freud: Clinical psychoanalysis in the school of Lacan.* New Haven, CT: Yale University Press.

Sears, R. (1985). Psychoanalysis and behavior theory: 1907–65. *A century of psychology as science,* eds. S. Koch, & D. E. Leary, 207–31. NY: McGraw-Hill Book Company.

Shakow, D., & Rapaport, D. (1964). *The influence of Freud on American psychology.* NY: International Universities Press.

Shipley, J. T. (1961). *The mentally disturbed teacher.* Philadelphia: Chilton Co.

Silberman, C. (1970). *Crisis in the classroom: The remaking of American education.* NY: Viking Books.

Silin, J. G. (1995). *Sex, death and the education of children: Our passion for ignorance in the age of AIDS.* NY: Teachers College Press.

Skorczewski, D. (2005). *Teaching one moment at a time: Disruption and repair in the classroom.* Amherst, MA: University of Massachusetts Press.

Smith, M. (1949). *And madly teach.* Chicago: Henry Regnary Co.

Sondheim, S. (1957). Officer Krupke. *West side story.* http://www.westsidestory.com/site/level2/lyrics/krupke.html

Sperber, D., & Wilson, D. (1986). *Relevance: Communication and cognition.* Cambridge, MA: Harvard University Press.

Spock, B. (1946). *Common sense book of baby and child care.* NY: Duell, Sloan and Pearce.

Strong, B. (1972). Ideas of the early sex education movement in America, 1890–1920. *History of Education Quarterly. 12*(2), 129–61.

Suppes, P., & Warren, H. (1978). Psychoanalysis and American elementary education. *Impact of research on education: Some case studies,* ed. P. Suppes, 319–96. Washington, DC: National Academy of Education.

Sutton, N. (1996). *Bettelheim: A life and a legacy.* NY: Basic Books.

Taubman, P. (1990). Achieving the right distance. *Educational Theory, 40*(1), 121–33.

Taubman, P. (1997). Autobiography without the self: Identity and aesthetic education. Presented at AERA, March 25.

Taubman, P. (1999). Silent voices, talking cures: Pedagogy as therapy, pedagogy as analysis. *The Journal of Curriculum Theorizing,* Editor's Introduction, 1–9.

Taubman, P. (2000). Teaching without hope: What is really at stake in the standards movement, high stakes testing, and the drive for practical reforms? Feature article in *The Journal of Curriculum Theorizing, 16*(3), Fall, 19–33.

Taubman, P. (2001). The callings of sexual identities. *Labeling: Politics and pedagogy,* eds. G. Hudak, & P. Kihn, 179–202. London: The Falmer Press.

Taubman, P. (2002). Facing the terror within: Exploring the personal in multicultural education. *Case studies in cultural transitions: Rethinking multicultural education,* eds. C. Korn, & A. Bursztyn, 97–129. Chicago, IL: Greenwood Press.

Taubman, P. (2006). I love them to death. *On the return of love and childhood: Psychoanalytic theory in teaching and learning,* eds. G. Boldt, & P. Salvio, 19–32. NY: Routledge Press.

Taubman, P. (2009). *Teaching by numbers: Deconstructing the discourse of standards and aaccountability in education*. NY: Routledge Press.

Thorndike, E. (1910). The contribution of psychology to education. *The Journal of Educational Psychology. 1*, 5–12.

Time Magazine. (1930). Mental hygiene. May, 19. http:www.time.com/time/magazine/article/0,9171,739253,00.html.

Time Magazine. (1956). The explorer. April 23. 70–78. http://www.time.com/time/magazine/article/0,9171,865301,00.html.

Tobin, L. (1993). *Writing relationships: What really happens in the composition*. Portsmouth, NH: Boynton/Cook.

Tobin, L. (2004). *Reading student writing: Confessions, meditations, rants*. Portsmouth, NH: Heinemann Press.

Todd, S. (2003). *Learning from others: Levinas, psychoanalysis, and ethical possibilities in education*. Albany, NY: SUNY Press.

Todd, S. (ed.) (1997). *Learning desire: perspectives on pedagogy, culture and the unsaid.*, NY: Routledge Press.

Toulmin, S. & Leary, D.E. (1985). The cult of empiricism in psychology and beyond. *A century of psychology as science*, eds. S. Koch, & D. E. Leary, 594–617. NY: McGraw-Hill Book Company.

Turkle, S. (1992). *Psychoanalytic politics: Jacques Lacan and Freud's French revolution*. NY: Guilford Press.

Tyack, D. (1974). *The one best system: A history of American urban education.*Cambridge, MA: Harvard University Press.

Tyack, D., & Cuban, L. (1995). *Tinkering toward Utopia: A century of public school reform*. Cambridge, MA: Harvard University Press.

Tyler, L. L. (1958). Psychoanalysis and curriculum theory. *The School Review 66*(4), 446–60.

Tyler, R. (1949). *Basic principles of curriculum and instruction*. Chicago, IL: University of Chicago Press.

Washburn, C. and Whipple, G. M. (eds.) (1939). *Yearbook on child development and the curriculum*, vol. 38. Chicago, IL: National Society of the Study of Education.

Watson, G. (1957). Psychoanalysis and the future of education. *Teachers College Record, 58*(5), 241–47.

Wedekind, F. (1995 [1891]). *Spring awakening*. Translated by Eric Bentley. NY: Applause Books.

Weidner, G. (1954). Group procedures modifying attitudes of prejudice in the college classroom. *The Journal of Educational Psychology, 45*(6), 332–44.

Weiner, J. (1995). *The lost drum: The myth of sexuality in Papua New Guinea and beyond*. Madison, WI: University of Wisconsin Press.

Weiten, W., & Wight, R. D. (1992). Portraits of a discipline: An examination of introductory psychology textbooks in America. *Teaching psychology in America: A history*, eds. A. E. Puente, J. R. Matthews, & C. L. Brewer, 440–56. Washington, DC: American Psychological Association.

Williams, F. (1926). The field of mental hygiene. *Progressive Education. 3*(1), 7–13.

Wilson, S. (1955/2002). *The man in the gray flannel suit*. NY: First Four Eight Windows Press.

Winnicott, D. W. (1968a). The use of an object and relating through identification. *Psychoanalytic explorations*, eds. C. Winnicott, R. Shepherd, & M. Davis, 218–19. Cambridge, MA: Harvard University Press.

Winnicott, D. W. (1968b). The use of the word 'use.' In D.W. Winnicott *Psychoanalytic explorations*, eds. C. Winnicott, R. Shepherd, & M. Davis, 233–35. Cambridge, MA: Harvard University Press.

Winnicott, D. W. (1968c). Comments on my paper 'The use of an object.' *Psychoanalytic explorations*, eds. C. Winnicott, R. Shepherd, & M. Davis, 238–40. Cambridge, MA: Harvard University Press.

Winter, S. (1999). *Freud and the institution of psychoanalytic knowledge*. Stanford, CA: Stanford University Press.

Wittels, F. (1931). Psychoanalysis for teachers. *Progressive Education.*, *13*(3): 238–41.

Wolpe, J. (1958). *Psychotherapy by reciprocal inhibition*. Stanford, CA: Stanford University Press.

Woodworth, R. S. (1929). *Psychology: A study of mental life*, 2nd edition. NY: Holt.

Wylie, P. (1942). *A generation of vipers*. NY: Farrar and Rinehart.

Yankelovich, D., & Barrett, W. (1970). *Ego and instinct: The psychoanalytic view of human nature*. NY: Random House.

Zachry, C.B. (1929). *Personality adjustments of school children*. NY: Scribner and Sons.

Zachry, C. B. (1941). The influence of psychoanalysis in education. *Psychoanalytic Quarterly 10*, 431–44.

Zachry, C. B., Kotinsky, R., & Thayer, V. T. (1939). *Reorganizing secondary education* NY: D. Appleton-Century Co.

Zaretsky, E. (2004). *Secrets of the soul: A social and cultural history of psychoanalysis*. NY: Alfred Knopf.

Zeichner, K. (2003). The adequacies and inadequacies of three current strategies to recruit, prepare and retain the best teachers for all students. *Teachers College Record*, *105*(3): 490–519.

Žižek, S. (1989). *The sublime object of ideology*. NY: Verso Press.

Žižek, S. (1994). *The metastases of enjoyment: Six essays on women and causality*. NY: Verso Press.

INDEX